THE
EMPOWER MODEL
FOR MEN

A GUIDE TO MORE CONSCIOUS LIVING

SCOTT E. CLARK

Bodhi Publishing Company, LLC
Phoenix, Arizona, USA

Published and distributed by Bodhi Publishing Company, LLC

Library of Congress Control Number: 2014939840

Tradepaper ISBN: 978-0-9903198-0-1
1ˢᵗ printing, May 2014
Printed in the United States of America

With Gratitude:

I wish to express appreciation to my family for their love and support. To my children - you continue to represent my greatest love and joy. To my friends, thank you for your encouragement, and for noticing the best in me. And for those who taught me, from their place of spirit or ego, I would not be who I am without you – so thank you for inspiring the words and message in this book!

A special thank you to Etana Holowinko at Society Jazz for the cover design and other technical and artistic contributions.

Contents

INTRODUCTION

"Our thoughts become our words, our words become our behavior, our behavior becomes our habits, our habits become our values, our values become our destiny"
- **Mahatma Gandhi**

I have learned that there are essentially three things necessary for a life well lived. One, we must live consciously. This means that we are taking responsibility for intentionally creating our life from the positive choices we make. Two, we must shift or raise our consciousness in order to elevate our perceptions, awareness, and alignment with our higher truth. And three, we must live and express our lives in ways that contribute positively to the world. The goal of ***The Empower Model for Men*** is to guide you along a path that supports growth and healing in order to experience a life well lived.

So, how is your life going? Do you feel truly empowered to make the choices that are most beneficial to you and those closest to you? Are you as focused on overall wellness, and is your life as balanced as you want it to be? Have you developed inner strength and inner peace that bring out your best in situations of conflict? Are you creating joy and cooperation in your relationships? Are you utilizing your unique gifts, talents, and passion in work that is fulfilling and rewarding? Are you living your highest purpose? Are you consciously living your life with the expression of unity, compassion, and equality for all people?

This book was written to help men change the "no" answers to "yeses". If you are looking to improve the quality of your inner and therefore outer life, the wisdom offered in the Empower Model is designed to guide, direct, and align you to your higher truth with the objective of achieving your highest potential.

On some basic level all people want to experience growth, love, freedom, joy, and prosperity. No matter how difficult an ending may be, we ultimately relish in the possibility of creating a better path for our lives. One year ends, and whether we experienced great joy or challenge in the previous year, we feel optimism and a breath of fresh air in a New Year that may bring all that we desire. This speaks to the power and strength within the human condition.

So we make our lists and resolutions, and strive with greater effort to be more focused and disciplined to change some behavior or condition. The problem, however, is that we are working within the same limiting belief system (education) and egoic framework that has convinced us that we can't have the quality of life we truly desire. We have not spent the required effort and intention in the necessary healing and re-education that will support an inner shift that then allows us to create the experiences and conditions we want.

We cannot fully live our true and higher purpose and potential until we understand and accept that this life is available to us, but only when we take the steps to create it. We cannot wait for others to ordain or approve of what we do, think, or say, according to their individual or historical standards and parameters. We can live a life that includes all of the desired qualities listed above without limiting or eliminating anyone else's opportunity to enjoy the same existence. We must learn who we are at the highest level, and then proceed down the path of personal and spiritual growth in order to develop the foundation of inner strength, guidance, and awareness that will then more organically facilitate the creation of a life lived on purpose; an Empowered life.

If someone asked, "Who are you?" or "What do you do?" You would probably give your name and your occupation. Within a normal social context this would be perfectly fine. However, I believe that we are entering an age where more men are looking to understand who they really are, beyond their name, job, and the various roles they have played in the past.

In order to evolve as a society it is clear that men need to take a more active role in their own inner and outer development. On a deeper level, the question of *who you are*, deals with who you are capable of being, why you are here, and how you define yourself and others. And the question about *what you do*, addresses the quality of the experiences you are creating, how you go about your daily life, and how you interact with others.

Both intuitively and experientially, I have felt for many years that I would be involved in supporting the raising of consciousness in men (though I knew not, how or when). I have always had an interest in personal growth and higher wisdom. Even while functioning in a career in corporate accounting, my greatest joy often came from supporting co-workers with insights and an intention toward helping them understand or overcome some life issue or drama.

In my personal time I enjoyed reading some of the more well-known spiritual gurus of our present day. I felt a great connection to this wisdom. I attended numerous classes, seminars, and gatherings where I soaked up the inspiration and spiritual truth that resonated with me. Yet like all people, I have had to try to understand their practical application while dealing with my own issues and challenges toward healing, growing, and shifting to a higher perspective and way of being in the world.

One thing that always caught my attention was how few men were attending these events, or otherwise focusing on their own personal and spiritual development. I am, of course, in favor of all people taking ownership of their life and truly understanding their capabilities toward creating a life of true empowerment. So I honor women for taking a lead in the shifting of the consciousness on the planet. But where are the men?

Our education and training has taught us to be more concerned with how things appear on the outside. We are less likely to ask for help or to take responsibility for healing our own pain. Our lives reflect the appearance of strength, which often manifests outwardly as force, but is masking an inner state of fear, weakness, and confusion. Men must begin to look more inwardly for strength, awareness, and truth.

This world is shifting. And this is a blessing (and a necessity); yet change is very difficult, especially when it is resisted. Men of the past have largely created the old world system which bestowed upon us certain definitions and egoic power. But like any system that is designed to control and undermine the rights of others, this system is now crumbling in favor of the evolution of humanity. We need to begin to shift in the only way that has lasting effect, and that is from the inside out. We cannot change our behaviors and attitudes without first developing greater awareness of our higher truth, leading to the inner healing and strength that will actually have the impact we desire.

Some will question the title of this book, and say, "That's ridiculous, men already have all of the power." In fact, I had two marketing experts say to me that "empower" is a term for women, and that most men are unwilling to admit that they are disempowered, because it would be admitting weakness. They suggested that I change the title to utilize terminology that would be more appealing to men. In the old world of ego domination, they were not wrong. So I briefly considered their opinion. However, through my inner meditation, I was quickly guided back to the understanding that on a higher level, all people need to be empowered. I was reminded that this book is more about the message than easy sales revenue, and that I would rather be slightly ahead of the curve with integrity, than catering to the status quo.

Disempowerment is not just being held down or held back by others, it is a lack of inner personal power. It is an internal quality that has been misrepresented as an external quality. When you look at life deeper, from a vantage point of higher truth, what the world has called power is often just ego. And it's an out-of-control ego at that. What the world needs is true empowerment for all, which implies a conscious connection to our true higher identity.

As men we need to relearn what power and strength really are. We need to open up to a shift that will actually bring us the qualities in life that we sought from the lies that ego told us. We will need a new kind of courage that is willing to look at our lives with complete honesty, and requires us to define for ourselves what will really bring us love, joy, peace, wellness, and abundance.

Over the past few decades, while I was studying this wisdom, I still could not always see how to make the shift in my own life. I resonated with what I was learning as truth, but how did I apply it? Intellectually, which is how most of us guys process, it all sounded good, but I still was struggling. Even while writing this book, ego was saying to me, "So what makes you such an expert?" Ego is the constant judge in our heads. And through this experience I have learned that I do not have to be an "expert", as defined by others, which in the extreme implies that one is all-knowing and infallible. I am merely intending to share my truth and light in service to the world. That is all any of us can do. How it is received by others is their path and purpose, and beyond my control.

I had to learn a new way of being that was not so connected to what I "thought" I was capable of based on my past. I needed to shift and heal within myself, not only to begin to overcome past emotional wounds, but also the false education and self-limitations that I had accepted. I was required to understand and accept who I really am, and begin to define my purpose and potential from a higher perspective. Over the past couple years I have applied the "principles" of spiritual wisdom into a moment by moment practice, in order to shift my outer experiences.

I recently watched, *The Matrix*, and near the end of the movie the character Morpheus said to Neo, "There is a difference between knowing the path and walking the path." I certainly believe that this is true for each of us who are trying to live our highest potential. I believe that personal and spiritual growth and development must be practical and applicable to us in order to be relevant. It was not until I began to walk this path that I was ready to share the higher truth in this book, and live this truth in my life.

We are all walking our path, and it is our choice of whether to choose to transform into our highest capabilities or to remain in the limitations of the known. I have experienced limited thinking and suffering similar to most other men. However, I now know that those experiences do not define me, and they don't define you either. I am not special because of my accomplishments or tribulations. Like you, I am special because as spirit, I am able to express my humanity while living the highest qualities for the benefit of myself and of all beings.

I have personally utilized the wisdom and tools in this book to begin to live more consciously, which means being more connected to spirit. The format of this book outlines this higher wisdom and insight, by specifically addressing most areas of our daily lives, within the seven steps of the *Empower Model.* EMPOWER is an acronym which spells out the words: Educate, Matter, Peace, Ownership, Wellness, Embrace, and Reward. This model was designed as a teaching tool in support of your inner healing, and the creation of the personal experiences you most desire. I have added Exercises at the end of each step (chapter) that may further support you in applying these teachings to your life. I recommend that you read the book in its entirety, then if so inclined, go back to work the Exercises.

As with all personal and spiritual growth, your results are up to you, so use your own discernment to determine what is most meaningful and supportive. But I would say that we are past the point, as men and humans, where we just continue down our current path of mere survival, blame, apathy, and suffering. It is time for each of us to take responsibility for our lives, in support of love and unity for all.

Regardless of our history, I have a great deal of faith in men. I have written this book because I believe that we are ready to evolve. I know that there are still many men who either think they are too smart for this spiritual stuff, or are too concerned with what their macho friends would think. I said above that the old world system is crumbling, but parts of it are hanging on for dear life. Everyone is living their own path, within their level of awareness, and they are certainly allowed to continue to learn in the manner that suits them. However, I also believe that there are a great many men who are ready to expand their consciousness, and live in the courage to explore their own highest possibilities and create a life that will support them toward fulfilling their unique purpose. I know that there are men who want to have more love and acceptance for themselves, and therefore stronger, more loving relationships with others. And I know that men are ready to develop true empowerment!

Each of the seven steps of the ***Empower Model*** is contained in its own chapter. Within and between the steps themselves, there may be similar concepts, ideas, and information, as it may reference a common topic that has a different perspective depending on the teaching model concept. For the most part, we men are logical thinkers, and things have to make sense on a practical level in order for us to truly apply them in our life. Yet, we also like to be inspired, as this relates to the most essential part of us that is "In Spirit". I will be sharing ideas that are intended to help you connect to the higher place within you that knows who you are, what you need, and why you are here. By combining these two essential points of view I hope to spur your interest in taking the steps to walk a more empowered path. I am asking you right up front to open your minds to new and expanded ways of thinking and seeing yourself and others.

One of the first things we need to establish right away is that I understand that at times I am going to generalize and categorize men as one group with similar attributes, qualities, functionality, and beliefs. I realize that this of course is not especially fair or accurate, since we are all various shades of gray. Yet for the purposes of assisting and guiding men to reach their higher potential, I am going to start from a basic framework that I believe reflects the majority of men historically. If you do not fit into the stereotype in a particular subject then do not own that. This is not meant to judge or demean anyone. If you have done any amount of internal work and feel more "enlightened" than these generic stereotypes, then be pleased that you are on a healthier path. But know that this path is on-going; there are levels beyond levels and there is always room for you to grow. Whether you just picked up this book out of curiosity and the concepts are brand new to you, or whether you have personally read numerous books on the subject, we are all on a path of growth and transcendence from our current level of awareness.

To be "empowered" needs to be defined, especially as it relates to men. Being "powerful" or seeking "power" is certainly not a new concept for us. It has been a primary objective since the beginning of recorded history. Bigger, stronger, faster, richer, smarter, etc. has defined the qualities that men have always strived for. And truly, bigger only really pertains to our egos. We are always judging ourselves and in competition with each other. And since there is always someone bigger, stronger, faster, richer and smarter than us, we have often plotted their demise so that we could feel more powerful. It is easy to see a history of corruption and violence toward others in order to make ourselves more important, or at least "better" than someone else. All of this is entirely ego driven, and as such is based in fear. This is not empowerment.

True empowerment seeks to discover and express the highest qualities within ourselves. And it comes from a place of higher integrity that supports the achievement of this level of strength and connection to purpose for all people. In order to reach this state of being we must focus on the process of inner healing and transformation. We must elevate our consciousness for the betterment of ourselves and all others.

Many men have exhibited greatness, made amazing discoveries, advanced brilliant schools of thought, created magnificent works of art and literature, and invented machines that have revolutionized how we live today. We have great potential! We have a great force of will and a logic-based mindset capable of solving any problem. If we were to shift to a higher level of awareness and perspective where our efforts are more supportive, creative, cooperative, and conscious, we would be men who are empowered. True empowerment is based in the higher qualities of spirit. We will actually be more confident because of the love we have for our true selves and others, instead of working so hard trying to appear important or better than others. We are actually stronger due to an inner strength that is now combined with our masculine energetic gifts.

No one is suggesting that men become more like women, or women more like men. I am suggesting that both men and women begin to fulfill the highest aspects of their being, which encompasses balancing the masculine and feminine energies available to all. I am also saying that we are all equal/valuable, and deserve to be empowered to strive for our greatest potential for joy, peace, and love. The Divine plan of mankind is to support each other and work together in order to function at our highest level as humans. Any thought, word, or action that does not promote this higher ideal is not the intention of the Universal Intelligence that created us, and is therefore less than what we are capable of, and designed to be.

The space between you and this higher ideal of life is where personal and spiritual growth must take place. The gap between your highest transformation and that of all other beings is the difference between the world we now live in, and creating a world based upon these higher principles. And the only way we achieve this level on planet earth is by each of us transcending our lower vibration to a higher one (ego-control to spiritual freedom). Don't wait for someone else to grow and change, and don't deny your responsibility because you can't "see" the whole world transforming. It does not take a shift in everyone in order for mankind to evolve; it only takes a majority to shift the energy to this higher vibration. We must be accountable for our lives and expressions of energy (thoughts, words, and actions); then generation after generation will grow up in a new, empowered program. You can see how our evolution to this highest vibration is possible. It matters not that we see this occur in our current human life.

The goal of this book is to offer re-training and tools that assist you in exchanging old ideas and habits for a new and more empowering way to see and experience life. You may have recognized that women have been far more interested and assertive toward growing and evolving than men over the past few decades. This is beginning to create an imbalance that is not good for us as a society that needs everyone functioning at our optimal levels. I believe that this is creating a great inner conflict in men, where they are lashing out with greater violence against women and other men. This fear of losing their perception of power is manifesting as force and it is not only not solving men's problems, it is harming other people. True growth requires sincere intention and true healing. It is my assertion that men are now ready to evaluate their lives and take the steps necessary to heal and grow.

As you read through *The Empower Model for Men*, allow the concepts to sink in and use your awareness to notice what you are feeling. This may be information that you are receiving for the first time, or wisdom that keeps coming around for you and has been trying to get your attention for a while now. Recognize that this is how spirit works, and it will continue to remind you of what you need to learn, do, or be, in order to heal and grow in some manner. Sometimes these reminders are gentle and other times not so much. Take this opportunity to listen, trust, and act accordingly.

On the other hand, you may read something that seems to go against your grain and may appear to contradict some strongly held belief. You may feel personally challenged and upset. Again, check into your feelings and try to figure out if the beliefs you were holding onto are from your higher knowing or are someone else's "stuff". Always decide for yourself what beliefs feel more empowering for you, and then choose those. Usually those things that give us the strongest reactions are the things that offer the most insight and opportunity to learn and grow. So don't summarily dismiss information that is new or different. Sometimes these new concepts can be incorporated into existing beliefs and fill in some of the missing pieces to the puzzle.

I love this quote by Bruce Lee, "A teacher is never a giver of truth; he is a guide, a pointer to the truth that each student must find for himself." In the end, you always get out of this process what you put into it, so if you approach the information in this book as a guide to your highest truth, you will certainly learn what is most relevant and supportive for you. Take ownership for your life and be empowered with diligence, strength, faith, and commitment toward creating a life more closely connected to your highest purpose and fulfillment. *Wishing you all the best on your journey!*

CHAPTER 1:
EDUCATE

"Yesterday I was clever, so I wanted to change the world. Today I am wise, so I am changing myself."
– Rumi

Personal and Spiritual Growth

Personal growth supports the creation of circumstances and experiences that promote a greater level of fulfillment in our lives and contribution to the world. It involves being accountable and taking full ownership of the choices you make on a daily basis. It implies that our time in this human life matters and should be lived with passion, urgency, and appreciation, for it is temporary and brief. It is not to be squandered or left to the designs of other people.

Spiritual growth involves the realization and acceptance of the truth about our higher nature. It requires us to go within, and beyond our physical senses, to further develop our connection to the Source of all life. It is an acknowledgment that we and all things are actually energy; therefore we are connected to Source and to all of creation (which obviously includes other people).

This confers the truth that we are all capable of living the divine qualities inherent in our existence, and we are to share them equally with all others.

Personal and spiritual growth work together. We are spiritual beings having a human experience, so in this human life we cannot have one without the other. Personal growth utilizes spiritual concepts in order to move beyond the energy of ego that has become pervasive in this physical world. It requires us to find within us the means to fulfill our human/physical needs while enveloped in our higher spiritual consciousness.

Upon incarnation, we release the memory of our prior existence, including our true identity, purpose, and plans for our soul journey; we are immersed into an ego culture and false education from the time of our human birth. Therefore, at some point on our journey, when we direct our free will toward an awakening to our higher truth, we will need to heal from the consequences of our false education, and re-learn (remember) our true path.

The steady application of this process of healing and re-training is what leads to personal and spiritual growth. I have endeavored within the **Empower Model** system to assist you with this process. Regardless of the teacher or method, this is an individual journey. The challenges are great, and there are plenty of ups and downs. However, the rewards of pursuing this path on a personal level, versus remaining stuck in an unsatisfying life, are immeasurable. You will find the means to truly love yourself, and therefore others. You will develop inner peace and strength that supports all of your relationships in a very positive way. And you will find the greatest possible fulfillment while offering your unique gifts, skills, and purpose in support of many others.

"Knowing yourself is the beginning of all wisdom."
– Aristotle

Understanding the REAL You

We have all learned to create the persona that we show to the world. This was developed over our lifetime of being influence by others. More than that, as men, we are influenced not only by those we directly associate with, but from an historical perception that has narrowly and falsely defined us. Maybe these definitions were once a truer reflection of the requirements of being a man in the world. However, this was still primarily based upon survival of the human form under the conditions in which humans existed in the past. Perhaps it is time to evolve and adapt to the needs of our present day.

So there is a belief that even from birth a boy is this, but not that, in order to grow into some previously defined and therefore acceptable parameter. Whether this is/was good, bad or indifferent is not really the issue. It is what it is, the past. What matters most is an honest evaluation of the present. The real question is if the old model still works today. Are men fully empowered to utilize all of their human and spiritual gifts for the fulfillment of their divine purpose and the betterment of humankind? Are we now functioning at our highest level? The real you is designed to be so much more than you may have realized.

In totality we are all both spiritual *and* human beings. It has correctly been said that we are spiritual beings having a human experience, and yet don't we focus nearly all of our attention on our humanity? This is somewhat understandable since this is truly the most fragile part of us, the part that is temporary, and the part

15

that is typically judged by the outside world. Yet we have the ability within us to develop both aspects of ourselves and in doing so attain so much more of what we really want in life, rather than simply focusing on the survival and acceptance of our human form. This is in fact the key to understanding the real you!

Now let's go to that false persona that has become our outward personality. Our perception of the world is largely developed as a direct reflection of the opinions, beliefs, judgments, fear, insecurities, and self-interest from those around us. We are not only influenced by our family, teachers, friends, neighbors, and clergy, but also from the media, national interests, racial history, etc. All of these outside sources are not a coincidence and are in fact designed to be part of your life path, but more about that later. So, all of these factors have shaped and molded you into the person you are today. Even if you have rebelled against or risen above some of these factors, you still have within you a deep-seated proclivity toward their views. This is why so many who exclaim that they will never turn into their parents or repeat certain patterns of behavior so often do. It takes more than a strong will and great intention to define and determine your own empowered life path. It literally takes a shift within that is preceded by a process of inner healing and growth.

What you need to know is that while all of this outside conditioning may reflect who you think you are today, at some point (hopefully now) it becomes your choice to accept it or change it according to the desires you want for your own life. The purpose of this book is to support you in understanding (or remembering) this truth, and then offer some practical steps you may take in order to examine and re-train your thinking toward creating the life that is most fulfilling to you. First, let's examine more thoroughly some of the factors that have led you to this point.

As children we are certainly the most vulnerable and impressionable to outside influences. How we react to these influences can vary according to the personality traits that we have decided to bring into this world to explore and experience. For example, two children can grow up in the same environment with similar outside stimulation, and yet they may react and develop very differently. Some of us are more sensitive, cooperative, and compliant, and others of us are more aggressive, combative, and independent. Yet in their own way every child is greatly influenced during their upbringing, and this has tremendous ramifications as to how they see themselves and the world around them.

The truth is that regardless of a shared environment, we each have our own unique gifts, qualities, and purpose. Unfortunately, when outside influences determine that some qualities are preferred over others, the potential for joy and success may be diminished in the mind of an individual whose skills are less appreciated. So in order to be accepted you may alter your true identity, and therefore limit your greatness. Of course, we are all here to share our truth and light, and to be the highest expression of who we came here to be. If you have suppressed or underdeveloped your greatest gifts, you need to shift your understanding of who you truly are.

Again, as children we are physically and emotionally ill-equipped to disagree with or defy adults, even if we have an inner calling that we know to be true, we will gradually learn to comply with others to the detriment of our higher knowing. This is significant because not only have we undermined our true selves in favor of other people's view of who we should be, but we have now also set a pattern of choosing to look for respect and approval from outside sources rather than within our own inner knowing. Even though we have come about this way of defining ourselves very innocently, it profoundly affects our experiences and life path. In our process of growing up and developing, we take in all of this information and energy. Some of it is useful and supportive toward building healthy self-love and self-identification, while other input simply tears us down and reinforces a false identity and negative perception of ourselves. And all of that "stuff" comes from other people. You can see how very quickly we forget our knowing of our spirits higher journey.

Those who have taught us were always coming from their place of awareness of who they thought *they* were. So there is no justification or cause to blame, judge, or criticize anyone else. If they could have done better or differently they would have. With much of humanity living in such an unconscious state it is no surprise that society has promoted the negative mental patterns of abuse, fear, discrimination, separation, selfishness, judgment, and hate that is so prevalent. This is why, and you will see it throughout this book, it is so important for each of us to become empowered in a way that develops love, unity, compassion, cooperation, and peace. This not only serves you with respect to the personal and spiritual growth you seek, but ultimately it is the only way for humanity to evolve and sustain life on this planet.

So the real you is not the accumulation of baggage you have picked up along the way. The real you is not your past at all, nor is it anyone else's expectations of you. The real you is a perfect, loving, unlimited, permanent spiritual being who in this very moment is experiencing life in a somewhat limited, temporary human form. The real you was designed to live and express your unique gifts and purpose, with joy and fulfillment. It is your opportunity and responsibility to decide how you are going to live your life, how you are going to see yourself and others, and what it is that you most desire to experience going forward. Your past has put you in real circumstances from which you must operate, but they need not define you or your potential.

"Who looks outside, dreams. Who looks inside, awakens."
- Carl Jung

The Difference between Spirit and Ego

Throughout this book I will refer to ego or spirit as a force or influence that may either control or support some aspect of our life path. Neither ego nor spirit is outside of us, doing things to us. They are terms that represent a pervasive quality within us that influences our energetic patterns. When we align with the energy of spirit we are connected to the life force that comes from Source, the higher, loving, permanent aspect of ourselves. When we are controlled by ego (ours or others), we reside in a state that is absent of spirit. From this place we struggle with the perception of impermanence and fear.

In the movie *Star Wars*, they talk about "the force", which is a subtle reference to spirit. Unfortunately, for most men the strongest force is ego. Ego defines our false, self-centered, and self-destructive nature. It is said that ego stands for **E**dging **G**od **O**ut. Others who do not understand this truth might say that ego is self-confidence, self-sufficiency, pride in accomplishment, or that it is our drive to push us to achievement. Yet in truth ego is a perversion of these things.

It is interested only with how things affect and impact us individually. Ego is extremely concerned with how we are perceived and judged by others. And while it is telling us what we

19

should be, it is also whispering, "You are not enough". It knows that it is only here for a short time since it is attached to the physical form and personality, so it will defend itself to the death (literally) to get the recognition and allegiance it thinks it deserves. And ego will attack anyone who gets in its way. Short-term gain is its preference, because once the temporary satisfaction wears off you are onto the pursuit of the next short-term pleasure. You are never satisfied or fulfilled because there is always someone else's approval to obtain, or another who has more stuff than you, and therefore by comparison, something more to attain.

This is where most people live their life. And certainly this pertains to how men have been taught to see their role in the world. Remember bigger, faster, stronger, smarter, etc. from the Introduction? We are so caught up in the physical. What something or someone looks like, the cost or value of some material object, or how much money or power we have over others. We have to win. And in this game there can be no winners without making someone a loser. Competition is fine, but ego is insatiable. And making someone the loser always creates suffering, and sometimes leads to hate, revenge, violence, or death.

Ego is in direct conflict with spirit, and the two are mutually exclusive. Spirit is the energy that connects us to Source and to all of creation. So when you are focusing on your spirit you are tapping into an unlimited supply of Universal love, peace, and wisdom that not only supports you in your human life, but is naturally compatible with the spirit in others. Ego tells you what you *want*, based upon what you perceive is missing, which you can only attempt to fill from the outside. You are driven by what others have, and what the world (media, advertisers, etc.) tells you that you should want.

Spirit knows what you *need*; in order to heal, grow, and transform to a higher state of being. Spirit is patient (because it always was and always will be) and loves you unconditionally, because it cannot do otherwise. Spirit knows that fulfillment and wellness come only from an inner connection and higher awareness. So while we as humans have largely ignored this ever present extension of Divinity, it nevertheless is always ready and available to assist us. It will not interfere with free will, so you must intentionally shift into this space of connection.

We all have ego, and so long as we are living this human life it is not going anywhere. However it is not necessary or beneficial to continually strive to claim superiority over others (in big or small ways) simply by a comparison of possessions or qualities. As you awaken to spirit you will still confront ego on a fairly regular basis, but you can see it differently. Just observe it and allow it to be. It no longer needs to run or ruin your life; it can now be a gauge to teach you where you still have some resistance to inner growth and are in need of further healing.

A large part of true empowerment involves developing the awareness to understand the motivation behind what we are doing and how it affects us and other people. By being present and aware we are able to make choices that support our highest good and that of others. If we are less attached to ego, winning can take on a whole new and expanded meaning. Your new mantra becomes, "this or something better, for the highest good of all involved."

We will talk about spirit and ego throughout this book, so you now have a basic understanding of the difference and where one leads to personal growth and the other supports selfishness, conflict, fear, and suffering. Some may think by choosing spirit over ego that they have to compromise their dreams and desires.

21

This is simply not true, though your ego will tell you this every chance it gets. In fact living within the context of spiritual awareness leads you to identify the things that are most important toward living in complete joy and fulfillment on a deeper more sustainable basis.

Learning to utilize this gift opens doors of opportunity that previously would not have been available because you are seeing through the unlimited vision of spirit instead of from the self-defeating lies of ego. Remember, spirit always says – "you are enough", while ego says just the opposite. As you move down your life path everything evolves and changes, life is fluid, so you will continually be checking in with spirit to evaluate and understand the best options. You will be tempted to fall back to the familiar voice of ego that's looking for the easy way out, the quick fix. And therein lies the challenge of the human experience for one who is on a path of personal and spiritual growth. Just know that the rewards are greater than you can now imagine on both a personal and Universal scale.

I like to summarize the difference with the phrase egoic control vs. spiritual freedom. Our ego is a thing that controls us by limiting our perceptions and possibilities, in line with outside standards, expectations, and comparisons. Spirit allows us to find, develop, and appreciate our own inner purpose, gifts, and passions, in support of creating and living our lives in greater fulfillment.

This is why people say they are "in-spired" when they have some breakthrough that offers bliss, fulfillment, and benefit to themselves and others. For now, in this re-education process, recognize that you have a higher aspect of yourself that is your true nature. Utilize your awareness in the present moment to consciously identify the force that is leading your thoughts, words, and actions. Are they supportive to your happiness, or are they primarily destructive? Ego thrives in an environment of unconscious living, which causes all of the suffering we experience as humans. Instead, be open, present, and mindful, and you will gain the wisdom to shift your life.

"The only journey is the journey within."
- **Rainer Maria Rilke**

The Development of Inner Strength in Men

Probably the greatest transformation needed for men as a group is to begin to shift more focus on developing inner strength. This is because we tend to be so focused on the external that our inner character is often underdeveloped. As a rule, men are overly concerned with outward appearance, with what things look like on or from the outside. We are visual creatures and on top of that, we are highly competitive. So we are continually striving for approval in the things that are more surface or superficial. It is not a giant leap of understanding to see how this often leads to our downfall. If we are under developed from an inner perspective, our outer strengths can become weaknesses. And in any case, we are out of balance which is always unhealthy.

Focusing on outer appearance is our preeminent disposition and in many cases our highest priority. We expend so much energy pursuing the things that are impermanent, transient, and always pass away. And we often spend so little time and effort on the things that matter most and are in fact permanent. Developing inner strength is not in conflict with our outer strength. In fact, it makes us complete human beings capable of even greater outer accomplishment. It is also the most critical part of personal and spiritual growth, and the qualities that will lead to us evolving as a species.

I am classifying "inner" as our spirit nature and "outer" as our human form and ego nature. Strength obviously refers to growing, healing, developing, utilizing, and empowering. Inner strength is where your true power lies. Outer strength is certainly useful for doing work of a physically-challenging nature, and when it refers to a foundation of good health for the body, it is very positive. But if not tempered with inner strength, it can be more of a façade that masks ego-control, or a tool for abuse and violence.

All people are concerned about their bodies, for health, appearance, attractiveness to others, and sometimes for our work. We clearly need our bodies in order for our spirit to experience life as a human. And there is an entire chapter in this book devoted to Wellness, including the health of your physical body. So I am not undervaluing the importance of the human form. However, for men it can become an obsession. Not only are we judging ourselves and each other by our physical form (and have done so since the beginning of time), but we certainly judge, classify, and objectify women according to their physical appearance as well.

We sabotage our self-worth or that of someone else every time we judge by these standards, which by the way, are arbitrarily determined by our culture. These perceptions are further promoted by the greed of companies that earn their profits by telling you that you are not good enough, unless you use their products or services. Every advertisement splashed with the image of beauty and youth that is unattainable by an overwhelming majority of the population is feeding our false identity and insecurity. This all fuels our vanity, which is ego run amuck, and we lose the truth of what really matters within this mindless pursuit of approval. This learned behavior and thought process are passed on from parent to child, from generation to generation. It is certainly not necessary to abandon our desire for outer health, beauty, or attractiveness; this is more about recognizing the greater value of the inner beauty that is our highest form.

Focusing on men as we are, not everyone can be big, strong, lean, tall, or able-bodied in comparison to some arbitrary scale, nor can we all rise to the same intellectual aptitude. And for those who believe that they embody any of these higher standards or qualities, without further contribution does it really have societal value, or render you more worthy or superior to another? It does not directly relate to your being more joyful, loving, peaceful, and compassionate. Plus, many of these qualities are temporary and fade away as you get older. Just as troubling (if not more so) is to judge yourself as unworthy for not having these "ideal" qualities. You need to shift your belief system to recognize your own inner value and strength. Judging anyone based on your feelings of jealousy or inferiority, is no better than someone who is boasting about their physical prowess. Wherever we are on this comparative scale, we all need to begin to develop and recognize our true value and worth, and place less of an emphasis on physical appearance. Inner strength is about accepting ourselves and others as we are.

Our physical qualities are largely determined by our parents (our genes) anyway. So what is your personal contribution to society, being physically attractive due to the genes that created your human form? Clearly I am saying all of this to make a point. There is nothing wrong with having the Adonis body and attractive features. Actually, your physical form was specifically designed as part of your life path, so it does serve a purpose. However, it does not give you any superiority over others or make you more valuable or more worthy of a healthy self-image. The most important and highest attributes come from spirit, which is a perfection that we all share equally.

So what about me? Like most, I grew up in an environment that greatly emphasized outside appearance. The description of a person nearly always included some physical attribute. My parents are relatively short, but they were fit and athletic. So that would describe me as well. My father would often appear enthralled that someone was over six feet tall and/or good looking. "He was a good guy, big guy - around 6'-4" I think", he would exclaim. My father has always been very competitive; he was a champion wrestler in school and a power lifter in his twenties. As a kid I liked to play sports, especially baseball and basketball, but I was relatively small. He wanted me to be bigger and stronger, so one of his ways of motivating me was to call me "weenie arms". Consequently, I was introduced to weight training at the gym at the age of 12, and still workout to this day. He grew up in a rougher environment and time than I did, so his perception of taking care of himself was to be tougher than the next guy. This of course is a way of masking our own insecurities and fear.

My father was teaching me to be a man in the world that he grew up in. He was teaching me in the way he was taught. It makes sense. This is a world where men are required to develop outer strength in order to survive and be successful (over the competition), and it is common and acceptable to display this by intimidation and physicality. Though at the time, much of this training was not supportive to my self-esteem, he was in his way showing love. I did the best I could to go along with this education, but within my nature I knew that this was somehow not truth for me. Might is not right, not for a society ready to evolve. This old way of thinking is very limiting to men, and damaging to humanity as a whole. It is based on ego, not spirit. While it has a tough exterior, it actually offers little value. It teaches that it is ok (and even necessary) to get your needs met at the expense of others. The fear is that you are not good enough or smart enough, so you must bully, intimidate, or otherwise bring down someone else to elevate your self-esteem. You cannot be empowered and at the same time functioning in fear.

When we have not developed our inner strength we teach people based on the perceptions caused by our own fear. We care about someone so we don't want them to suffer from the things that scare us. But what impact does this have on the student, or on the advancement and empowerment of men? You are actually teaching them to be afraid of the same things you are afraid of, instead of encouraging them to heal from this false perception. As a kid, in the process of developing my own identity and self-esteem, this old way of defining and limiting men was disempowering. I think it encouraged me to try to fit in to other people's model for approval, instead of developing my own innate strengths. Mainly, I just felt like I did not belong. It is far better to encourage an individual to be their best in a way that supports their specific goals, gifts, interests, and personality. A healthy society needs all of our greatest contributions. I love my parents, and this is no indictment on them, they were great teachers for me, it's just an example of the importance of shifting our focus to inner strength.

I think that my story is one that is very common for men, many of us were taught to judge ourselves and others by what's apparent on the outside. This often leads to some form of dysfunctional thinking or behavior, where we either over compensate in some unhealthy way or we feel lost and depressed. We must begin to develop within ourselves more value in our inner qualities, through the process of personal development; in doing so we will raise our level of awareness and appreciation for all that we have to offer the world. In this process of personal growth, we are learning to understand, accept, and develop our own inner value and strength.

I know that women complain about body-image and judgment, but as men we are in the same boat and have, in fact, created most of the problem. I also have noticed that as women have developed more masculine qualities based in ego (not spirit), they now more freely and publicly judge and criticize men's anatomy and attributes, just as we have done to them for so long. I think that this is a pendulum swing in the other direction, but none the less a setback in consciousness for women. For the sake of empowering ourselves and all others it is time to shift our focus to the inner qualities that will support the manifestation of the outer experiences we all want. Don't we all want to be loved for who we truly are, to experience true inner peace, and to feel unity and connection with all of life? Deep down within our soul we all want to contribute to a world that provides and supports the highest qualities of life for all people.

Inner strength starts first with your intentions. Why we are doing things is often as important as what we are doing. Do we truly have a passion for this pursuit, or are we participating in order to gain someone's approval? Is this activity healthy or is it creating suffering and confirming our need for inner healing? Are we doing something that is bringing harm to someone else, which is masking our own lack of self-value? When we are doing the things that support our personal and spiritual growth we begin to gradually eliminate the things that are most harmful to ourselves and others. It then becomes about doing healthy things for the right reasons.

There are things that we need in order to satisfy our requirement for physical survival and desire for comfort, and there are things that we need in order to enhance our experience of love, peace, wisdom, and joy. The pursuit of these things brings about the experience of the full life we are here to live. However, our love, peace, wisdom, and joy are internal gifts, and as such must be developed within. Any effort to seek these from external sources is ultimately futile. To the extent that we exercise, practice, and develop our spiritual gifts, will determine our level of inner strength.

This strength will not only affect how you treat other people, it will eventually dictate the quality of the people and experiences that will show up in your life. Your joy, self-love, confidence, and empowerment will not be dependent upon what someone says or does to or around you. You won't need to react defensively or attack verbally or physically. You more easily setup the boundaries that support your wellbeing, and when people push your buttons you will not need to take it personally. This is because your happiness is not dependent upon their approval or opinion of you. When you develop these skills and qualities you will bring great benefit to yourself and others, as now your efforts and intentions are more productive and positive. This all requires great strength, and it is absolutely within your ability to live this way.

In order to utilize the highest aspect of yourself, which is spirit, you must begin to focus more attention and awareness within. And this starts by being more present. The goal is to intentionally connect with your spirit for guidance, peace, wisdom, and strength. While we are always guided and supported in our lives by an unseen spiritual team, living more consciously means to actively participate in our lives on this spiritual level. This is not an outward display for the sake of impressing or convincing others. It is a solemn inner process. We are the ones who have to choose to receive and then honor our intuition. Our outer experiences are offered up as a teaching device, designed to show us what we need to know about our inner development (or lack thereof). But if we just move through life acting and reacting without ever being fully present, we will surely miss these messages of truth – this is the definition of unconscious living.

Building our inner strength requires us to do something really radical for most of us, and that is to create space for reflection and honest self-assessment. But what if you stop *doing* for a minute, won't the world as you know it come to an end? Well, isn't that the point? To get a different result you must do things in a different way. Our ego nature has told us we must fight and struggle, primarily based upon physical or mental exertion in order to gain anything. It is more natural for us to try to control all of our outcomes in this manner, which also includes trying to control other people. What we find, if we are being honest, is great stress and frustration that things are not turning out the way we want. And even when they do it is not so satisfying because we will soon move on to the next battle. Perhaps there is some joy mixed in when for a brief moment things work out or we find some external escape. But mainly it is constant striving and doing. **What is most needed in your life, when creating a shift to more conscious living, is equal parts being, allowing, and doing.**

Inner strength requires that we first learn to accept our life as it is. This is, in fact, not a passive attitude. We take the steps necessary to fulfill our plan and purpose, but we must understand that not everything we desire will bring the desired reward. And we must not (should not) control other people to get what we want. In all that we do we intersect and integrate with the will and life path of others, so sometimes the outcome of our efforts will not produce the fruit we seek. Our inner strength comes into play in that when this happens we are not defeated because we are learning not to define ourselves by external circumstances. We also can accept that since we are all connected on a spiritual level, when one benefits we all benefit, and we can find joy in someone else's happiness. And finally, we know that since we are divinely guided and our intent now is to follow our highest path, something even better is on its way. If you just get pissed off and yell and scream whenever you don't get our way, you make yourself miserable, you make others miserable for being around you, and you totally miss the point of the lesson. This is a shift to greater spiritual understanding, awareness, and evolution. We cause so much unnecessary pain and suffering to ourselves and others simply by our childish behavior and resistance to developing our inner strength.

Throughout this book we will talk about various methods and practices for developing this inner strength. But for now know that this is a shift from false perception to higher truth that will make all of the difference in what you create in your life and how you experience it. They call it a spiritual **practice** for a reason. There are no quick fixes, and nothing to believe in or do that will instantly transform you. It takes a conscious effort that is gradual and on-going, with continual tests that will show you where you still need healing and practice. This effort requires a balance of being (which is internal) and doing (which is external). There is no greater challenge than personal /spiritual growth, and no one can do it for you. But it is the only thing that leads to the greatest joy and highest fulfillment of the life you are here to live.

"Winners compare their achievements with their goals, while losers compare their achievements with those of other people."
— **Nido Qubein**

The Higher Purpose of Competition

As I have said before, men love to compete. It is in our DNA, yet even more greatly pronounced by our ego nature, which needs to judge and compare. Historically we have competed for the best physical form, for achievement in sports, for jobs and money, for women, and more. Since we have judged our success by external rewards, our primary reason for competing is based in comparison to others. And while we like to accumulate these "trophies", we are rarely satisfied for long because we crave the attention or praise that comes with the next victory. Once again, the ego is leading us to pursue things that, by comparison, make us feel better about ourselves, without necessarily healing or changing anything. This has a temporary effect, and may completely ignore the higher value available to us.

The higher purpose of competition is to participate, learn, grow, and express our gifts. Truly the value of the competition takes place within us. We must first decide what we are interested in (what are our gifts), we must be motivated and goal oriented to grow and improve, we must learn and practice a skill (which requires sufficient effort), and we must engage with others in order to test our growth and proficiency. The point is always to give your best effort, in order to grow and expand your energy, while contributing value to your life path and the world. It is more than the traditional definition of trying to be better than another person or team.

The outcome of a contest will give you a clue as to where you can go from here; which is the point of personal growth. Did I accomplish my goal? And do I now decide to pursue a new goal? Or do I now know more specifically where I can improve? They say that we learn more in defeat than in victory. If your reason for competing is personal growth, then this is true, but if you are just in it for the attention or accolades you will probably not learn or grow much either way.

I have always loved sports (playing and watching), and am a baseball fanatic. I admit that I still feel some pride when my fantasy baseball team wins the championship (I know, nerd alert!). And on the golf course I can feel the elation of a good shot or the disappointment of a poor one. This is because I am interested in doing my best, and it is fun to succeed. But my winning or losing does not have to degrade, destroy, or diminish the others participating in the sport, or in life. And the same is true for the teams I may root for. Truly, we are defined more by how we treat others in and around the competition than whether we win or lose. So as long as we are developing our inner strength and are conscious about the way in which we utilize our external gifts and outcomes, we can easily and rightfully enjoy the competition. And just as importantly, we can feel joy in the victories that others experience, because it is easy and natural for us to also support their growth.

By definition a contest is a test performed with/against others. When we are focused on personal growth we will find great value in the contests that relate to fulfilling our higher purpose. And this always involves supporting others on their highest path as well. So whenever you are competing, do it with integrity. Whether it is a hobby or a professional competition, or if you are competing for a new job or a promotion, or if you are "competing" for someone's affection, do it with the highest

33

integrity. If you cheat, trick, or manipulate others in order to "win", you have not served yours or anyone's highest interest. The victory will create consequences somewhere down the path that will necessitate experiences for the purpose of learning that will likely be unpleasant.

A real life example of this, which is currently in the news, involves baseball players who were caught using PED's (performance enhancing drugs). The temporary "benefit" from cheating may have garnered better contracts and statistics, however, the penalties incurred caused a loss of income and a damaged reputation. The truth is that these are only the public consequences, but I suspect that there is a great deal of additional fallout that these players will experience on a personal level. Ultimately, our mistakes are not about punishment, they are about recognizing our lessons on a deeper level, seeking atonement, and choosing a higher path.

This is not just about sports, though sports are significant in our culture (especially for men), anything we strive for as a goal can be looked at as a competition. Again, this is because the contest takes place primarily within ourselves and is about personal growth. For instance, I have written this self-help book with the intention of serving those who may benefit from its message, and for the goal of advancing my own personal growth. Maybe the author of the book next to mine on the shelf has a similar desire, with a slightly different message and audience. Some may think we are competing, but in my world I am not limited by the idea that some will choose to buy the other book instead of mine. I know that those who resonate with the energy of my book will be drawn to read it. And for those who choose the other book I am equally supportive. As the reader, this is your path, and not mine. I have fulfilled my part in achieving my goal by creating and publishing the book, any additional benefit that may come my way is very appreciated, but incidental.

While you are determining your goals, which should reflect your highest desires, choose to pursue the things that bring you the most value. A contest always involves others, some you want to work with or be with, and others you will compete against. It is most beneficial that you always treat others with kindness and respect, the same things that you want them to show you. Whenever possible strive for the win-win. You benefit most from the value of the experience, so be defined as one who does their best, and who grows and improves while supporting others in the process. The journey is always more important than the outcome.

"It is not easy to find happiness in ourselves, and it is not possible to find it elsewhere."
- Agnes Repplier

A Greater View of our Life Circumstances

What about our life circumstances? We were initially placed or born into a specific family, which provided the genetics that primarily determine our physical, mental, and emotional qualities in this life. Plus, this family taught us certain values and beliefs, and gave us our initial socio-economic structure. Additionally, we were born into a geographic location that gave us a nationality and local affiliation, as well as more education about values and beliefs. We were also born into a specific time in the history of mankind, which has countless ramifications in our daily life. So life is a game of chance, whatever hand we were dealt, that's just how it goes. Luck of the draw, right? That sounds pretty disempowering and fatalistic to me.

Our initial life circumstances seem to give us some kind of parameters that would suggest the value or opportunities we are to have. If there was no spiritual aspect of life, that would be hard to argue against. In fact since so many people over time have believed this (even those who considered themselves religious), it is easy to see how we have created so much separation and division in the world. The whole structure of a caste system is based on this principle. For one born into "unfortunate" circumstances, physical survival would be the primary objective. Your chance at happiness would be based upon the life circumstances you were born into. And for those less fortunate, well, too bad, thanks for playing the game. The "haves" would rightfully be superior and feel either pity or disgust for the "have-nots". And the "have-nots" would be inferior and feel envy, jealousy, or hatred for the "haves". This might even cause wars, violence, discrimination, corruption, greed, gluttony, poverty, famine, etc. Oh wait, it did! And what about the physical life that ends relatively young, they did not even get a full opportunity to play the game.

This view of humanity and of the world is not sustainable. And it is not truth. We must all begin to recognize and access the higher aspects of who we are. We are spiritual beings having a human experience and it is time to shift into that higher state of knowing and being. Is life easy in this world we have created? No. Can it be better? Yes. Let me give you another view of your life circumstances that is much more empowering, and is in alignment with Divine truth.

Since our spiritual nature is permanent, and did not start with this physical incarnation, you have been in existence on the level of spirit beyond time and space. From this situation you decide when you are ready to have another human experience (incarnation). It is believed that there is a system for this and that you are Divinely Guided and supported in this process by enlightened energy beings. Together you review your lives and determine what it is that you want to experience in order to learn, grow, expand your light, and otherwise ascend to a higher vibrational level. The human experience is designed to further expand the soul; it is not necessarily designed for your comfort and popularity.

All of those initial life circumstances that were described above were decided by you on a soul level. That means that your parents, genetics, family, geography, and birth date are all a part of the life path *you* intended to experience on this soul journey. This was no accident. How you deal with these circumstances and what you decide to experience as you progress through life is up to your free will, although, with awareness, you can always access your spirit for guidance. In addition to learning and growing, your life design factors in a thing called karma. Just as the decisions we make and the things we do in this life have consequences in this life, sometimes these consequences do not manifest (or come into balance) until a future life. Therefore, it is necessary to experience aspects of life and interaction with certain other individual souls, in order to restore balance and a deeper soul contribution. Sometimes these karmic experiences can feel either joyful or very challenging. However, this is always meant to support the growth of the soul, and never to punish, though this is largely misinterpreted by the ego.

Regardless of what you might think about your life circumstances, you are here on purpose, in order to fulfill your spirit's plan for growth and ascension. We have all had many lives in various dimensions, and have experienced human lives in each gender, various nationalities, religions, etc. Some souls who have otherwise completed their evolutionary tract, have agreed to incarnate into this world purely for the purpose of supporting humankind in both vibrational and material influence. When we have awakened to this higher understanding, it becomes quite unreasonable to look upon another person with hatred just because they have different circumstances than us. Instead we can have compassion and appreciation for the challenges they have assumed in this life in order to advance their soul.

"Knowledge comes from learning. Wisdom comes from living."
Anthony Douglas Williams

The True Value of Experience

Your experiences are Divinely Guided and on purpose. They come from spirit and offer you great insight as to your state of being. I say that they are Divinely Guided because they are always consistent with spiritual principles. They are consequences of your energetic expressions. When some people think of a Divine presence or interaction they think about something outside of themselves – "God" intervened. But I am claiming that each of us, within our own Divine connection to Source, is fully equipped to function in this capacity at all times. Yet unfortunately we are often unaware of this process and ability.

Our experiences are more than just objective events that happen in our life. They also include our intentions, our perceptions, our feelings, and our energetic reaction. In the moment we are creating an experience (large or small) we are expressing various qualities on the level of energy. All of this is manifesting into what we experience with our physical form and senses. When we are only aware of the outcome of the experience in terms of getting what we want or don't want (pleasure or suffering), we are missing a tremendous opportunity to recognize what is going on within us on a deeper level. The reason that this is so important for everyone is that if we are not functioning on the level of awareness we will continue to require a repeat of the same experiences until we finally realize the lesson being taught.

This is the difference between living consciously or unconsciously, between being empowered by spirit or enslaved by ego. Ego abides in a world where things happen to us. If we are fortunate enough, hardworking, and follow the rules established by others, maybe we will have more "good" experiences than "bad" ones. But this is a naïve view of what is really creating your experiences. Again, this is judging the value of an experience based upon the outcome, which may be somewhat outside of our control.

One reason why the outcome of our experiences is outside of our control is because we are intersecting with the expressions of energy that are manifesting the experience of the person(s) we are interacting with. We cannot all get what we think we want all of the time. Especially when so many are functioning primarily from their ego, which is only interested in our own selfish desires and survival. We then take the undesired outcome and turn that into frustration, disappointment, anger, stress, etc. If we happen to get the outcome we want, there is still a lack of peace because we are concerned about either the consequences of getting our way, or what the result will be in the next experience.

With a spiritual approach to experiences, we can look for the value in all that shows up in our lives. We can understand on a deeper level that we are attracting external experiences that are in alignment with our inner state of being. If something unpleasant comes to us, and we have a negative reaction, we know that we are in need of some form of inner healing, and possibly a change in our thinking or behavior. If an unpleasant experience occurs, and we remain unattached to our ego, we can move on down the path with acceptance of what is, while taking whatever positive actions we can take. If we have a pleasant experience, we recognize a validation of a positive state of inner being (with respect to the subject of the experience). You can see that, from this approach, all of these experiences now have great value. All experiences from this standpoint are received with appreciation for the opportunity to learn and grow. And gratitude is always an energy that inspires the greater qualities we are seeking.

This is where wisdom is attained from living. This shift requires a consistent development of personal and spiritual growth. The words on the page are information that leads to knowledge, but applying this knowledge in your life leads to wisdom. I think that you can see that when one is living from a place of wisdom (or at least the intention of seeking wisdom) they are in a position to create experiences and opportunities for living a more empowered and joyful life. We are not relying on luck, nor are we waiting or wishing for someone or something to save us. We are fully capable and accountable for the life we lead and how we experience it.

Now you see the value of your experiences from a higher (spiritual) perspective. What about the experiences themselves? The way our soul chose to learn, grow, and expand at this time is by experiencing life in human form. So clearly our experiences have tremendous value far beyond the immediate and temporary impact to your egoic perception. We came into this world at this specific time to experience our unique life path, as have all other people on the planet.

While we are each on our own path, there are many similar patterns of experience that most, if not all, people are here to experience. We usually define ourselves early on based upon the input from others. And then at some point, when we are in a greater position of influence over our own lives, we are given opportunities to overcome these false and limiting beliefs about ourselves. Perhaps we will recognize our true value, discover and develop our unique gifts, transform into an empowered being, create and live a joyful, peaceful life filled with love, and offer higher service to others. The choice is always ours. Regardless of what initial life circumstances we agreed to before birth (or how it compares to anyone else), this is the path of a soul that is ascending.

Once we are born into human form we lose our memory of our true identity and our soul journey. We are operating from free will, but our spiritual nature is always with us. Many people never get past the level of mere human survival. Others progress along the continuum until they succumb to too much resistance (ego). If you are reading this book there is a good chance that this teaching resonates with you, and your spirit is guiding you to keep going toward the recognition and accumulation of greater wisdom and completion of your higher purpose.

If you need to look back at some of the more significant experiences in your past for the purpose of healing, then do so. But I suggest that you do this with a new, more empowered mindset. You may have felt like a victim, where it appeared that someone brought you great pain, harm, embarrassment, or some other suffering. Or you may have regrets or remorse about the suffering you think that you inflicted upon someone else. Or maybe the experience was an accident, disease, or loss of someone close to you. The healing that is required is for you to see these experiences for what they were, and not continue to "carry" them with you under a false and disempowering misconception.

The truth is, that on a soul level, you were guided to your experiences to learn and understand about where you need more healing, self-love, wisdom, or a shift to a higher perspective in order to fulfill your soul's purpose. Even experiences that seem horrific on a human level have their foundation and motivation from a perspective of spiritual truth for the people involved. You can accept this as a learning tool for expansion and growth, or you can reject this and relegate yourself to overwhelming fear, anger, pain, and confusion. "Why" cannot always be explained in terms that our human mind can comprehend, without considering a more expansive viewpoint. Remember, our human mind (in this respect) is a compilation of the misinformation and therefore false teaching of our lower ego form. Sometimes you need to use your logic to uncover or discover the means to find the healthiest viewpoint for yourself and others. Yet in order to see a higher truth you need to access a higher perspective.

Since your experiences are a reflection of your inner energetic state in a specific moment in time, they are designed to have a limited shelf life. Once we see the value of the teaching we are free to heal, grow, and create new, more empowering experiences from which to continue our journey. Holding on to a past experience is a choice! Utilize your higher awareness to glean what is most beneficial, accept the way in which the lesson came to you, and release it with thanks and appreciation. You are on a higher path now toward creating the life you most desire. Stop giving attention to the things you do not desire. Recognize your higher purpose in creating the experience, which helps you define yourself as one who is empowered with Divine creation. Now

42

utilize your gift for greater healing, self-love, and service to the world.

This healthy perspective will build an inner strength and energy that will be felt by those around you in a very supportive way. By healing ourselves (including our beliefs and perceptions) we are of greater value to others as well. You can see how this new perspective would offer a superior platform from which to manifest more joyful, supportive experiences. It is a matter of expressing a higher energy.

"If you are depressed you are living in the past; if you are anxious you are living in the future; if you are at peace you are living in the present."
– Lao Tzu

Living in the Present Moment

Who we *are* is defined in each present moment. Who we *were* is in the past, and who we *will become* is a dream full of possibilities yet to be lived. So our true power for creating the life we want happens in the present. Therefore, place your focus and highest intentions in the present moment. If you don't like who you were, based on some experience from the past, move your consciousness into the present and be who you *do* like.

Whether we are intently involved in personal growth, which often represents a substantial change and transformation from who we previously perceived ourselves to be, or we are currently living the healthy balanced life that brings us the greatest joy and satisfaction, present moment awareness is key. We are most conscious (connected to spirit) in the present moment when we are "noticing" our life in whatever situation or experience we find ourselves. This noticing supports us in fully living each moment. And in doing so we are aware of our thoughts, actions, and choices, and how they impact us and others.

This takes steady practice and is a process of re-training our minds. In the meantime we will surely go unconscious quite often, and fall into our old habitual patterns. However, with awareness we can quickly regain our present moment noticing and once again live more fully and intentionally. This will require us to slow down and be more mindful.

In Buddhism, mindfulness is the third tenant in *The Noble Eight Fold Path*, and is at the heart of the Buddha's teaching. Mindfulness is remembering to come back to the present moment. The practice is to find ways to sustain appropriate attention throughout the day. Right mindfulness accepts everything without judging or reacting. The point for us is not to worry about achieving full attainment of mindfulness, but instead to make progress with the sincere effort of utilizing our full attention.

When we are able to begin to live more presently, we have greater power toward actively creating our lives. Everything we do can take on more significance because we can do more things that are in alignment with our higher purpose. Sometimes finding more joy in our lives requires us to do things in our life more joyfully, as opposed to looking for something new to come along and *give* joy to us. We are now more aware of when we are doing our best or when we are just doing enough to get by. Personal and spiritual growth is about being and doing on a higher level, for the benefit of ourselves and all others. When we are noticing all that is happening within and without, we are *being*, which is, consciously speaking, higher than *doing*.

Being more mindful of the present moment will also help us in our relationships. We can be more attentive and supportive to others as we will now be more aware of our surroundings and connections to those around us. When we are spending time with our loved ones for instance, we are more available to give and receive on all levels. Our communications will become so much more effective, as you are now more willing to listen. When you are each present for the other you will both feel more respected and valued. If you want one key to a more successful, fulfilling, and loving relationship, this is it. **Be Present with each other!**

Being present reminds you to breathe, to allow and accept when something undesired is happening outside of your control. And it allows you to take appropriate positive steps (thoughts and actions) when you can improve your situation. Being present supports your relationships with friends, family, co-workers, and others. And it allows you to notice your thoughts if and when they turn negative or disempowering. You now have the opportunity to change a thought or activity to something more supportive.

But most of all, being present allows you to connect to your Divine Source. Whether you are in meditation or doing some routine activity, you can still the mind and seek guidance from spirit, leading you to greater power in the present moment. Utilize this time to get clear within your intentions about how to proceed in whatever situation you would like clarity of truth. When your mind is stuck in the past or too focused on the future, you will miss the truth that you are being shown in the present moment. So always work toward being more present and mindful in all you do.

"If you would create something, you must be something."
- **Johann Wolfgang von Goethe**

You are able to Create the Life you Desire

I am sure that you have heard the saying, "Thoughts are things", and that your thoughts manifest into your physical reality. As was discussed earlier, our initial life circumstances are the external reality of our physical existence in the early stages of life, and this was planned prior to incarnation. As we grow beyond our childhood years, our free will takes on a more direct consequence in the manifesting of our external reality. At this stage we have been primarily developed and defined by our environment, with little if any conscious connection to our true essence and spirit journey, yet we are now exercising our independence and believe that we can make choices in support of our own wellbeing. So we are busy creating all that shows up in our lives from a mind that is run by ego and unaware of its great potential for manifesting what we truly want in life. Since much of what shows up feels negative, we tend to support the false belief that things are *"happening to us"*.

Naturally we create many learning experiences that involve trial and error, along with the requisite amount of suffering and drama. Many people never leave this track, and never realize their true higher potential for creating a life filled with the qualities we all desire. Others have awakened to a higher understanding of their life purpose and inherent creative power. With proper understanding they can design a pattern of thoughts that support the creation of that which they desire, and with present moment awareness they can observe their thoughts and, when necessary, re-align them with their higher purpose.

According to Jerry and Esther Hicks in their wonderful book, *The Law of Attraction*, "The more you come to understand the power of the Law of Attraction, the more interest you will have in deliberately directing your thoughts – for you get what you think about, whether you want it or not."[1]   All that shows up in our external life is actually a reflection of what we are thinking, feeling, and believing on the inside. It is merely a mirror image. Therefore, the true reality is in the energetic seeds that created the outer images. This is true regardless of the experience that shows up. And this is why we are totally accountable and responsible for our lives. We cannot blame God or other people; it is all on us. The greater the awareness and acceptance of this truth, the more able you will be to take the steps necessary to fully and consciously create the life you desire.

We must start where we are, meaning we are only able to conceive and manifest from our current place of consciousness. As we grow and transform into a higher realization of our true purpose, plan, and beingness, we will utilize our gifts to create and manifest life experiences that are far more rewarding, fulfilling, and satisfying. People create the external experiences that reflect their inner values and self-belief. In order to create experiences and circumstances that reflect a higher spiritual value and fewer limitations, we must develop ourselves internally. This takes specific and intentional action, and is a requirement for the personal and spiritual growth for which this book strongly advocates. We can only manifest that for which we are in a vibrational alignment or match.

Accordingly, when we are struggling, we tend to continue to create similarly challenging experiences, because that is where we are energetically. So we need to shift into a higher vibration in

---

[1] The Law of Attraction, by Jerry and Esther Hicks – excerpt from page 31.

order to create new, more empowering experiences. We can do this consciously and intentionally, hopefully before, and not after some devastating event. This may be a shift in your thoughts and willingness to love and care for yourself, or it may be to associate more frequently with others who are more positive and supportive, or it may include a change in lifestyle and healthier practices. These are all things that are discussed in this book. To the extent that you develop yourself internally in connection to spirit, you will be more able to create the life you want.

A Guide to Manifesting Your Highest Desires

There is a wealth of information available that details the wisdom surrounding this process. Here I am listing and summarizing some of the key steps:

1. Clearly conceive of what you want to create in your life.

While utilizing your own discernment, consider what you want to create or experience in order to bring the desired higher qualities into your life. Consider the consequences of your desire, as best you can, in order to be very clear that this is truly what you want. Do not rush this process. If this is a significant desire it is recommended that you meditate on it, ask for guidance in order to gauge how you "feel" about this choice. Then listen to any intuitive input.

Always seek to manifest only that which supports your highest good on your path of fulfilling your highest purpose. We never want to try to create things that are not consistent with this perspective, and we never desire harm to another.

2. Call upon your Divinity and utilize your faith and creative ability.

The natural law will manifest according to your thoughts/energy, to either bring what you want or don't want. Calling upon your Divinity brings support and alignment on your highest level. You are calling in experiences that promote spiritual qualities (love, peace, wisdom, joy, prosperity, wellness, etc.), so always access your Divinity.

We must believe that the possibility exists within us to manifest or receive this outer experience. I can envision all day long about dunking a basketball or playing major league baseball, for example, but I know that this is not going to happen. But I can manifest experiences and people that support higher love, peace, and prosperity, because I believe that this is within my ability to create.

What you seek is not being given to you; it is being *created by* you. There is a difference. Know that you are capable, as one created in the image of Divine Source, to create these higher qualities in your life. Release the idea that only "God", as an outside source, is capable of creation. Own and call upon this ability within yourself. This is what has always been intended for us to realize and accept.

3. Place or fix your sincere and fervent energy upon manifesting that which you desire.

Intentionally and consistently apply your expressions of energy (thoughts, words, and actions) on what you WANT to create. Be very careful to not maintain your expression of energy on what you DON'T want. Your expression of energy creates a vibration that goes out into the Universe seeking a match that may manifest into your physical reality. So the thing is first created in an energetic field of intention and unlimited potential.

You cannot manifest that for which you are not a vibrational match. So in order to attract certain things of a higher nature, you may need to shift your energy to a higher vibration. This is a great reward and benefit of personal and spiritual growth. Your desire will manifest into physical form at the appropriate time according to spirit, not your ego. This always proves to be a good thing. If everything we wanted at a particular point in time was to instantaneously manifest, we would create great chaos in our lives. So stay with your expression and it will appear when/if it's supposed to.

One very interesting factor in manifesting that which we think we want, is when our minds are fixed on two outcomes that are mutually exclusive. Part of you really wants to bring in this new experience, while another part of you is equally content without this manifestation. These two thoughts and desires will cancel themselves out, and no changes will occur. So back to step one, be very clear about what you *really* want, otherwise you may be frustrated with the results of your efforts.

4. The importance of your feelings.

Feelings are a higher energetic vibration than thoughts, so when manifesting what you want, endeavor to reinforce your thoughts with feelings. Conceive of the thing with your thoughts and intentions, but express and notice the feelings of joy, peace, or enthusiasm that either reflect your sincere passion for the thing, or the feelings you expect to have when the thing shows up. This adds power to your creative forces.

As a reminder, negative thoughts and feelings are energy as well, and work to manifest in their lower energy form. So be careful about holding strong fears, or placing your attention on the things that frighten or anger you, as these feelings add power toward creating what you don't want.

5. Utilize your awareness and mindfulness.

Train your thoughts to consistently reflect the desire to be manifested. This requires your ability to notice your thoughts on a regular basis. As a society with growing attention deficit this can be challenging for many. But if you consistently move from desire to desire, never staying on one thing long enough to solidify the attraction, it will be a difficult thing to manifest.

Notice if conditions exist that would rightfully cause you to alter or abandon your original desire. Energy flows and life changes, so as you evolve you may find a desire that supersedes your original plan.

Notice all that shows up in your life that may be connected to your manifestation. The steps leading to the manifestation may come in the form of an opportunity that suddenly appears, or a person you meet, or a powerful insight you may have. Don't miss these clues, sometimes additional steps are required of you in order to shift to a vibrational match. Things don't always materialize out of thin air (though they might).

6. Hold your thoughts while shifting and walk through the accompanying sensations.

They say, "Feel the fear, and do it anyway." This will often be required when while transforming your life you attempt to create new empowering experiences and circumstances. Change is not easy, it may require you to let go of some old established habits and comfortable ways of being and feeling. Yet since you cannot create anything that is not a vibrational match, change on a deep level is sometimes necessary. So you must stay with the uncomfortable sensations while you are developing more familiarity and comfort with the new conditions. Otherwise you will revert back and settle for old patterns of thought and experience, even though less than what you initially intended to manifest. You are literally creating a shift or expansion of consciousness, which in turn is manifesting your desire. So stay with the process, and step into that new reality.

Again, there aren't any shortcuts, so place your primary focus on personal growth and inner development. Your ability and opportunity to manifest what you want in your life will grow from a position of greater consciousness. Incidentally, as you develop, you will notice that your focus will be less on what you can manifest for yourself (or ego), but instead on how you can flow through life with a positive radiance that naturally brings joy, peace, and love to yourself and others in your world.

"The greater danger for most of us is not that our aim is to high and we miss it, but that our aim is too low and we reach it"
- Michelangelo

A Lesson on Spirituality

As we continue to set the stage for the following steps in the ***Empower Model***, I think that it is important to provide some education or clarification regarding spirituality. Sometimes people are turned off by terms that they don't understand or they misinterpret. You do not need to become *spiritual*, because, as one who comes from Source, you already are. It is not about doing or believing anything; it is about recognizing your higher truth and living from this place. You only need to expand your consciousness to allow who you truly are to shine through. People often confuse spirituality with religion. Religion may be a subset of spirituality, or it may be a limiting belief system that separates people from connecting with others and from their true Divinity. It all depends on how they are living or applying their teaching.

In truth, spirituality is the way in which you connect to Source (some call it Universal Intelligence, God, Tao, or whatever other name you prefer). This may be supported for you in a church, synagogue, temple, your home, in nature, or anywhere else. In other words you do not need a certain place, guru, or religious leader in order to practice spirituality. This is a personal connection between the Divinity within you and the Source of all that is, and beyond the consequences of our human delusion, it is always in alignment with the unity of all of creation.

It is important to make clear right now that it is my assertion that you have all of the power within you, as one created by Source, to walk your path as Source. We all do. This is why and how we are empowered to create our lives in such a way that we are truly fulfilled, and a blessing to all others. This will of course contradict some religious dogma and tradition. However, my intent is to open minds and hearts, not to offend. In my view religion may support your spirituality if: 1) it guides you to recognize your inner divinity; 2) it leads you to recognize the highest value in yourself; and 3) it leads you to recognize the highest value in ALL others.

I am teaching this higher education in order to share wisdom that leads to personal growth and healing for those ready to accept their own power. My purpose is not to condemn established religious models. I would hope that each person would decide for themselves what is appropriate for them. As we know, each tree will bear its own fruit. The fruit of the Universe is Love, Light, Peace, Joy, Unity, Equality, etc. If these are the qualities expressed by you based upon your religious practices, then you are bearing Holy fruit. If not, then you may want to take an honest look at the tree.

When one accepts that their spiritual nature is inherent and available directly, they understand that no one else is responsible or even capable of healing and growing for them. In the process of your creation, Source designed you to have all of its gifts. Many are just now learning this, and thereby accessing this power to grow, transform, and transcend. Within the model of free will, the choice to accept or reject our birthright is always up to us.

If you recognize your spiritual nature you may gain access to wisdom and healing that supports a life lived on a "higher" level. If not, you live your life based upon the whims of ego and free will, and you get what you get. But in any case, you started in a spirit form, were born into a human body with free will (while

54

maintaining a connection to spirit), then you leave your body and return to a purely spirit form. So it makes sense to not leave out our spiritual gifts within this thing we call a human life.

One of the real challenges to the fulfillment of our highest potential is a matter of education. Many have been taught that God is out there (somewhere) and in some way controls things (us and our surroundings). We are blessed or cursed, rewarded or punished, which again takes all of the accountability out of our own hands. So why ever take responsibility for our own healing, growth, and wellbeing. This teaching seems to say, "live any way you want, regardless of how it impacts anyone else (or planet earth), and then pray for God's mercy or blame God if you don't like what's happened". It seems like a life run by individual selfishness, non-accountability, and the whim of "God", who by the way is defined differently by different people all over the world. This is a very disempowering way to look at spirituality.

This is why many have abandoned religion as fallacy or been frustrated with it while trying to reconcile it to their inner truth and reality. When I hear someone say, "I don't understand why God would ....." (Fill in the blank), it makes me a little crazy. God is not doing or causing terrible things, and God is not doing or causing miracles. Instead, Source created miracle workers (us) and set them free to create a world whereby the spirit (or soul) would be able to experience life in a human form. God did not make you sick, injured or healed, born with mental or physical disability, wealthy or poverty stricken, tall or short, a certain race or gender. Otherwise I would be a bit ticked off with God for making me 5'-8", instead of 6'-2". Whatever your circumstance in life, you created it! And you can choose to understand the value of what you created, and from that position, learn, grow, transform, and transcend, as your spirit intended.

55

Spirituality is the understanding and the process by which we personally recognize and develop our connection with our spiritual nature, and grow into our highest potential. This understanding reminds us that all beings are connected in this way, and all are here to fulfill their spiritual journey. Since we are all functioning on varying levels of understanding and awareness, we see a very diverse world of humans. Any one of us can choose to recognize our higher purpose, and then focus on our personal growth, and any one of us can completely dismiss this as possible, relevant, necessary, or true. That's the beauty of free will; it supports our individuality within the context of spiritual law. However it is my contention, and a commonly-accepted principle, that we do not avoid learning our spiritual lessons, and therefore will continue to return to earth school as often as necessary. No hell or other eternal punishment, the Universe operates with love, not fear or hate.

I am offering the ***Empower Model*** teaching as a way of helping people remember who they really are, and that they are here on purpose to fulfill a higher mission. You have been designed with more gifts and abilities than you may know, that will not only facilitate the creation of a more joyful, loving life now, but also will support the growth and expansion of your soul. Utilize this time on earth wisely to bring a positive outcome for yourself and all others.

Chapter 1 Exercises

Exercise 1:
Journal your life story, in as much detail as you want, from as early in life that you want. Whatever feels relevant or significant to you is what matters. You are objectively identifying your life circumstances and the experiences that have taught how you perceive yourself and others today. Notice how you describe and define yourself, does this tell you something about your self-image?

See if you can recognize a higher purpose or value for having experienced this early education. Identify the experiences that support what you want more of in your life going forward, and what lessons taught you what you do not want in your life now.

Exercise 2:
After completing Exercise 1, where you have looked more objectively at your past, now begin to contemplate and consider what you most want to create or manifest into your life. Within an internal meditative process consider the qualities that most resemble your ideal life. You may journal or document some specific events or outcomes that you want to create in order to experience these higher qualities.

This could be as broad or specific as you want but in order to bring in the spiritual aspect (and the highest outcome) you want to identify positive qualities over specific things. Maybe you want more fulfillment and success in your career, or a loving relationship (or more love in your current relationship), or more wellness, peace, balance, or abundance.

Now, follow the steps listed above in the "Guide to manifesting your highest desires". Begin to shift your awareness and thereby your consciousness to an acceptance of the qualities you are manifesting. Begin to "see" this as your new reality. You are now planting the energetic seeds that are shifting your inner vibration to be in alignment with your desired manifestation.

CHAPTER 2:
MATTER (YOU)

"There are no extra pieces in the Universe. Everyone is here because he or she has a place to fill, and every piece must fit itself into the big jigsaw puzzle."
– Deepak Chopra

What Does "You Matter" Really Mean?

Since this is a book about personal and spiritual growth leading to more conscious living, you know that we are going to take this to a different level of understanding. In the first step of the *Empower Model* it was important to be **"Educated"** and to provide some context from which the other steps may unfold. It is appropriate now to explore the second step which is **"Matter"**. It goes beyond some of the traditionally accepted definitions.

Once again we must explore the spirit vs. ego dynamic in order to properly convey our truth. Spirit is the force that promotes healing, growth, expansion, wellbeing, and a supportive connection to others (Unity). It is the higher aspect of our life force and being. Conversely, the ego is our lower base energy that will always persuade us to focus on our perceived human limitations, and separation from Universal love and all other beings. Spirit supports the truth of inner strength, which expresses outwardly as unconditional love and compassion, and ego supports an outer appearance of strength while masking inner weakness and fear.

This distinction speaks to all people, but maybe more directly to men. *You matter* because of all the amazing things you have specifically come into this life to explore, experience, and learn. This only occurs in a state of complete freedom, recognition, and alignment with the higher aspect of Who You Are. *You matter* takes on a higher meaning as you continue to grow, transform, and overcome the challenges you have created with false and limited thinking. When living this higher path you are healthier, stronger, and more capable and inspired to live consciously for the benefit of yourself and all others.

In *You Matter*, I am offering the empowering statement that everything you do and everything you are truly matter! It matters to your spirit, because you have specifically chosen this life path with the sincere intention of completing this soul journey. Therefore, it is important to now begin to understand this unique path and purpose you have designed. This is worthy of your examination and attention, and supersedes your focus on mere survival. And *You Matter* because you are an integral part of the fabric of all of humanity. We all have a significant role to play, and we can either enhance the higher energy of unity and love, or we can deplete this energy and create chaos and further separation. Again, we are always choosing between spirit and ego. We are all light bearers, and the amount of light we will shine is dependent upon our living more consciously, and expressing this higher energetic vibration into the world.

You Matter does not mean that you are better than or superior to other people. It doesn't mean that only your needs matter, which is the selfish approach many have taken. When you are functioning from your higher awareness, your needs, along with those of others, may be met in a supportive way with greater ease. *You Matter* is a call to tend to your needs in the healthiest of ways, which uplift and empower you while adding your light to the world. If you are continually sacrificing your own needs you may be limiting or neglecting the higher opportunities for growth and healing that your spirit is offering you. While truly being accountable and responsible to those in our lives that require our assistance is commendable, we often take on other people's burdens and that becomes an excuse for avoiding taking the steps we need to experience the expansion of our own soul. We, then, miss the opportunities to reach our highest potential.

When speaking directly about men it is a bit of a mixed bag. Most are highly responsible, and function with at least the intention of high character. Yet we sometimes get lost along the way under the weight of our self-imposed responsibility, need for control, and lack of higher understanding. It is largely a matter of education in wisdom, and then practical application of these truths into our lives. This is why it is critical for men to learn and practice the education and tools of personal and spiritual growth that will support us throughout all of life's circumstances and experiences. Knowing that *You Matter* will help you to use your discernment while contemplating various choices and creating your close associations. For many, NOT knowing that you matter is a reminder of your deeper need for inner healing.

We all experience those times of fear and doubt, and it helps to remember that you do matter, and just to do your best. If you are stuck in a dark place in your life where you do not see a way out, please remember that *You Matter*. Even if you are in a space of sincerely questioning this truth, do not give up. You just have to take things from where you are. Each new day offers an opportunity to gradually heal and release the darkness. Do not look for a complete instant transformation, this is not realistic. Plus, patience is part of the healing process; it is a pillar for offering kindness to yourself and others. Know that this process is on-going. The most important thing is to look for the next step on the path to healing!

Your inner beliefs have created a circumstance that is unacceptable to you, and the good news is that now that you see this, you hopefully are willing to change these beliefs. I have been there myself, and I truly believe that most (if not all) of us can relate. The outer experience is not the same for everyone, but the inner space of pain, despair, and hopelessness is universal. It is a great catalyst for seeking a more empowered life, and can guide us in fulfilling our highest potential. When you have shifted out of this dark space and begin to create a better life you will look back and be ever so grateful for not giving up. You will now have so much appreciation for the blessings in life that you would have otherwise missed. *You Matter* so much that you need to find your way through the darkness both for the positive things you will experience in the future, and for the benefit you will bring to those you have not yet met.

Then of course there are many men who feel like they matter to the exclusion of any semblance of integrity, accountability, or concern for others who are rightfully relying upon them. Unfortunately, they cast a negative perception upon all men. This way of life not only shows great disrespect for others, but great disrespect, weakness, and lack of higher awareness within themselves. This is an example of someone controlled by ego, who has lost their way or knowing about their true identity, their spiritual essence. We all struggle with this from time to time, and it is usually a matter of degrees. No one can throw stones and be overly critical of others, we all have ego in us, and so there is always room for growth and greater love.

While others (especially women and children) seem to feel the brunt of these men's actions, behavior, and attitude, it really expresses a sad state of affairs for these men personally. They are truly lost, and without an understanding of how to heal, are lashing out at the world, and specifically anyone who dares to care about them. They do not know that they truly matter. We are all spiritual beings having a human experience, and this is no different for those who appear to be living lives that are in complete denial of this truth. On a spiritual level they have the same qualities of goodness, but they have lost touch with this aspect of their nature. We cannot give up on those who seemingly have given up on themselves, but our part is to support with compassion and to be an example of one living in spirit. Our job is **NOT** to heal them, enable their behavior, or allow ourselves to be abused and disempowered by their energy, words, or actions! Only they can heal themselves.

If you have lived in a truly selfish and destructive way, recognize this within yourself. You are spirit first, just like anyone else, so you always have the capability of choosing to heal, grow, and walk a higher path. Because of the intense false education you likely received, you may have deeply ingrained destructive habits and coping mechanisms. The truth is not that you are bad, but that you are in need of healing and re-training. You have an opportunity to transform into a more conscious man who may have many great and wonderful qualities to share with the world. You may be required to demonstrate a substantial amount of change in your life in order to facilitate the inner healing and shift to spiritual freedom. But your spirit is always there to support you.

Your intentions for personal and spiritual growth are for you alone. You recognize an intense desire to create and live a different life, one that is in greater alignment with spirit. While assistance and education are available, only you can walk this daily path. Therefore, you can only do this for yourself; which can only happen once you decide that *You Matter*. You cannot do this for anyone else, or for purposes of salvaging some aspect of your current life. Often, drastic changes are necessary in order to separate us from the negative energy that permeated our past condition. You need a clear space from which to rebuild and reconnect to Source, and the deeper and more pervasive your wounds the more this is true. With healing and accountability you will be able to shift to a truly empowered life that brings higher qualities for yourself and others.

You Matter is most relevant as an agent of significant inner change for those who have grown to feel unworthy of self-love. The message of the **Empower Model** is designed for healing and growth, they always go together. On a deep level we all need to know how much we matter. We matter enough to heal and grow, to transform and elevate our awareness of our true value and contribution to the world. You may have model good looks, and all of the material possessions you could ever want, but that's not what really matters. Those things pass away and by themselves do not provide real value or happiness.

When we know how much we matter, we will treat all others like they matter! And how we treat others is a direct reflection of how we truly feel about ourselves. This is why it is critical to work on our inner development and stop judging value from outside appearances. You can see that from the platform of the **Educate** step, which helps bring a new more empowered understanding of *who we really are*, the next logical extension is to

64

treat ourselves and others within the context of the higher wisdom of **You Matter.**

"My life is my message."
— **Mahatma Gandhi**

Your Purpose is to fulfill your unique Human and Spiritual Plan

We talked about the **"Real You"** in the **Educate** chapter. In every aspect of personal growth it is critical to first uncover the real you, then develop the real you, and finally express the real you to the world. The real you is in alignment with your spirit, which has designed your current life path. This life path has put you into circumstances and situations from the time you were born that have in many ways been challenging. This serves the purpose of providing the lessons and opportunities whereby we may learn and understand on a deeper level the value of our spiritual truth. It is in the overcoming of these challenges that often times facilitate the wisdom and healing to transform from a place of perceived limitation to a place of expansion and growth. The power of transforming from a lower, false self into your true self (a human being living their spiritual purpose) supports you in the ascension of your soul. Had you not designed a life path that put you into the position of dealing with these challenges, you would not have known the full spectrum of the human experience in support of your soul's growth.

So we get here, and grow up physically with the education of our environment. Often this is quite contrary to our true nature and gifts. Again, we chose this to experience growth. Virtually all of us will conform for some period of time as a way of fitting in, surviving, and gaining approval. We develop in ways that are not our true self. Though on a deeper level we are mostly unfulfilled and unsatisfied, we begin to identify with this false self. As this continues for longer periods of time we may find that we are very disconnected from our true nature, and we may deny our potential altogether. It is possible for people to complete their human life without ever really identifying with their true higher purpose or fulfilling their spirit's objectives.

As we are evolving as men and as a society, I believe that younger men will understand and connect with their true selves at an earlier age than ever before. This is incredibly significant for them because this is how we are most able to fulfill our soul's purpose, and in doing so bring the most benefit to all. We cannot have lasting inner peace and joy until we are functioning in this way. It is also a positive development in that the amount of our life span spent suffering in experiential lessons against their true nature is significantly lessened. So not only will they experience less pain and suffering, but will more quickly reach a place of understanding and awareness that is most supportive toward attaining their highest potential.

Wherever you are in this place of living your false self or recognizing your true nature and gifts, this is where you start growing and developing from this moment forward. Would I have liked to be at this place in my life in my twenties or thirties instead of my fifties? Absolutely I would. However I needed to experience many challenging lessons between these time periods. This included a couple marriage relationships that ended in divorce, several job changes, and many other lessons, some enjoyable and some very difficult. All of those experiences taught me who I really am, and prepared me for living my true life and purpose now. They taught me that my life path cannot be satisfying or fulfilling until I decided it was time to honor myself, know that I am enough, and know that *I Matter*. Regardless of your circumstances, it is not too late for you to learn, heal, grow, and transform. The plan of spiritual law is perfect. I continue to evolve and transform according to my level of awareness of truth and my courage and willingness to live it. Again, had I been ready sooner it would have happened sooner. This is true for everyone, which is another reason to have compassion for all people.

The truth is that we usually know our truth before we are willing to change our lives to be in alignment with our truth. However, we think that we can straddle that line of "safety", whereby we can do the things others want us to do in order to be loved and appreciated, and then maybe we can dabble in our truth on the side. Unfortunately, this is not how spiritual truth works. You are either choosing spirit or you are choosing ego. And when you play with fire you will get burned. If you are trying to play it both ways, while on some level knowing that you know better, start preparing for the most challenging of experiences designed to show you that there really is no safety in choosing ego (even though you thought there was). If necessary you will be required to receive experiences that will bring such a high level of suffering that you will then have no choice but to honor your true self and choose spirit.

I had to experience this level of devastation in my life, where I knew within my being that something was not good for me, but I did not listen. At the time I had sufficient knowledge of spiritual matters and was at a very peaceful and powerful place in my life. Sometimes you don't know how bad or how low things can get until you are fully immersed in darkness. I chose ego when I let myself be enticed by someone, and then I gradually gave away all of my power to them. If you will let them, there is always someone who is happy to take everything you have. This goes far beyond the material things which can be replaced. Suffice it to say it took many years to overcome (heal and grow). And there were many times where I really wondered why I mattered and if I should stay in this world. As I look back from here, I know with all of my being that this person was one of my greatest teachers. I needed to learn the consequences of not fully loving and honoring myself on such a deep level that I not only would grow personally, but that I could relate to the deep suffering that others experience by doing the same thing. I truly believe that those who have overcome the greatest obstacles or lessons have the highest potential for the greatest service to the world. I have learned that I truly *Matter*, not only for myself and for my loved ones, but for all of the lives I will touch on this journey. However, in order to truly make a positive impact in this life I must be who **I AM** (Divine Presence).

As it was for me, these transformative experiences are a blessing, though they will not feel like it at the time! If you decide to learn this way, you too may spend years recovering and healing. So my advice is to listen to your inner knowing and begin to shift in earnest with the highest intentions of claiming your true self. This is how much it matters to live and be who you truly are. Only you know what is in your best and highest interest. Listen to this knowing, and honor it. You will be given opportunities to fall back to ego and let suffering back in. But don't let it (no matter how enticing the teacher). From this place you are moving with the Divine Force that flows through all of creation, instead of moving against it, which, as I said, has dire consequences.

"You change your life by changing your heart."
– Max Lucado

It Matters that Men Heal and Evolve

In order to live, be, and express your amazing spirit in the form you have chosen in this life, you must be willing to live your higher truth. In order to truly do this you must accept and release the past as the learning experience that it was. You now step into the present with an open heart, and fresh eyes, trusting your higher knowing as you take each new step from a place of empowerment. There are still many learning opportunities ahead, but you now know that they need not defeat you, and in fact are shaping you into the *Being of Light* that you are.

As a man writing this book, and for the men reading this book, we have chosen to incarnate (and hopefully awaken) in this day and age. This does not mean that we haven't lived in many other previous ages, we most assuredly have, but this is the time period for the world we currently inhabit. This is significant because it is important for us to remember that we are setting the tone for the identity of men now and in the future. When we think of men (or women for that matter) in a stereotypical way that represented decades or centuries past, what real relevance does that have to the evolution of humanity?

Maybe there was once a valid reason why men were the way they were. They were created to be bigger and stronger physically, so it made sense that they would track and kill the food, and be the protectors of the family. And since women bear the children, it made sense that they would be more nurturing than men. Then eventually men used these characteristics to track and kill other humans so that they could take more land, more wealth and resources, and build empires unto themselves. Then men made the rules of politics and commerce in ways that ensured that they would be in control; and not even all men, just men of certain nationalities, races, or religions. Like it or not, this is the historical path that has led us to today.

So now in this day and age do we really need to continue to replicate this model? I don't know about you, but I haven't been required to track and kill my food, ever. Maybe we are bigger and stronger as a group, but if that just leads to domination, destruction, and abuse over others, how does that fit into an evolving planet? I am obviously focusing on some of the negative consequences of the historical male pattern, such as aggression, avarice, domination, cruelty, abusiveness, and discrimination. And that is because these negative qualities, which exist energetically in the collective consciousness, do not reflect spirit; therefore we must heal and grow in order to transcend these traits and create better conditions for all of us. As men of a new, more enlightened age, we need to be more conscious and empowered in ways that are in alignment with our higher nature. It is our individual and collective responsibility!

On the other hand, we can emulate the positive qualities from men of past ages. Many men have been staunch promoters of the very ascension to the higher living that I write about. And in fact men have brought many things into this world that are very good and necessary. Due to the inquisitive and assertive nature of man, the world has been explored and analyzed from every angle. This includes here on earth, from the highest mountain tops to the depths of the oceans, and throughout the solar system. It also includes exploration in the field of quantum physics and all of that which makes up matter to the tiniest detail. We have music, art, architecture, mathematics, medicine, and technology at whatever was the most advanced stage at the time. We have in fact invented many great things that were not designed to kill other people. It's just that we have tended to go where the money is. And the money is always where the power is. And the power is always in the hands of those who make the rules and have the most might. And there you are, back to where we started.

All of these qualities we call negative have been a pervasive part of the human experience. Sadly, these negative qualities have also been portrayed in the name of religion for thousands of years. So be very careful when you point to your religion as your spiritual practice, know within your spirit that it is promoting Divine qualities and not ego-based qualities. Our history largely reflects a legacy of humans driven by ego instead of spirit. Unfortunately, this is still the case today. And while it may be less accepted than in the past, it is not uncommon for man to act in similarly cruel and ruthless ways. There can be no hiding under the old outdated models; we must be fully accountable for healing and correcting our thoughts, actions, and beliefs.

All of this to say, it is imperative that we as men begin to explore and develop our inner strength and healing. We must truly live in the truth that we are both spiritual and human beings. This is what is most needed in the world today, and this is the time that we chose to be on the planet. So we need to step up and be accountable for the solutions of the time. We all need to be the leaders who are establishing a new and higher standard. Let's start by taking inventory of our own lives. It matters less about what your brother does, heal yourself, and exude the peace and strength that will heal the world. We can only change ourselves. And when enough of us do this, the tide will turn and the new model for men will be one of great inner strength, compassion, peace, and wisdom.

As you are now firmly on this path of personal and spiritual growth, begin to analyze your thoughts, words, and actions. This requires you to be conscious and present in the process of observing and noticing. Pay attention to your thoughts, if they do not reflect self-love and love for others equally, change it to something that does. If words slip out before you are able to change your thoughts, that are hurtful or angry, follow up with words that are more loving and supportive, and if appropriate, apologize. And if your actions do not reflect the appropriate qualities of your spiritual nature, make amends, and develop greater awareness and mindfulness in order to improve going forward. This is what being conscious means. You do things intentionally, but from a place of love, peace, and unity.

Your only obligation is to start from where you are and step onto this higher path, your true spirit journey. From there you will need to apply consistent practice, which supports your healing and training, as a way to facilitate an inner shift. I know that you will find so much inner joy in this transformation, because it is more gratifying than the temporary pleasures you previously sought that never really provided lasting happiness. In doing this inner work you are creating great and lasting benefits for yourself and others. **This is why you matter greatly to the world!** And you will now attract others who are on a healing, loving path, and together you will not only enjoy life on a deeper level, but will combine to offer great assistance to many.

"Life isn't about finding yourself. Life is about creating yourself."
– George Bernard Shaw

Choosing your Roles Consciously

Let's talk a bit about roles; we all choose to play many of them in our lifetime. Some roles are defined by us, some by other people in our lives, and still others by society. Some feel "forced" upon us and outside of our control and others we just back into. Yet, ultimately, everything comes into our lives of our own choosing.

Our roles usually come with a title, such as father, son, brother, husband, boyfriend, boss, employee, teacher, student, etc. Many of these titles come predefined with the expectations of meeting some societal standard. If we don't know that we matter, we can get lost in "playing" these roles, instead of utilizing them to support our greater fulfillment. You say, "I am a father, son, brother, husband, etc." It's not really who you are, it's just a role you are playing. However, unless you are consciously choosing your roles and defining them in a way that is most personally beneficial for you and the other people involved, it will be very difficult to find your true power and support this area of your life in the highest manner.

The true power of You Matter is that when you are living your higher truth you are Enough! The primary role we were born into is that of male, which of course was not a conscious choice (at least on the human level). So we are not consciously choosing this role, but we **can** consciously choose how we experience it. In many respects this role comes pre-defined (just as the role for women is pre-defined) in ways that can be quite disempowering.

In actuality, all people were created to be whole beings, yet societal expectations have burdened us with perceived limitations. As men we have primarily been brought up to withhold our feelings, define toughness as domination or control over others, and to never appear as weak. So we avoid opening up to our true potential for love, joy, peace, and wellness by avoiding being vulnerable. The problem is that it is in the facing of our vulnerability that we not only connect with others in the most meaningful way, but we also are empowered to heal, grow and evolve. And when we do not face our vulnerability, or are otherwise unable to live up to the narrow definition of a "strong" man, we fill this space with shame. Shame is a very disempowering emotion that directly brings us into the experience of pain and suffering. And shame is always telling us that "we are not enough".

The truth is that the narrow definitions of others can prevent us from living the full embodiment of all that we are here to be. I suggest that as a way of living more consciously you expand this concept of male to incorporate that of being "wholehearted". Also, wherever you can, allow yourself to step up with the courage to be vulnerable. Watch how your life will transform, and the fear of being exposed will dissipate, and you will step into your highest truth.

Often times our true identity gets lost in our identification with the roles we play. We are so engrained to care about what we look like to others that our ego wants to give the appearance of successfully portraying society's definition or expectation of one fulfilling a certain role. When we consciously choose our roles, we move into alignment with our highest power and integrity. As a result, our joy, peace, productivity, passion, and fulfillment are now offered as a higher purpose and are worthy of our time and effort. In this way, we are in a position to bring great benefit to others as well.

When you consciously choose your roles, you can know with great clarity that you and all you do truly matters, not only to yourself but also to others in your life. When we choose to accept roles merely for the purpose of succumbing to the wishes of others, or from a place of fear, you will soon find that the choice to not honor yourself will bring suffering to you and others. You can only give so much effort toward something that is not in alignment with your true nature and purpose. In this case, the energy cannot be sustained at a high level indefinitely. Eventually you will not live up to the expectations of those involved, thus disappointing both them and yourself. I am sure that you can recognize this truth from your past experience.

After graduating from college I started my work career, and I entered the business world as an accountant. My roles while offering this service took on various titles over the years, from Accountant, to Accounting Manager, to Assistant Controller, to Controller, to Vice President of Finance. I played these roles within various companies and industries, always in small to medium sized organizations. Some roles change as a natural progression of our skillset, some we change for the opportunity of increased benefit, and some end due to circumstances outside of our control. I have also witnessed many who have stayed in roughly the same role within the same company for many years. My guess would be that this is partly personal preference and partly a lack of inner belief in their ability to grow within themselves and contribute in new or different ways. They may not yet know how much they matter, and how much they are capable of doing. The point is, whether you stay in one job you love for many years, or you seek opportunities to expand and experience new things, always choose through an empowered perspective that supports your highest good.

I am now expanding and shifting my career roles to include titles like: Author, Teacher, Speaker, and Life Coach/Mentor. This is a progression and a conscious choice which has included much transformation in support of inner healing and growth in pursuit of my higher purpose. The impetus of this transition (which is always ongoing) was first to connect and align with my spirit nature. This led to discovering my higher purpose, and developing my opportunities to support and assist others in this process of growth and healing. It is always necessary to do the inner developmental work first, when shifting and expanding to a new and higher role, in order to maintain your integrity and truth. You are most empowered and fulfilled when you shift for the work (service), and not just for the material benefits.

It is not always easy, but sometimes you have to be aware enough to see the truth, and strong enough to honor your truth. In the end you are always striving to create growth and harmony. You Matter is largely dependent upon you caring enough about yourself to begin to define what is most in alignment with your true power, purpose, love, and inner calling. This is not a selfish perspective; it is an honest and empowering one. This leads to you creating the most joyful, loving, and beneficial life you are here to live.

With a new focus on your personal and spiritual growth leading to the fulfillment of your highest potential, begin to look at all new experiences, opportunities, and challenges from this empowering perspective. We are constantly receiving new information designed to teach and guide us to our highest path. Here are some questions to answer: As I release my past false identity, and connect within, who am I? What is it that I truly enjoy in my life that will also assist me on this higher journey? What is my plan for personal growth? What are the roles I may now accept that support this plan? With your awareness and courage you have the ability to consciously choose your new roles. These new roles will help facilitate a shift to a more awakened, fulfilling life.

So how do you handle the roles you are currently playing that began while in a past unconscious ego state? Some roles can be instantly released, whereby you may now shift to a better role. Other roles require a period of time for a proper completion, due to certain commitments you have made. To the best of your ability, honor these temporary commitments to a conclusion that displays your highest integrity. You now understand your level of connection to others as well as yourself. So as you are shifting internally and preparing for a new role, ask your spirit for the guidance and assistance to be fully supported in this process. Still other commitments are on some level lifelong. Yet, even these change over time, so use your higher awareness and guidance to assist you in remaining empowered within these changes.

The roles that we choose are opportunities to discover our true power, and to reveal this power in support of others. If we choose a role from ego we are primarily concerned with what we can *get* out of it. When we consciously choose our roles from spirit, we know that we are opening to the best and highest path, so we more easily focus on what we can *give*. Our greatest success always comes from giving. And empowered giving always leads to receiving! As we have discussed, our ego is concerned with self-preservation, while our spirit is concerned with expansion and unity. As we begin to release the hold of ego (fear), we more easily trust in the process that is supported by spirit that brings the highest benefit.

At times we find that we have so many roles that it is difficult to function optimally within all of them (or any of them). Those of us residing primarily in ego are overwhelmed, dissatisfied, critical of others, and stuck in disempowering life circumstances. This often leads to emotional pain, disruption of roles, and suffering for you and the others involved. Inner development and growth are so very important in creating life circumstances that support our journey. When you find that you have more on your plate than you desire, your inner strength is paramount, and your determination to do the best you can, with acceptance and peace of what is, will support you. Then, when you are able to make adjustments in your life to a path that promotes greater wellness and balance, you will have the awareness and courage to set better boundaries and make new, more empowering choices.

"If you haven't the strength to impose your own terms upon life, you must accept the terms it offers you"
– T.S. Eliot

Being a Conscious Partner Matters

Our personal partner relationships provide an exceptional opportunity to learn where we stand with respect to our own inner healing and consciousness. Most often our fears, insecurities, and the false education of our ego nature will come out in our interactions with that person whom we have chosen to share our most intimate space. Developing our personal growth and healing is very difficult within these partnerships, though with great awareness and intention on the part of each of you, it is possible.

Ideally, we would do this work within ourselves prior to manifesting this type of relationship. However, we always create the opportunities to learn and grow based on our current level of awareness, from whatever situation we find ourselves in the present. So where you are in this moment is perfect for what you need to learn about yourself. Work from where you are, and utilize your highest consciousness to heal and grow within the context of partnerships.

It is always up to you to create your roles, and to find your healthy place within them. If you have chosen the role of husband or partner in a personal relationship, recognize your responsibility to be authentically who you are. This is an opportunity to discover your true power, and to reveal it in support of your wife or partner. Who you are and how you participate in this relationship MATTERS! You must be honest with yourself, and you must each communicate truthfully, in order to heal, grow, and receive the highest benefit of the partnership. Without complete honesty and integrity, the relationship is a ticking time bomb. It is only a matter of time before it blows up.

Remember, in this book I am not talking about just surviving; I certainly would not want you to believe that suffering is your lot in life. We **must** be accountable for our own truth, healing, and growth. If you want a fulfilling, loving, joyful relationship, your thoughts, words, and actions matter. With the intention of giving and receiving the highest love, and the action of communicating truthfully (not manipulatively), you have the opportunity to evaluate this relationship in the most empowered way. Then, make the choices that are most beneficial to all involved. Your goal is to each be in alignment with your individual spirit nature and path, while coming together to add support, companionship, joy, and wellbeing to the other.

As often as possible, focus your highest attention and awareness on your partner and the energy between the two of you. If there is tension or uneasiness, you will feel it. Start with addressing this energy before thoughts, words, or actions become unkind or cruel. Remember that your partner is a very strong mirror for you. So when you recognize unloving qualities in them, on a deeper level you likely are being shown that which is unloving within yourself. Additionally, if you are critical or unkind to your partner, you are merely identifying yourself as one who is judgmental and cruel; there are no higher qualities or justification in your words and actions that intentionally harm someone. Instead of holding yourself accountable, you take it out on your partner. This is why your inner growth and healing is so vitally important to the peace, love, and joy in all of your relationships.

As we have discussed before, your higher awareness will allow spirit to be present, where previously you may have been unconsciously leading with ego. When you feel challenged, you have an opportunity to experience peace and joy with your partner by recognizing the arising ego before it escalates into its various negative qualities. Then with this awareness, openly and honestly discuss the issues. Everyone has a potentially different point of view, neither right nor wrong, just different. Sometimes it requires some amount of compromise, but honestly, more often than not it is merely the absence of truthful communication. We are too afraid to reveal our true feelings because our ego always wants to control the outcome. This is manipulative and unsupportive to the true healing and growth that spirit is guiding you toward in any particular experience or situation. You cannot have authentic love within your relationship without being truly honest.

Consciously function at your highest level with respect to your partner relationship. Of course ultimately it takes two people to function in this way, so you never can be assured that any such relationship is always going to support your higher path. You cannot control your partner, nor are you responsible for their growth and healing (only they are). From the place of your highest truth and knowing you will have the best opportunity to be a happy, fulfilled person and a loving partner. And, if necessary, you will be in the most empowered, healthy place from which to transition out of a relationship that is not going to support you in this way. Again, be honest with yourself, and courageous enough to make the choices that are most beneficial for your higher wellness. By avoiding your truth you are not changing anything, you are merely postponing the inevitable conclusion, which will likely be far more difficult and challenging.

If you are single, and desire a relationship, your focus on your own higher truth will create an opportunity to partner with someone who supports the life you want for yourself. Always begin manifesting your intentions from this premise. After that, you must sincerely desire to be a loving partner for someone else. If this is not the case, you may need to reevaluate your reasons for desiring a partner relationship. A healthy person never seeks a partner in order to "complete themselves", take away their own loneliness, or provide what they think is missing.

Honor yourself by choosing a partner that is compatible with your highest desires, and communicate these desires with them truthfully. Of course in order to do this, you need to first develop your own inner healing and higher knowing of what supports your highest path. Remember, you are choosing a partner that supports you in the healthy, joyful life you are here to live; not for the temporary satisfaction of your ego. Choose from your own empowered place, not from ego, weakness, or

81

perception of lack. When you have love and respect for yourself, you will attract someone who recognizes these qualities within you, and within themselves. From this place you can grow together, fully supporting the other on your higher paths. You will more readily accept them as they are without wanting to change them to suit you. You are being accountable for your own happiness, and therefore have so much more to share with your partner, and they with you. This is an example of consciously choosing your role as a partner.

With respect to relationships, never allow anyone to force or pressure you. Anyone can be in a relationship, but to be an equal participant in a truly loving, healthy relationship means that it supports your higher love and growth. The same is true with marriage. Being married does not make it a good relationship. If you established that you are in a loving, supportive relationship, and getting married further supports your connection and plan for fulfilling your higher purpose, then this may be the best choice for you. But do not be deceived to think that you **must** be married in order to "legitimize" your love. This is an outdated model that has proven to be untrue. Being empowered to live your highest love, joy, and fulfillment means that you get to decide what is best for you. When your focus is on continuing to develop and sharing your highest love, you will create the greatest commitment to yourself and your partner. This supersedes all legal contracts.

If you find that your highest truth is supporting your greatest growth at this time without you being in an intimate partnership, than honor that fully. *You Matter* begins with taking care of yourself first. It is vitally important that we take responsibility for our own healing and growth, and often times the best way to do this is in your own space. If we are paying attention, we all will learn a great deal about ourselves while in relationship. Yet in order to utilize this wisdom and transform into a higher awareness and understanding of our path, we need the space to just be who we are, and honor ourselves fully.

If we jump from one relationship to another, how will we actually begin to apply what we have learned in order to grow from the experience? We will just be looking for the next person to fix the problems within ourselves that proved troublesome in the previous relationship. Of course this makes no sense, but we probably all have done this before. Now that we are consciously choosing and creating our empowered lives, let's be wiser in this process. We need to experiment on our own to find out what it is that truly propels us to our greatest joy and purpose. Additionally, we must learn to discover how wonderful we are, and love ourselves fully from within. You are now accepting that You Matter, and are therefore, worthy of love, with or without a partner.

This can be the most productive period of personal and spiritual growth if you will apply yourself for this purpose. Being alone does not have to mean being lonely. You can and should develop great friendships that will support you on your path, and bring great fun, joy, and fulfillment. I have personally been in this place for the past few years, and the transformation has been remarkable. I have never been so secure and accepting of myself, and I have never had so many wonderful friendships. I continue to transform from someone with many self-imposed limitations to a person who is creating, expressing, and living my higher truth. I have also moved to a greater heart space, which balances my customary mental/logical approach, and has brought me to a healthier and more balanced state of being. My spirit knew that I needed this space in order to make the necessary shift that is leading to fulfilling my highest love, joy, peace, prosperity, and service in this life.

83

It is not always easy, for we are conditioned to think that something is wrong or missing when we are not sharing our life with a partner. My goals and perceptions about relationships have changed. I now know that the most important part of a healthy relationship is the level of my own inner health. I know that I do not "need" another person to make me feel loved, valued, or whole. I Matter to me (spirit), to those closest to me in my life, and to the world at large, by fulfilling my calling to share my unique gifts, love, and light. I know that, should the Universe present me with a partner who has achieved a similar level of personal healing, adds to my joy and love of life, and provides that "spark" of chemistry that is undeniable, I would enthusiastically connect with her.

"The most precious gift we can offer others is our presence. When mindfulness embraces those we love, they will bloom like flowers."
– Thick Nhat Hanh

Being a Conscious Parent Matters

As a way of assisting the world in shifting to a higher path for humanity, your role as a parent is paramount (if this is part of your life path). You must **consciously** choose to be a good parent. If you are not ready to choose this, then take the necessary precautions to make sure you do not go blindly into this critical role. For many people this is one of the most challenging roles you can undertake, and it is one of those roles that lasts a lifetime. Your best success as a parent comes directly from your own level of inner healing; therefore, your efforts toward personal and spiritual growth are extremely beneficial to you as a parent, and to the development of your children.

Being a good parent requires the highest degree of unconditional love that you are likely to encounter in any human experience, over a long period of time. But it is more than being selfless; it requires that you educate your children with the wisdom of true empowerment, and the consciousness of unity. It is time that kids learn at an early age that they matter and that all other people equally matter as well. As men we must all take our responsibility as fathers to a new level. We can now express both our feelings and our strength, so that our children know that this is ok for them to do as well. Guide them to find their true path and purpose. They are not subordinate to you, in fact their path and potential is likely greater than yours (due to the time they have chosen to incarnate), so encourage them to shine their light.

Unfortunately there are no rules stating that only healthy, awakened people can procreate. If you have not entered the role of parent from a conscious place, please utilize this opportunity to take your own personal growth and healing very seriously! As you are reading this book I hope that you understand that you absolutely have the power to do this. Too many kids have been damaged by unbalanced, ego-based parenting. As parents we are responsible for the safety, education, and development of the most vulnerable among us – the children.

Please know that from whatever level of awareness your parenting skills were based, you did the best you could at the time (past tense). Parents are people, and people are in need of healing. Sometimes we carry guilt for the things we did or didn't do, but this serves no useful purpose. You start from where you are, and right now you have every opportunity to be a more available, supportive, and loving parent.

I was parenting during specific times when I was experiencing great personal challenges. I can now recognize things that I wish I could have done better as a parent. However, my love for my children never wavered, and I know that I did the best I could within my level of awareness and consciousness at the time. I do not live with regrets, instead I offer them all of my love and support in the present from a healthier place. It is important to be real with your kids, not to burden them with your problems, but to teach them that when life is difficult, you deal with it, heal, grow, and move forward a better person. Life is not a Disney movie, and they should not expect that everything will always be easy and accommodating.

Whether your children are infants or adults, they will always look to you for love, approval, support, and guidance. Let them know how much you love and value them exactly as they are. They do not need to be or do anything to "deserve" your love. Be proud of their accomplishments, even if you do not understand their path. This kind of support may transform their lives beyond anything you can do or buy for them. Don't wait for them to take the first step, this supports your healing as much as theirs, so be bold, listen to spirit (not ego), and be there for them always.

Because of the level of commitment and unconditional love required, it is a difficult job even for those who *are* conscious and awakened. Due to the constant nature of their needs, you must make this role a priority, and yet you are trying to balance it with many other "priorities". Thus the child-rearing role may suffer due to a lack of time and energy. For a parent that is functioning almost exclusively from ego, the children are receiving very little value, and you are likely implanting them with emotional challenges that may take many years to overcome. When parenting from a healthier spirit based energy, do the best you can within your highest intentions. That is all you can do. Beyond that, be honest with them, explain that you are doing your best. Depending on their age they may or may not understand (or respond kindly), but in the long run they are learning the responsibilities of being a loving adult.

Sometimes we are functioning at our highest level and yet we may not be able to support a child's unquenchable thirst for the latest toys and material things that "the other kids have." Where possible, explain your commitment to loving them and providing their basic needs first, and that these other things are optional and unavailable at this time. One day your honesty and trust in them will be rewarded. In the meantime, continue to make wise decisions without being swayed by the whims of your children who due to no fault of their own have been saturated by media marketing. Obviously, this is most prevalent during the Christmas holidays, but there is no good reason to be fiscally irresponsible.

Training in appreciation and moderation starts young, so help them to learn the higher lessons of family, loving, and sharing, instead of buying their approval. The value or quality of your parenting is not dependent upon the quantity and cost of the gifts you buy your kids. If you spoil them when they are young, they will develop expectations of materiality and entitlement when they are older, and then may suffer the same guilt and lack of control as you do, when parenting their own children. If you are wealthy enough to spend much for gifts, consider teaching them the joy and value of giving and serving those in need. A conscious parent is always teaching their offspring higher values.

By far the best parents are those who have developed a sufficient amount of personal and spiritual growth so that they have an awareness of how their energy affects their children (and others). Plus, they find healthy ways to care for and heal themselves instead of taking out their frustration on their youngsters. This is as true for men as it is for women. Men do not get a pass when it comes to parenting. Your highest focus and care must be given in each present moment, whether you are working, parenting, or other activities. And keeping in mind that your personal wellness and balance is extremely important, "other activities" takes a back seat to parenting.

For too long it has been accepted that this is the job of the mother. So now many men are hesitant to be true loving parents, and women have moved equally into the workforce. What about the kids? A single parent household should mean that the children live with their unmarried parents' alternately; two loving, healthy households. A healthy and interested male parent is a must (if, in fact, one is part of the family structure). There seems to be a growing trend for the father to stay home to raise the children. There is nothing wrong with this, so long as this is a conscious choice designed primarily for the welfare of the kids. No matter who (if anyone) is "staying home", make parenting the priority.

Women have the right to add career to their life path, and typically have been more successful than men in balancing work and parenting. Men have an obligation to add "being a loving, supportive father" to their life path. This not only requires a shift in a societal view but also an inner energetic shift for men to accept a more nurturing, unconditionally loving aspect of their total beingness. As spiritual beings it is in us, and the world needs for us to grow and balance our energy in order to shift to greater peace, wisdom, and love for all people. Men matter greatly in the highest development of children for future generations. We have seen what the world has created with the old model. As we shift and evolve to a higher level of consciousness, men need to be more concerned with other beings on an emotional level.

We need to raise young men who are capable of utilizing all of the healthy aspects that we are blessed with. This involves the attainment of inner and outer strength, intelligence and compassion, determination and acceptance, and love of self and all others. I believe that there is a great future in the evolution of men, and that is the purpose of this book. We all need to awaken, discard the limitations we have put on ourselves, and become more of what we were designed to be. I assure you that women have been evolving far ahead of us, which is wonderful for them and society. By contrast, men have become a bit complacent and disinterested in this respect, relying on our eroding might and position.

We must add the more supportive, nurturing qualities, first within ourselves, then outwardly toward others. This must be applied to our children as fathers, and to the education of raising our sons. Men must be able to hug their youngsters and say "I love you", every day that you are together. And this includes sons as well as daughters. Every child must know that their father loves them; they need it and they deserve it! The world needs us to step up, and move into the light of our higher truth.

Let's utilize these higher aspects of who we are toward guiding and supporting our children. Meeting their physical (material) needs is a given requirement, and it is our job to do the best we can, though in the new family model, women are now equally able and obligated to support these needs as well. We need to shift how we look at our children. To begin to understand what they need in order to best develop the qualities and skillsets that support their unique gifts as it will be applied to a more loving world.

Let us never again teach a child to judge, discriminate, or hate another human being because they look, think, or act differently than us! We need to teach them the values of unity, peace, kindness, and love for all; not just from our words, but more importantly from our example. And we must teach them about self-love and self-respect. It is not about what "things" you can buy them; instead what matters is how they ultimately feel about themselves that will lead them toward fulfilling their highest potential. As parents we can either uplift them or damage them in this respect. Whether you are parenting individually, or as a couple, please recognize that you matter enormously in the lives of your kids. The evolution of humankind and the ascension to a new age on earth depends upon what and how we teach our children.

"Effort only fully releases its reward after a person refuses to quit."
– Napoleon Hill

You Matter Enough to Heal from Abuse

As human beings we are spirit (whether or not we are aware of this) and we are ego; we are both light and darkness. To the degree that you are primarily functioning as one or the other will determine the quality of the majority of your experiences. When we are unconscious (caught in the web of ego), on some significant level we likely will attract others who are unconscious. The combination of two such people interacting on a regular basis can lead to a combustible situation.

On the level of energy this is unavoidable so long as we have lost sight of our true nature. In any moment we have the opportunity to awaken and make empowering choices toward improving our inner perception, and thus changing the dynamic of an unhealthy situation. If we are unable to do this, we typically will need to experience the consequence of suffering on some level. This suffering is not punishing us, it is teaching us. Then once again, we have an opportunity to heal, grow, and shift toward spirit.

These lessons always involve others. We are brought together in order to assist the other in some form of healing (which may even involve a karmic balancing from a past life). If this were not so, we would have no use for this interpersonal experience at all. Sometimes our interaction with someone feels heavy and slightly uncomfortable, but without an awareness of your own energy and intuition you may overlook these signs and continue down the path of this higher lesson. Therefore, the energetic signs are likely to manifest into a more obvious external expression. There may now develop more frustration, disappointment, and even anger between the parties. This is due, in part, to how we are interpreting their behavior, and also because, on some level, we know that we are not honoring our self. And yet, if we are still choosing to be closed off to the spiritual truth we are being shown, we may continue further into more aggressive and harmful territory.

We have ventured into the darkness of ego that is fighting for survival with this other person. We become offended by them (their words and actions) and defensive towards them (from their accusations). At this point both parties are in danger of resorting to some form of abuse upon the other (emotional, verbal, or physical). Had we previously chosen to connect to spirit, we would need no part of this. We would know that this is not our higher nature, that we love ourselves, and that we matter enough to choose a different path. We would not attach to the opinion or accusations of someone who is not acting from a place of consciousness. We certainly would not so adamantly try to make a relationship "work" that is heaped in dishonesty and suffering.

But since we have chosen to stay in this situation, we are in need of the lessons and consequences that will ultimately be rendered. We may feel we are victimized by the other, and that we have lost something of great value (money, possession, pride, reputation, etc.), while gaining pain and suffering. In truth, everything that we perceived as gain or loss was only temporary, and related to our false identity and sense of security. We were fighting for the things that we ended up losing, when we actually could have kept those things, plus avoided pain and suffering if we would have followed and trusted our spirit enough to choose differently.

So having ultimately chosen this experience what did we learn? It turns out that if you are able to truly and honestly analyze the full experience from a place of awareness and ownership, you will see that you stayed in the relationship/situation to more fully understand where you need inner healing. And it virtually always speaks to a need for greater self-love, inner peace, and self-reliance. You have a false perception of yourself that you are somehow unworthy of a healthy loving relationship, or that you cannot survive at a healthy level on your own. Your ego says, "You don't matter, you are unlovable, and you are not enough". What a harsh self-condemnation, no wonder such an extreme experiential lesson was offered for the sake of healing.

Spiritual healing is always the answer, because this addresses the inner belief system that is manifesting your external experiences. When you know that you matter, you are worthy of love, and that you are fully capable of independently living an empowered life, you will choose very differently. You will no longer lash out at anyone else who may be pushing your buttons; really they are acting as a mirror or teacher showing you where you need inner healing. You will develop the inner strength to be able to walk away from a hurtful or unkind expression from someone, without resorting to striking back with words or violence.

If you are currently in such a volatile relationship, please recognize your need for personal and spiritual growth and healing. This is the primary lesson in that situation for you. The second very significant lesson is that you cannot control or save the other person – ever! So do the healthy, empowered thing that you need to do for yourself. If the other person is unwilling to be truly accountable for their own healing, you do not have anywhere to go with them but down, into greater ego darkness. Do not stay and fight with them, instead choose to honor yourself and move on. Rebuilding from a place of greater awareness and freedom is the best option for healing, and creating the life you desire.

Once you have survived and moved on from such a challenging relationship, work through the re-training and tools as described in the *Empower Model* teaching. As quickly as possible come to terms with the higher truth of the experience, and how you may greatly benefit going forward. As will be discussed in the Peace chapter, come to a place of forgiveness for the "teacher" who on a soul level served you well. Be sure to do the work leading to more consciousness before you begin to pursue any new relationships. You want to experience a significant amount of wellness and peace within yourself, without the need for additional abusive relationship training.

If you are a parent and have expressed aggressive or harmful energy toward your children, you are in need of inner healing. It is never ok to abuse another person, especially a child. If you need to seek this necessary inner healing through counseling and/or coaching please do so. You may have had your own childhood abuse experiences that have translated into unhealthy patterns as an adult. You need to heal; you need to find forgiveness, release guilt, and gain the higher awareness necessary for you to change your behavior. If not, this will continue to haunt you and keep you from experiencing a life filled with the higher spiritual qualities. And of course it will scar your children, and reinforce false ego training leading to patterns of suffering in their life. Take your life and responsibilities seriously enough to support your own healing and wellness, as well as that of others around you.

Chapter 2 Exercises

Exercise 1:
List and evaluate the various roles that you currently hold.

- What is it that you like best about these roles?
- Do you feel fulfillment (joy, bliss, or enthusiasm) when experiencing this role?
- Do you feel that this role is a good fit for what you want in your life going forward?
- Now, what roles are troublesome or unsatisfying/unfulfilling?
- Can you identify where you may need to shift your perspective or otherwise heal in order to have a different experience in this role? Or is this a role that no longer serves your higher purpose?

Choose any new roles consciously, meaning participate fully in creating roles that are fulfilling and rewarding to you.

Exercise 2:

Write or journal a couple paragraphs about why you think you matter. Pay attention to how easy or difficult this is for you. Can you hear your spirit voice? Can you hear your ego voice? Which one is most dominant? Become aware of these two aspects of yourself; spirit is empowering and expansive, while ego is disempowering and restrictive. Make the effort to notice, nurture, and reinforce spirit.

CHAPTER 3:
PEACE

"Until people find inner peace, outer peace is unsustainable"
– Scott E. Clark

Inner Peace Defined

The third step in the *Empower Model* addresses **Peace**, and more specifically, Inner Peace. Our level of inner peace reflects the quality of our mental and emotional state of well-being. While inner peace is thought to relate to relative stillness and calmness, its attainment is by no means a passive pursuit. It is my contention that for the majority of men inner peace has been highly undervalued, and very challenging to achieve.

In a society where aggression is often seen as a valued and admired quality for men, the consequence of this has created the world in which we now live. It's interesting how we constantly complain about the violence in the world (and in our own neighborhoods), yet peacefulness in men is often discouraged as weakness. For many in this country, the answer to more safety is more guns, in order to protect ourselves from the "other" crazy and violent people. How about we start to look at the false training that has led not only to the aggressive nature within us,

97

but also the desire to eliminate other people as a way to fix our own problems? We cannot continue to function in the old world order; instead we must be willing to make powerful and significant changes within ourselves. The optimal state of being is one of "empowerment", which utilizes inner peace, and does not seek to reduce the opportunities and quality of life for others.

The term "Peace" also relates to our quality of safety, or a lack of war, violence, fear, and anger ("aggression"). This pertains to countries, governments, political parties, religions, businesses, and personal relationships. Until people find inner peace, outer peace is unsustainable. They say that it is merely human nature to act aggressively and violently. Is that supposed to make it acceptable? Is there nothing we can do to evolve? Often our objective as men is to "just get things done"! Knowing that there are often significant consequences relating to what we do, and how we do it, maybe we can begin to evolve into a higher approach.

History would certainly show that we have demonstrated violence and anger upon each other since the beginning of recorded time. Man has even turned God into a violent Being (as a representation of us), according to some scripture. The purpose of evolving as humans is to begin to demonstrate, with our expressions of energy (thoughts, words, and actions), that something better is possible. And not only possible, but necessary. Personal and spiritual growth within a significant percentage of the population will shift the world to a vibration of inner peace. When we are functioning from this baseline, the quality of and reverence for all life will render our current way of being unthinkable. This is likely not a fast process, but it is the only way. As for those of us on an awakened path, we are willing to be responsible for developing our own inner peace, and sharing this quality with everyone we meet.

Whether or not we see a transition to a peaceful world in our lifetime is irrelevant. We cannot wait for others to change first; we must be willing to lead. In any case, we know that by doing so our lives take on a healthier, happier quality. Inner peace is the resulting effect of developing your connection to spirit. A lack of inner peace is only "human nature" because for too long people have primarily identified with ego-control and not spiritual-freedom. Again, when ego separates us from connecting with spirit, we are only concerned with getting what we want, even if we have to take it from someone else. So when two or more ego-based entities are at opposition while "wanting" the same thing (or one side wants to take something away from the other side), this aggressive nature is typically invoked. Sometimes this leads to a heated argument and other times it leads to mass killings.

As long as we are attempting to solve our perceived problems with aggression, instead of focusing on inner healing (which is at the root of all problems), we will continue along the path of suffering and destruction. As always, it is up to us individually to heal, grow, and transform. This would be a major step in the evolution of humankind. So when I said earlier that shifting to a state of inner peace is not a passive pursuit, I meant it. It takes great effort, persistence, awareness, patience, compassion, and wisdom. The effort is not one of gritting your teeth, and forcing an outcome by the sweat of your brow or the balling up of your fist. The effort is in *releasing* the arrogance and false teaching of the world (ego). Inner peace and inner strength go hand in hand. It takes great inner strength to react to the ego of another with calmness, acceptance, and compassion, where in the past you may have been insulted, defensive, and then attacked in any way you unconsciously felt appropriate.

For all of us, developing inner peace is an ongoing pursuit. However old you are, is likely how long you have been developing your false ego-based understanding of yourself and others. So let's be real, based upon your intent, effort, and spiritual practice, your goal is to *gradually* shift into this higher perspective. This is what we mean by the term "personal and spiritual growth", it is a growing, relearning process that is life changing and empowering.

If you were looking for a quick fix, or for someone else to do the work for you, you have come to the wrong place. The good news is that if repetition is the best way of learning, you will have plenty of opportunities to "practice" within virtually every relationship or experience that you encounter. And the really good news is that while these learning opportunities never go away completely, as you shift within to a higher perspective, you will have more people show up in your outer life that reflect this peace and support.

> *"Smile, breathe and go slowly."*
> **– Thich Nhat Hanh**

Peace or Suffering is a Choice

In their basic forms peace and suffering are mutually exclusive. With every situation or experience, you have within you the power to choose peace or suffering (spirit or ego). You are empowered to create the life you choose and you are here on purpose to fulfill your highest human and spiritual potential. It's just a matter of making a conscious choice to do so.

Your choices lead to future experiences, but sometimes your choices involve seeing a situation or experience in the present moment with a higher awareness. The act of choosing to see things from this higher awareness fills you with empowering opportunities. This is where peace happens, regardless of the situation. On the other hand, when you are living unconsciously, you are unable to see that you have choices; your awareness has been limited. You engage the situation, as if on autopilot, and you just walk right into suffering. You may feel like you had no choice, but you always have choices when your nature shifts to inner peace.

Sometimes the feelings or the situation may be too intense to experience peace. In this case do your best to focus on a neutral mindset. If a choice for action is not necessary and you are dealing with a stressful feeling or mental self-judgment, make the choice to find positive reinforcement or at the least distract yourself from anything negative or harmful. Living more consciously is a lifelong practice, so do not think that this should happen overnight or that anything is wrong with you when you are struggling. Just do your best. As I have said, finding true peace is not a passive activity. Utilize the tools, teachers, coaches, programs, and methods that work best for you. Always have compassion for yourself! Find that special feeling of empowerment when you realize that you have made a choice that directly led to peace instead of suffering. Remember that feeling, and do this as often as you can.

"I've learned that people will forget what you said, people will forget what you did, but people will never forget how you made them feel."
- **Maya Angelou**

Shifting Awareness from Head to Heart

Inner peace, as a quality of life and connection to the Divine within us, is more of a feeling, a knowing, and a positive energy. It is not so much a thought, or something to be analyzed and explained like a mathematics equation. This is true for most, if not all, spirituality. For the most part, it cannot be measured with man-made instruments, yet for those who experience and utilize these qualities they are experiential and extremely real. When I reference the head, I am talking about the thinking mind; the heart refers to our feeling emotions and not the organ in the middle of our chest. The head wants to judge, compare, critique, and fix. While the heart wants to accept, allow, support, and love. They each have their place in the world, but the development of inner peace requires more heart.

Many men have been raised primarily to be more comfortable thinking (or acting) than feeling. I am not talking about openly weeping at the slightest disturbance. I am talking about noticing what is happening within us; and recognizing that how we feel is telling us something important that we should pay attention to. This is information that can be utilized to bring healing or benefit on some higher level.

I, myself, am not especially openly emotional. Outwardly I typically function within a fairly controlled, logical framework. However, in this process of shifting to greater consciousness, I have learned to utilize this objectivity with awareness. I now notice that how I feel about a situation or personal connection, on the level of energy, is teaching me a great deal about what is truth and healing for me. This information that is coming from within (heart space) is real truth, before my mind can change or manipulate it to appease my ego.

As men, we are sometimes told, "just toughen up" (literally or figuratively). This is code for keep your feelings bottled up inside, and keep up a strong exterior appearance. It has been labeled weakness for men to express how they feel. This "training" often leads to withholding the energy of emotion until it has to come out and be released forcibly. Sometimes this release is expressed as violence or other inappropriate behavior.

Our head will often over analyze and over think everything. We like to plan things out as a way of controlling outcomes in our perceived favor. This closes us off from the magic that happens when you allow things to take a more organic course. There is certainly a place for planning, but don't ignore the process of life that is flowing around and through you. Flexibility and change are required in order to achieve most optimal outcomes. Heart activity deals with the energy of emotional truth that can be accessed to a high degree through a spiritual practice, and of course, awareness is where we primarily place our focus and attention.

In developing inner peace we must begin to move away from thinking about every little detail and nuance, and open our heart space to start feeling more. I correlate the mental functions primarily with our human form and survival; absolutely required to sustain this life. But it is limited for the purpose of our spiritual connection, both to the Divine and to all other beings. Knowing is a deep feeling or truth that goes beyond analytical thinking. This *feeling* opens us up more to consider the consequences of our

103

expressions of energy upon others. We may become less calculating and more compassionate. It is much easier to be present when you are in your heart. When stuck in your head you can easily be reliving a memory or anticipating some future potential. Life is happening right now, and so is inner peace, if you will allow it.

This needs to be part of the evolution of men. We must begin to look upon ourselves as significant, vital, and worthy of healing, and connect with others from a healthy strength. From a place of higher energy (whether or not this is communicated verbally) our love and consideration for others will be received. Heart space supports the context of unity, where we are all here to live in peace, harmony, and cooperation. How we actually go about creating this new world will of course utilize both our heart and our head. When I talk about personal and spiritual growth as a way of reaching our highest potential, this is what I mean. We must utilize the best human and spiritual qualities that support our highest purpose and function.

We would be hard pressed to function in this world strictly from the heart. But when our mental faculties are combined with a sincere integrity and desire for the wellbeing of all, we will experience the wholeness in which we were designed to live. This obviously is not a male/female thing. Many women live in their heads, and some men have great compassion and understanding of their spiritual capacity. However, I think that finding this proper balance is more of an issue for men than women. As one who has outwardly functioned and expressed more from an intellectual and analytical perspective, I know that maintaining this balance and freedom to open my heart is critical for my growth and healing.

The issue is not that we don't have the emotional capacity to understand on the level of feeling, it is more a matter of shifting our priority and focus within. The place where the healing and growth happens is when as a man you can accept that it is not only ok, but vital to your wellbeing to recognize and express your inner truth. In the context of spirituality, it is not a matter of memorizing the words of wisdom expressed by others that offers any real value. You must be able to feel your truth within your being. If you allow it, which is a shift in awareness, you will know when something resonates with you as true or not – but go beyond your thinking mind. If something is not true for you, just allow it to be without attaching your energy. If you recognize a feeling or knowing within, that in any way supports and raises you energetically, then you will want to listen to that and explore it further. This is the inner focus that brings healing on a life-changing level. Again, it is more about feeling than thinking. Feeling is in the present moment and is unlimited when fully allowed to be experienced. Thought is based upon prior knowledge and is often, therefore, limited.

When people ask you to accept something on faith they are asking you to put aside a purely analytical process and be open to exploring something based upon feeling and energy. Some people sense energy very strongly, for others it is very subtle, and still others seem to have no conscious awareness of energy at all. Where you are in this level of consciousness and sensitivity to energy varies widely among all people. If you are on a path of healing and growth that is improving the quality of your life, then that is what is most important. Don't get hung up on your level of sensitivity to energy, and don't compare yourself to others; it is not a competition.

Based upon my training, personality, and gifts, I like to combine the unseen principles with the more tangible outcomes when explaining personal and spiritual growth. I hope that you have noticed this in the writing thus far. Being an accountant for 30 years has taught me to be practical, structured, and organized as a way of thinking and being. While I have experienced tremendous personal growth by balancing my life from both a human and spiritual perspective, I understand that for most there must be a payoff that they can grasp with their minds. Yet faith is an essential and valuable tool in that it allows us to open up to unlimited possibilities, to things greater than our education and personal experience, and to a higher purpose for our life.

For example, the writing of this book required my being able to function at a high level both from my head and my heart. The process of being structured, organized, and disciplined was essential to creating an outline, editing, and handling all business aspects of self-publishing. The actual words in the manuscript came from an allowing within my heart space (spirit) to open to something beyond the known within my mind (this is higher wisdom). Spirit also supported me in this process by blocking a critical mind that would often tell me I can't do this (ego), or the energetic expressions by other people that I should be doing something else (more profitable).

While living in this physical world we must fully realize the value of our growth in our daily lives. We must re-train our mind, improve our thoughts, shift our awareness, and take daily steps toward developing a healthier, more joyful, and fulfilling life. This requires that we utilize our spiritual gifts as well as our more human qualities of logic, analysis, structure, and effort. Many spiritual teachers (gurus) live in such a heightened state of spiritual connection and sensitivity to energy that they are primarily unrelatable to most people. While they serve their purpose on the planet, I recognize and prefer to teach that this process of transformation from ego to spirit, within the human experience, is a gradual and on-going pursuit that must have relevance to our physical lives as well as the ascension of our soul.

I always felt things deeply, and had great interest in things beyond what my senses could determine, but I kept this mostly to myself. I learned that it is "safer" to stay in the box of the known, and to outwardly show less emotion than I was feeling on the inside. Ultimately this is very unsatisfying and inauthentic; it is based in fear. Being overly analytical withholds opportunities to feel and experience the wonders of life just as they are, and not according to some perfect mental plan that never materializes. We can get caught up in paralysis by analysis and limit our exposure to discovering our truth organically. Instead of putting our heart out there in relationships, we might hold back, afraid to be vulnerable, and risk the other person not really knowing how you feel. We also hold ourselves back from being leaders and difference makers; always the student, never the teacher. Well, I have news for you, we are all here to be leaders and teachers in some capacity.

Opening up to my heart space, and allowing myself to be ok with being more vulnerable and expressive, has created a more authentic life. I am now functioning from my head and my heart. I connect with others in a more supportive way, because I have compassion for them and I can feel their pain, yet I am also objective in analyzing and understanding where they are in their healing process and where my support may bring benefit. Does this mean that I am always right? No, but my intentions are always coming from a higher place. I can also more easily feel and support other people's joy, and express my own. I am always learning from every person and experience, but I am now also a teacher, awakener, writer, and mentor. I was never one who felt the need to express my opinion about every subject, nor am I "in love" with the sound of my voice, so speaking up about my truth is quite the transformation. We offer our light and love into this world from our heart, not our head. But we do not need to lose our head in the process, the shift I am talking about moves us toward balancing the head and the heart.

Shifting your awareness from your head to your heart is not only for those of us who have tended to over think everything. Other men leap into action, constantly on the move, with seemingly very little thought processes. Actually, that's not quite true. They are thinking and moving, but primarily for their own benefit, exclusive of the impact it has on the feelings of others. In this case it is still vitally important to begin to shift and develop more awareness into heart space. Only your thoughts, feelings, and actions that bring benefit to all have any real value.

If there is a lack of compassion or empathy for others, then there is an unhealthy imbalance, and a human in pain. The heart space is considered the seat of the soul. So while this is not a literal physical manifestation, it implies that our spiritual connection to Divinity and permanence resides in this place within the body. Shifting our awareness to this higher truth may support us in being more conscious of how all beings are affected by our expressions of energy (thoughts, words, and actions). However, a person who is lacking compassion and empathy for others is likely in need of a great deal of healing and re-educating before they are ready to focus on opening the heart and developing inner peace.

Always know that it is to your highest benefit to be who you are. And know that by shifting more awareness to your inner connection you can be more aligned with your highest potential. Doing so will give you great insight as to your true gifts, purpose, and path. Stifling your feelings will always lead to limitation and suffering. We are all here to thrive and be the culmination of all that is possible. So utilize all of the clues that are trying to guide you to a higher way of living, both for yourself and others. As you develop the quality of inner peace in your life, you will have accepted your higher truth, and now can relate to, and accept others in a loving, compassionate way.

"All difficult things have their origin in that which is easy, and great things in that which is small."
– Lao Tzu

The Power of Forgiveness

I believe that, at least intellectually, everyone is familiar with the term and concept of forgiveness. But the true forgiveness that has the power to change lives must come from your heart space and not your head. We can say it, we can think it, and we can think we mean it, but until you feel it deeply within your level of knowing (truth), you are not yet there. When you reach true forgiveness there will be a strong inner peace surrounding the person or circumstance for which you are offering forgiveness. This does not mean that you are ready for round two with them. Use your higher discernment, attained through your experience, to determine if there needs to be any further association.

This forgiveness is not dependent upon its acceptance by someone else. True forgiveness is for you, and not for anyone else. It need not even be expressed to the other person to have benefit to you. No one else has any power over you that you do not choose to allow. If you feel that someone has brought harm to you in any way at any time in your past, there is nothing that they can do to take away that experience. Therefore, there is nothing

109

more required from them pertaining to that situation, or your healing. How they deal with their transgressions is their lesson and life path. That is part of their journey, not yours. If, however, you sincerely feel that by expressing your forgiveness to them it will help them release their guilt and suffering, then this may be appropriate. But make sure that you are doing this for their benefit, and not some kind of ego gratification for yourself. A truly spiritual act does not require an audience.

Whatever harm that you feel they may have brought into your life can only be carried on and perpetuated in your present life by you. So when you can forgive others on a deep level, you are accepting that what was done is done. You are choosing to no longer suffer as a victim, and are now moving forward in an empowering way. You are now freed from this past lesson. As a memory it may occasionally come back into your thoughts, but you can now recognize it for what it was and simply release it. This present moment releasing serves to confirm your inner strength and peace. In truth, you are acknowledging yourself and others as humans who sometimes make mistakes, or otherwise act from an unconscious place (disconnected from spirit). This is true compassion and higher wisdom in action.

When we don't come to this higher perspective, we may assume a victim stance which is a real hindrance to personal growth and healing. As a way of not taking responsibility for ourselves we derive great false power in blaming others for the experiences in our lives. Spiritual principles dictate that we attract into our lives that which serves the greatest opportunity for healing, growth, and truth. Every experience is designed to teach us how to be more loving and empowered in who we truly are. Sometimes these lessons support and encourage us along the path we are on, and other times they will abruptly redirect our life toward the higher path. When we choose to follow ego, we will attract the experiences and associations that lead us down the wrong path, and into suffering. Whether it rises to the level of victim depends upon our perception of the experience.

Anytime we can blame an experience on someone else we are not going to learn the higher lesson involved. So while the ego is satisfied that it did nothing wrong, you are setting yourself up for more such lessons, or at least on-going suffering from the original lesson. Either way, you cannot grow and transcend from the experience. On some level you are held down into that negative energy space where you will most assuredly attract more of what you don't want. Being empowered means to be accountable and responsible for your choices, thoughts, feelings, and opportunities. Growing and developing to the healthy space whereby you can accept your role in any experience, and then release it without holding blame, is life changing in leading you to your highest personal and spiritual potential.

The biggest part of forgiveness is in forgiving yourself. I have had some of these life-altering experiences where I was abruptly and harshly redirected away from the wrong path, as I am certain you have experienced as well. The fallout and consequences can be quite painful and may have an impact on your life for years to come. At first, it is natural to feel victimized and angry. But relatively soon it shifts to guilt, embarrassment, and yes still anger, but now it is directed at yourself. You recognize that you allowed and even participated in these experiences, often against the warning of your own inner knowing (intuition). And then, ego runs with this self-tormenting scenario. We all know how easy it is to beat ourselves up for the poor choices we sometimes make, or anytime we are disappointed in our effort or outcome.

Forgiving yourself is one of the most significant opportunities for healing. Our ego says, "You made a huge mistake, and look what you got!" But spirit knows that you made a choice (while unconscious) to have an experience in order to learn your truth. No judgment, no punishment, simply an opportunity to learn and heal. Had you been aware of your higher truth in those moments, you would have made a different, more empowering choice. You would have chosen to love yourself enough not to engage with another person who is also unconscious. Forgive them, for they were merely your teacher, and they themselves were disconnected from their spirit. Forgive yourself, because you chose that lesson in the only way you knew how, so that you could begin to heal.

What if you were the one being accused or you felt responsible for harming another? From the standpoint of all human interaction, we all judge an experience from our own perspective. In other words, we look at our own experiences from how we are affected. This could either be somewhat objective or completely delusional, yet either person can claim their perception as their truth. This often relegates the shifting of blame to being unreliable. Therefore, the real value in the experience is to show each of us where we are in connection to spirit. If while unconscious (disconnected from spirit), you chose to engage with someone else who is also unconscious, then you each participated in this experience for the purpose of facilitating a healing and a re-connection to your spirit. Whether you are able to choose to honor this lesson and shift in a positive direction going forward is up to each person individually. However by doing so you will develop more compassion and love for yourself and others, and create the higher awareness that will support you in making more empowered choices in the future.

Whether the "harm" came last month or decades in the past, take this opportunity to receive the healing you desire and need, and offer a full heartfelt forgiveness to yourself and any other person involved. Again, it does not condone anyone's inappropriate and unloving actions, it does not need to. Only ego is concerned with the perception of fairness, guilt, judgment, or retribution. Your spirit understands the higher value to be gained by all parties involved. As we have previously elaborated on in good detail, life is more than this physical body in this particular lifespan or incarnation. Always shift toward love and a release of the things that are not of love.

During the writing of this book, Nelson Mandela, the former President of South Africa transitioned (passed away). One of the most amazing enlightened men of any generation, Mr. Mandela was a prime example of the power and goodness that comes from forgiveness. After speaking against and challenging the brutal and unconscionable acts against the black South Africans, Mr. Mandela was imprisoned for 27 years. He was finally released in 1990 at the age of 72, and became a central figure in ending apartheid by working together with his former captors in creating a new inclusive society. In 1993 he was awarded a Nobel Peace Prize. And in 1994, at age 76, he became the first democratically-elected President of the Republic of South Africa. What an amazing life story and example of transforming from your experiences and living your higher purpose for the betterment of mankind.

Some things can only be explained by this higher truth. Events happen every day that seem unfair, unjust, and perpetrated by one person or group against another "innocent" person or group. The truth is that even if you cannot satisfactorily explain it in human terms, the holding on to hatred, fear, and suffering serves no beneficial purpose. Forgiving and releasing this consuming negative energy supports us all in moving forward in the most empowered way.

Another example of forgiveness comes from a good friend of mine. As a young child she was abused and molested by her step-father over several years. As she grew into adulthood, she appeared accomplished on the outside, but had many unresolved issues within. These experiences as a child were affecting her self-image and accordingly the choices she made as an adult, especially in the area of personal relationships. She went through counseling and various studies for many years, but it was not until she focused within to her spiritual power that she was able to find the healing that changed her life. And a significant part of that process occurred when she was able to fully forgive her step-father.

She now understands the value of this experience in teaching and shaping her toward the fulfillment of her higher purpose. And she is a coach to women who have experienced abuse (as well as any other afflictions) who are working through the process of healing in their lives. Through the inner work she has done, she has transformed from a victim to one who adds great light, love, and wisdom into the world. You can certainly say that as a human child she did not choose (or deserve) that experience, but as a spiritual being here to learn, grow, and fulfill her unique purpose, is it not possible that this was designed to bring benefit to her and others. So next time you hear about some such tragedy, have love and compassion for all involved, and also consider that there may be a higher purpose that is being served in their lives.

"Every time you are tempted to react in the same old way, ask if you want to be a prisoner of the past, or a pioneer of the future."
Deepak Chopra

Non-Reaction to the Ego of Others Supports Inner Peace

Begin to claim your inner strength while interacting with others. It is not always easy (especially at first) due to our long history of "defending" ourselves from the perception of being attacked. This is the clash of two egos creating drama and suffering. Of course, if real danger is present you must always take steps to protect yourself. When you can achieve a state of non-reaction to the ego of others, you have taken a very significant step toward realizing your true power. You are also demonstrating self-love and you are teaching love to the person who is acting from their ego.

There are two key points to consider: 1) recognize in that moment that the other person is a divinely created being that is simply acting out from a place of their own ego (fear) instead of from their Divinity; and 2) You always have a choice to connect with your spirit and choose inner peace instead of being offended or harmed. If you want to be empowered always choose spirit. If you choose ego (which is a choice to disconnect from spirit) you will create more fear and suffering. There are no winners in a confrontation of egos.

I have already talked about the truth of who we are. If our thoughts, words, or actions are steeped in fear, selfishness, hate, judgment, or insecurity, it does not change who we are. We judge ourselves all of the time, but we are never judged by Divine

115

Source, who knows from where we come. As an extension of our Creator, we have the choice of seeing only the Divine in others as well. If someone is acting from their place of ego and separation, and being unkind toward you, they simply were unable or unaware of their ability to act from their Divinity. We don't have to like their behavior, but in recognizing their suffering we can and should have compassion for them. This is the "turning the other cheek" that Jesus spoke about.

Maybe someone put us down or said very hurtful words. Does this make it so? With greater inner strength, we define ourselves, instead of allowing others to define us. And though we are not infallible, we are always striving to do our best, so let's now see ourselves in the highest light. It always feels better when someone praises us than when they are critical of us. But either way, their words do not define us. That is why all of the lessons in this book deal with finding and realizing your own power, from within yourself (which is spirit).

One of my all-time favorite books is *The Four Agreements*, by Don Miguel Ruiz, which I highly recommend to all. The second of the four agreements reads, "Don't take anything personally". Regarding this "Agreement", Don Miguel says, "Personal importance, or taking things personally, is the maximum expression of selfishness because we make the assumption that everything is about "me"... Nothing other people do is because of you. It is because of THEM. All people live in their own dream, in their own mind; they are in a completely different world from the one we live in. When we take something personally, we make the assumption that they know what is in our world, and we try to impose our world on their world."[2] I think that sums it up pretty well. Allow others to be in their space

---

[2] The Four Agreements, by Don Miguel Ruiz, excerpt from page 48.

without acting upon the desire to correct, fix, or attack them, and without feeling like you need to defend yourself.

We always have a choice of how to react. The more time you have spent serving ego the more likely that your immediate response will be to return the perceived attack. As you are now developing a spiritual connection and higher understanding of yourself, you will begin to respond more quickly from that perspective. As always, awareness is critical. When you are fully present and a situation arises, you can recognize this as an opportunity to make a conscious choice that will be more beneficial to all involved. If you immediately feel the heat of anger, stop and take a deep breath or two, just to get the space you need to connect to Source. In truth this person is providing a teaching moment. If their words trigger an emotional reaction in you it will show you an area where there is still some fear or doubt within you. Though it does not feel like it, this is really an act of kindness on their part (on the level of spirit). They are mirroring aspects of you that are in need of healing.

You can begin to see that with a higher perspective of who you are and your potential, everything can take on a different meaning. The other option that most people take is to get heated, become offended, insult them back (with either words or thoughts), and argue back and forth. Now you both feel insulted. Plus, you may feel bad about yourself because secretly you believe that what they said is true. Ego always leads to drama and suffering.

When you choose to honor yourself and others there is a very different outcome. First, you kept a potentially volatile encounter from escalating. Second, you held a peaceful view of yourself and the other person. Third, you can decide if what they said has any merit for you. If it is completely untrue or

117

unfounded, don't attach your energy to it – let it go peacefully. But if there is some truth that you may wish to utilize to improve in some way – humbly thank them (even if it was not delivered in a kind or gentle way). Fourth, you have acted as a spiritual teacher to the other person.

Remember that, like you they are spirit, the difference is that in that moment they chose to separate from their spirit. Your action as a response to their unconscious behavior is a mirror showing them the truth of who they are. This is how we begin to heal the world, by teaching through the example of our lives, the higher nature of *who we truly are.*

"Happiness comes of the capacity to feel deeply, to enjoy simply, to think freely, to risk life, to be needed."
– **Storm Jameson**

Creating Peace in your Relationships

In the **Matter** chapter we talked about the significance of being a conscious partner, and that healthy people make the most joyful and fulfilling relationships. So your greatest opportunity for a loving relationship is to develop your own inner love, healing, and growth. Of course, we may already be in a relationship, and besides, we are always on some level working on this inner development. Therefore we are often in the position of working on ourselves while in a personal relationship with another person.

We usually think that we come together for purely human reasons, like physical attraction, personality, intellect, common interests, etc. But more than that, it is the energy between you,

118

and the soul's purpose that attracts the two of you together. Energy is often hard to explain in human terms. Why am I drawn to her, but not her? They are both cute, fun, and interesting, but I'm really drawn to that person. There is somehow an opening energetically for you to connect with each other. You are definitely being brought together for some higher purpose. It could manifest as a temporary companionship or friendship, a long-term partnership, or anything in between, but in any case, there is always a connection and a sharing of energy.

While it is true that each of us are on our own life path, on the level of Divinity we are connected. So when the frequency of your energy is telling the Universe what you need/want, it will match up with the frequency that our partner is transmitting. You have come together to support each other in learning and experiencing something of value on a spiritual level. Sometimes these lessons ultimately manifest as great love, joy, fun, and passion (which again, is largely a factor of our level of inner healing). Other times we must learn through pain, fear, doubt, and suffering. It all depends on our consciousness or wholeness, and what we have decided to attract for the purposes of our own inner healing.

Within the truth, that other people reflect to us our deepest thoughts/feelings about ourselves, our partner will likely be a walking/breathing extension of our inner self. Your life path is ultimately about taking responsibility for your own healing and growth in order to reach your highest potential for love, joy, and expansion. Therefore, what are you to think about the interactions between you and your partner? Is it predominantly happy, joyful, caring, and supportive? Or is it mostly joyless, draining, combative, and disempowering?

119

Be careful to not confuse your temporary circumstances with the energetic interaction between you. As energy and experience ebb and flow, you may presently be involved in challenging experiences, or you may find a relatively smooth patch where things seem to be easy. This will naturally have an impact on your relationship. However, your interaction, independent of your circumstances will tell you a great deal about the energy that is being exchanged between you, and therefore, the purpose and true value of the relationship. Do the energies of trust, support, encouragement, and cooperation with each other exist? These are the healthy qualities that determine a positive relationship under any circumstance. With your higher awareness you will know the quality of the energy between you.

Only you can control how you want to experience your life, and you have no control or authority over your partner. Within a relationship if you generally feel supported, appreciated, and understood, you will feel the Divine love energy between you combine and expand. This empowers you not only as an individual but as a couple, to manifest your highest desires for a happy, fulfilling life.

Conversely, if you typically feel unsupported in being yourself, unappreciated, unrecognized, and misunderstood no matter how you try to relate, then you will continue to feel your love energy being withdrawn from you. When people remain in this type of relationship, determined to "make it work" no matter what, they will invariably "lose their power". And this leads to all kinds of suffering. Depending on your level of awareness and accountability to your spirit, you may not recognize the energetic signals that you are being shown. Without honest healing work, you will likely experience the manifestations of losing your power, as the emotions of sadness, disappointment, defensiveness, frustration, anger, and indifference.

Honestly work within yourself and with your partner to discuss, contemplate, and understand what may be the internal cause of the challenging emotional interaction between you. All of our experiences are lessons, so what is the lesson of this relationship. How can we utilize our partner (mirror) to better understand our need for love, healing, and inner peace. With this higher wisdom, we must lovingly express our needs to our partner (without any blame) and ask for their support, while taking the responsibility to transform and grow within. And we must allow our partner to do the same thing. This does require a level of awareness and detachment, as you are not only tuning into your higher knowing yourself, but you must be willing to accept the truth that comes forth for your partner as well. Your application of inner strength is essential. You want to expose absolute truth in order to create the freedom necessary to reach your highest potential for growth, love, joy, and inner peace for yourself and for the relationship!

If you are unsupported in your effort to take this level of accountability for your wellness and happiness, or if your partner is unwilling to examine themselves on this level, you would be wise to seriously consider your options. At this stage you are probably not remaining together for the purposes of spiritual growth and expansion. You are likely together for reasons that seem justified by ego, and centered on fear. Maybe deep down you don't feel that you deserve better, or that you are not fully capable of surviving on your own, or you have pressure from outside parties to stay together. You can clearly see how none of these reasons are empowering or sustainable for someone who really wants to experience a happy life. You may continue to co-exist within this unsatisfying life circumstance, but for many this will naturally escalates into a fierce battle of egos, leading to great bitterness and even abuse.

121

Abuse is the condition whereby two unhealthy, unempowered people are so intent on getting the other person to be who they want them to be (to compensate for the inner healing they are unwilling to do themselves), that they will resort to unkind, cruel, or inappropriate expressions of energy (thoughts, words, and actions). They are not taking responsibility for their own healing, so instead they are trying to survive by taking out their frustration on their partner. Subconsciously they are pulling their partner's energy because they are so disconnected from their own higher source of energy, spirit.

Abuse in personal relationships is a pandemic in our world. Even to this day some cultures continue to denigrate and disrespect woman to a level that renders their behavior medieval and unevolved to the point of living in darkness. So perhaps this discussion is beyond their consciousness level. Consequently, I am focusing these words on those who have a true belief in equality in relationships.

The face of abuse, if you will, has been physical violence by men against women. This has been a significant societal problem throughout history. In the past, much of it related to the displacement of power between men and women. Due to this circumstance, a false concept of power was developed and carried out by men, assuming that they were somehow superior to women, much the same way that slaves were abused and mistreated by their owners. Certainly this need not be promoted or accepted by anyone on any level today. We must now be the example of people living more enlightened lives.

So as equality is gaining hold, I believe that the dynamic of abuse is changing as well. In a partnership of two adults, both individuals are contributing and participating to the ongoing energy exchange dynamic. The truth is that both men and women are equally capable of abusing their partner, and while physical violence gets the headlines, and is often the final step, mental, emotional, and verbal abuse is far more common and extremely disempowering. This is not just a "men's problem" it is a problem for all people.

A healthy, peaceful relationship requires two people who are healthy and peaceful within themselves. This does not mean that everything flows smoothly, and we are always happy and smiling at each other. After all, we ultimately came together for purposes of growth, healing, and expansion. It does mean however, that we acknowledge our own responsibility for giving ourselves what we most need, in order to be healthy and peaceful. In this relationship, our partner is loving and caring for themselves, just as we are for ourselves. Each of you, then, is adding love and light to your partnership, and the energetic connection between you.

We now can easily add support when our partner has a slight depletion due to some temporary circumstance. It is in trying to fill the entire void in energy, of someone who is completely unconscious, that it becomes very unrealistic and exhausting. Yet I am sure that we all have attempted this. We have expectations that someone will act in a loving way, when they have consistently shown us the contrary, and have made little or no effort to be responsible for their own healing and happiness.

Many men, me included, have been guilty of trying to rescue a partner. It is fine to recognize the good qualities in someone (deep down we all have them), but it is actually irresponsible to dismiss the glaring problems that may prove to be so personally damaging to you down the line. You cannot heal a damaged partner! As a counselor or coach you may be able to assist someone in their healing process, but this is always done from a healthy professional distance. It's time to be responsible enough to accept the truth about others, and to love yourself enough to do the inner work which leads to choices that support a life of empowerment and reward – **you are worthy!**

When you are doing the spiritual work within yourself you will now be aware of what it is you need in order to heal, and you will be demonstrating your willingness to be accountable for your own happiness. You and your partner do not have to live within the same level of awareness and consciousness; however you each need to recognize what it is that you need in order to create the healthy, loving, joyful life you desire. The absolutely essential factor is that you are completely honest with each other. This is the only way that you have a chance to come together in true support. If you honestly determine what you need for yourselves, and find that your paths of fulfillment are totally incongruent and incompatible, then with the highest truth and integrity you need to make a different choice. But this decision need not be made without a full accountability and understanding of your needs for inner healing and growth.

The shifting to greater consciousness implies awareness and connection to our highest spiritual truth. Within the arena of developing inner peace, as applied to fulfilling, loving relationships, we, as men, we have one more obstacle. We are and have always been very testosterone-driven creatures, and as such, our awareness and higher judgment may be impaired to our detriment while in a predominantly egoic state of being. If we want to change the path that has brought suffering in the form of misguided relationships, we must develop the inner strength to gain greater awareness of how we are affected by this issue.

For some it is more of a problem than for others, but it is likely that each of us has been guilty of poor judgment for the sake of a physical/sexual attraction. As men this can be our true weakness, and I assure you that this is not lost on women, especially the women who have learned to use this power as a trap to devour their prey, which of course is due to their unhealthy inner state. As we know, like energy attracts. Over the ages men have freely followed their "passion", and have propped up women as sex objects, so we have set our own trap. We must use our higher awareness to avoid this pitfall.

When you make the decision to connect with a partner based primarily (if not exclusively) on sexual attraction and intimacy, without fully considering the myriad of other more relevant factors regarding what constitutes a healthy, loving relationship, you cannot be too surprised when things end badly. Let me lay it out plainly. Are those moments of sexual pleasure worth trading your overall happiness and wellbeing? Do you understand that the consequences may be far reaching and very destructive? Is it more important to you to have a physically beautiful partner in order to satisfy your ego, or a partner that has inner and outer beauty sufficient to satisfy your soul? Do you want someone to lust after who is happy to use you for what she can get, or someone who truly loves you for who you are? As I am writing this I am reminded of the movie "Shallow Hal", which has a very powerful message about the true inner value in people. The choice is always yours, just be aware of what you are actually choosing, your inner peace and happiness is at stake.

Knowing that sex is an important factor, a better way to approach the decision of partnering with someone is to determine what are your true needs, desires, and boundaries. If all you really want is a meaningless fling, then you have your answer. However, you must be honest about your intentions with your partner. But, if you are looking for a partner with which to establish a mutually-beneficial, loving, joyful, and supportive relationship, then you must really understand if this person has the qualities you need to deliver what you are looking for. Again, utilize your past personal experiences as lessons; listen to your inner knowing and do not let yourself be deceived. People will show you who they are, and if you are going to ignore this truth, then you are choosing disappointment and suffering.

Men are certainly not absolved in all of this. First, we are not above displaying our most desirable assets with the intention of persuading a woman to fall for us. It is natural to want to "put your best foot forward", and certainly that is better than leading with your wounds. However, we all need to be honest with each other and not try to deceive a potential partner by presenting some false persona or withholding extremely relevant information. There is no victory in conning someone as a basis to start a relationship. The second point is that, in the end, we are each personally responsible for ourselves. Therefore, it is up to us to go into these situations with our eyes open and utilize our highest discernment. The better we know ourselves and the more self-love and healing we have developed, the better are the chances that we will present a positive and honest view of who we are, and attract someone worthy of our love and attention.

If you are currently in a relationship that is loving and supportive, then point your "passion" toward your partner. Use your inner strength to detach from the seemingly unlimited provocative outer distractions. Honestly communicate your intimate desires with your partner, and learn to understand hers as well. Then together you must make the effort to find the greatest connection that satisfies each of you physically, emotionally, mentally, and spiritually. This is a significant part of a healthy, loving relationship, and for most people is a balancing act. Our energies are typically scattered in many directions, so while you don't want to over-emphasize your love making, you certainly do not want to ignore it either.

In order to attract a peaceful relationship, one in which you support each other fully without the need for drama and other emotional setbacks, first develop your own inner peace. If you are currently in a relationship that is lacking such peace, look within yourself first and stop blaming your partner. You are responsible for you, so do the inner work to fully understand your role in your own happiness or unhappiness. With this wisdom in place, communicate honestly with your partner as to the things you are working on for the sake of your own healing. When you need their support, ask for it in a gentle loving way (do not accuse or blame them). Some of what you need may require that your partner make some inner changes, in order for the relationship to work for you. Be embolded to express your thoughts and feelings with your partner, and really tune in and listen to (and feel) how they respond. From here you will have a stronger basis for evaluating the higher quality of the relationship toward supporting your path of inner healing, peace, love, and joy.

"The healthiest response to life is joy."
– Deepak Chopra

Do You Want to be Right or Happy?

One of the great sayings is, "If you want to be happy you are feeding spirit, and if you want to be right you are feeding ego". This is a tremendous example of developing inner peace. As you are working to advance along your higher path of personal and spiritual growth and healing, you will begin to recognize that you are more secure and comfortable with who you are and what works best for you. This is inner strength, and you are now not as susceptible to the opinions of others as you once were.

People will interact with you from whatever is their level of consciousness. If they are disconnected from spirit, and in need of inner healing, they will likely try to draw you into their drama and ego struggle. This is how they survive, without really taking responsibility for themselves, they will try to suck your energy - they are called "energy vampires". These are not bad people, they are merely in need of healing. They may in fact be people you like or even love - family, friends, etc. When you are in your space of inner truth you have a bit of a cushion of protection, whereby you may be able to look upon them, not with judgment or anger, but with compassion. Depending on your level of consciousness, this may last a couple seconds or remain indefinitely.

These people are always providing us with an opportunity to choose spirit instead of ego; therefore we can look upon them as our teachers. I think it is clear that this is a much higher view than getting angry, defensive, or thinking of them as a pain in the ass. With this brief cushion of protection you may breathe and gather yourself before your ego can arise to say, "Hey! You are wrong, and I am right." It could be an opinion or criticism, but some words or attitudes will easily fly by, while others will push some sensitive buttons and really get your attention. This is when you must take notice, they are pointing out some inner belief you have that is still in need of healing (that you are probably not even aware of).

If someone calls you an idiot for doing or thinking something, you have a couple ways to react. One, you can say, "no, I'm right, you're the idiot" and then get into a verbal insult contest. Now, both of you are unhappy and depleted energetically, because you were each serving ego and not spirit. Historically this has been the first instinct of the old school macho man. Or two, you might have a knowing deep within that you, in fact, are not an idiot, and being connected to spirit as you are, you feel no need to attach any significance to their words or return the attack to this person. You are left clear, energized, and peaceful within your being. And you feel no need to judge them harshly for their inner weakness.

In a third option, you may be connected to spirit, and feel compassion for the other person without the need to retaliate. But what if being called an idiot (or some other demeaning name, such as: lazy, stupid, weak, boring, ugly, etc.) is something that has been ingrained into your mind over many years and has attached to your self-esteem and identity? You likely have made great progress in redefining the truth of your inner knowing of whom you really are, yet there may still be some remnants of inner poison. You will likely feel an energetic heat rising from within. But, instead of defending yourself to this person, utilize this experience as a way to recognize that you are still in need of some self-love and healing in this area. Then take the inner steps necessary to re-connect with spirit and further support your healing and growth by remembering your higher truth. This simple act of recognizing with awareness this false self-belief will begin to foster a level of healing. You are shining the light of truth upon a place of darkness, thus the darkness may be eradicated.

Of course in all three examples of how you might respond to the ego of others, the view point of the other person is entirely their own belief, and has no basis in truth. More than that it is likely a reflection of how they feel about themselves. Therefore, when we respond in kind, we are revealing how we feel about ourselves in that moment. Again, developing inner peace is not a passive activity. It takes great inner strength and wisdom in order to love yourself enough to not be adversely affected by the unconscious expressions of others. Add to this that you are showing them compassion, and a proper example of a more loving way to be in the world. You are now being a *Peaceful Warrior!*

I have been speaking primarily to your inner and energetic reaction to the ego in someone else. However, if you are in any physical danger you must act appropriately to hopefully retreat, or if necessary, defend yourself. Most of these situations are entirely avoidable when you begin to become empowered in your life. When you cease to think of yourself as a victim you will tend to remove yourself from a potentially victimizing circumstance before the conditions may even arise. Additionally, you can access a higher level of discernment when you are connected to spirit in the present moment, and avoid most dangerous situations altogether. We learn our lessons through experience, and when we are functioning on a higher level of awareness it is rarely necessary to learn our lessons through great suffering and harm. Though there is a higher purpose in all experience.

It is worth mentioning that this concept of choosing to be happy or be right has great relevance in the male/female dynamic. We so often think and relate on such a different level, largely because we have both operated in such an imbalance of masculine/feminine energy, that we foster much misunderstanding between us. Functioning differently does not by itself have to cause such suffering. Notice how often we choose a partner that seems to be very different from ourselves. However, when our egos are routinely operating within the interaction and communication of this particular dynamic, you have the potential for fireworks. We have been falsely educated to think that it is more important to stand our ground, be right, and get our way. If instead we focus on acceptance of our different views, and allow each of us to function within our own truth, we would be using a spiritual approach to come together in peace. Of course, in a personal relationship it is required that both individuals learn to take this empowered, loving approach.

"Greater than the tread of mighty armies is an idea whose time has come."
– Victor Hugo

It's Time to Stop the Bullying

It's interesting that bullying as an attitude and activity has been prevalent as long as there have been humans, but now, all of a sudden, there is a big push to draw worldwide attention to the harm that this causes. This is a very good sign for the world. There is much happening on the level of energy to awaken this world right now, and I know that personally the time has been ripe for me to write and disseminate the message of personal growth and healing for men. The world is more ready than ever to receive and implement higher wisdom for the sake of greater consciousness and unity.

In a more civilized world it seems obvious that bullying other people is wrong and counterproductive to the wellbeing of all involved. With greater development of inner strength and peace, the need or even the desire to abuse and/or manipulate anyone else would be non-existent. It takes only a basic level of awareness and understanding to notice that bullying comes from inner weakness and self-loathing. A healthy human being lifts

131

others up, which is what we naturally do when we begin to live more consciously.

Developing this inner peace in men is such a healing gift to all people. The old stereotypical bully was long on aggression and short on inner strength. Maybe they were bullied and made to feel like they did not matter, or were otherwise insufficient to excel without bringing others down. When you can look beneath the surface to the underlying problem for all afflicted people, instead of just judging them by their actions, you can have compassion and a sincere desire for their inner healing. They are living a life dominated by ego (fear), which not only disturbs other people, but inhibits them from recognizing their true higher path and purpose in this life.

The reason that this issue is so prominent in society at this time is that this is a two-fold problem that, of course, is part of the bigger issue. First, as I have said, this is a cry of help for those who feel justified in mistreating others in order to feel some kind of warped power for themselves. The second problem is that we as a society of humans have allowed, accepted, and encouraged this behavior. My father tells of a story from when he was a young boy, where his grandfather told him that he would give him a quarter if he would beat up some (random) kid walking down the street. This of course sounds barbaric. This is only a few generations removed from today. But even now there are school yards and parks that promote such cruel and unevolved thinking. Of course now through technology we hear about cyber bullying that has brought great harm and even death to some fragile psyches.

This is now the age when people individually and societally must come to a greater healing and respect for themselves and all others. The world is diversifying and globalizing, which means that there are many more lifestyles, beliefs, nationalities, and desire for personal freedom interacting than ever before. The time is now for us to be accepting of all of these brothers and sisters who have just as much of a right to happiness, love, peace, and prosperity as we do. It is time to open our hearts and our minds, to practice personal and spiritual growth for our own benefit and that of others as well.

Our world is evolving, and those who continue to judge, discriminate, bully, and condemn others who look, act, or believe differently than they do, are beginning to stand out and show their ignorance and weakness. They are no longer the majority, and like the dinosaurs, soon will be extinct. Where they once may have ruled from the bully pulpit, with a secret underbelly of hypocrisy and vile behaviors, their attitudes now seem archaic and baseless. This is as it should be, we all must accept our true higher nature and begin to act and think within the framework of unity.

If you bully, you are not tough, you are just under evolved. If you are being bullied you need to know that you matter and that you are worthy of better treatment. That starts with self-love, which can be developed even if you do not feel loved from your outside environment. If you need physical protection, get help. But a major step in your development is to stop being the victim in your own mind. If available, get the counseling or coaching help you need, but take ownership of your own life and wellbeing. You are not here to be judged or crucified by anyone else, so be the first to take a stand for yourself.

This will continue to become easier as more of us awaken to support those who struggle to support themselves. Like a team, society can be judged by its weakest link. Those of us who are strong must lift those in need, not trample them as was done before. What could be a better use of your gifts, talents, and resources? Utilize your inner peace to have more compassion for other people, and use your inner strength to maintain your own empowered position in life.

Chapter 3 Exercises

Exercise 1:

As a way to overcome the mental and energetic blocks from the past you may need to utilize the tool of forgiveness. **Look deeply at any fears or resistance that may be blocking you, due to the fact that you are still holding pain, anger, or blame against someone else for their mistreatment.** Remember everyone is a teacher to us, and our experiences are designed to show us where we are still in need of healing.

Fully consider what you may have learned about yourself, as a result of dealing with this person, which may serve you well in the future. The lesson is/was for you, so utilize this experience for growth. **Next, hand write a letter to this person (you will not send it) to forgive them and yourself for any experience in which you perceived pain and suffering. Express your gratitude to them for having been the teacher that taught you xyz (whatever the specific lesson was). Thank them, bless them, and then release them in love.** The point is for you to move forward to create your ideal life, and not continue to carry within you the lower vibration of fear or anger. Now you may safely destroy or dispose of the letter. Repeat this process for anyone who you are still allowing to have a negative impact upon your personal power.

Exercise 2:

Sharpen your higher awareness by noticing the energy of your interactions with other people (do this over a period of one week). Document any significant findings. Work to develop your inner peace by allowing others to have their space to express their truth (or opinion). Notice the urge to judge, correct, or even

135

condemn others. Allow your truth to be expressed without the need to defend it or convince anyone else.

Simply noticing the ego in you is a significant step toward reducing its power. It is your spirit that is the noticer, so you will be shifting more attention into this powerful space. The goal is to be happy in who you truly are (remember, you are enough). The ego wants to be right (in comparison to someone else) but this will not bring peace or happiness.

CHAPTER 4:
OWNERSHIP

"You must take personal responsibility. You cannot change the circumstances, the seasons, or the wind, but you can change yourself. That is something you have charge of..."
– Jim Rohn

Personal Responsibility

One definition of ownership is – "Belonging or relating to oneself; that which belongs to oneself." In the ***Empower Model*** the only thing which you truly own is yourself. At least it's the only thing you own that really matters. Your material possessions serve only a temporary purpose, and you cannot own another person (though sometimes people act like they do). When I talk about taking ownership of yourself, I am talking of course about your life, and all of the ways in which you express it.

With respect to this life that you "own", the key point in supporting personal and spiritual growth is to begin to take responsibility for it. With the background of shifting your awareness and understanding of who you truly are, and what you are capable of, your actions may now more easily be directed to the things that bring greater love, joy, peace, and fulfillment. Your thoughts, words, and actions may now be more supportive of other people as well.

The mere act of being born into this life confirms ownership; however, it is then what you do with your life that determines its growth and potential for adding or detracting from the light in this world.   Personal responsibility is synonymous with accountability.   Once we become accountable and responsible for our expressions of energy in a higher manner, we will be able to create a healthy life that flows with the higher energy of spirit.

Personal responsibility implies more than just working hard to support a lifestyle and a certain material existence. It also places higher standards on how you interact with others, and how you think about yourself and others. Taking ownership of your life within a spiritual context means to acknowledge where in your life you are in need of inner healing; where you are disconnected from spirit. The ego thinks of ownership as possession. It says, "I own this life, and I will do whatever I please in order to get whatever I want. How it affects you is really not my concern." When you see it like that, doesn't it seem harsh and excessive? Yet when you look at any conflict between you and another person, that is what you are saying. Too many men have had the, "it's my way or the highway mentality". This is the thought process made manifest in this world by most people. We can certainly continue down this path, and continue to create the conditions we see in the world. Those with the strongest egos will control the rest, and both will suffer.

Ownership from the standpoint of personal responsibility, which is supported by spirit, recognizes the need for each of us to care for ourselves, but from a place of balance and wholeness.

Spirit says, "I am most empowered when I create the conditions in my life that support my wellness on all levels, within a larger context whereby I add my light and love for the benefit of all beings." Clearly, if we, as individuals, lived our lives according to Spirit's definition, instead of egos, the vibration of all life would be substantially higher. We would be living the new age on earth that we were designed to experience.

The first step in taking this higher ownership is to make a completely honest assessment of your life, both the various individual aspects of your life, and your life as a whole (the micro and the macro). You must do this exactly where you are right now; this is your starting point. Whatever has occurred in your past has already been experienced and has combined to create your present life circumstances and outlook. Here we are dealing with the perspective of coaching as opposed to counseling. We are not concerned about going back and re-living your childhood or past trauma. This is not to say that there is not value in this, but from the standpoint of assessment and establishing a baseline, you are determining where you are now and not how you got here.

If you need professional assistance, please get it, but this is a personal exercise that only you can determine with complete honesty. No sugarcoating, everything that exists in your life right now has been created by you! This also means that whatever you create going forward is because of you. **Now that is ownership!** No blame or guilt for things that are now unsatisfactory, and no useless boasting or excessive pride for the things that feel satisfying in your life. At this early point of analysis we are just being objective, without assigning emotion. Go to a space, both externally and internally that allows for the greatest peace and calm. Connect with your Divine nature and ask for guidance and assistance in support of this step in your personal and spiritual growth. I recommend utilizing your spiritual nature *and* your reasoning mind in order to combine both wisdom and knowledge (heart and head).

You can create a chart to document what you determine to be your current circumstances in the key areas of your life, for example, health, work/service, relationships, family, friends, hobbies, spiritual development, etc. Now on a subjective scale (1 – 10) rate your level of satisfaction in each of these areas. Only you can determine this rating. No one else can decide your value or the satisfaction in your life. From the framework of this analysis, you can see the areas of your life that may be the most out of balance, and in need of healing. Any area of our life that is unsatisfying, which could mean anything from feeling disappointed, to manifesting great pain and suffering, is pointing to something that is either receiving an insufficient amount of healthy attention, or too much negative attention.

Next, take time to contemplate or journal about the current conditions within a specific aspect of your life that you have rated unsatisfactory. For example, you may want to improve your health. Think about why this is an area that needs improvement. Maybe you are getting sick often, or you notice that your energy is low, or you want to be more fit, etc. Or your dissatisfaction might be work/career. Maybe it is too stressful, or it is unfulfilling, or unrewarding, etc. In this first step we are determining our level of satisfaction (or dissatisfaction) in the various areas of our life, and considering what it is that we feel is lacking, or otherwise suppressing our happiness.

The second step in utilizing personal responsibility for healing and growth is to begin to consider and determine the specific conditions that may begin to shift us to a greater level of satisfaction within this aspect of our life. From here, what steps can we begin to take right now that would empower us toward creating the outcome we desire? Ultimately, we want to bring in the Divine qualities of greater joy, love, peace, abundance, and fulfillment into our life.

We started with an analysis that gives you an objective view (using your subjective standards) of the areas of your life that need some kind of change in order to improve the quality of your life. In order to create change, action is always needed. An action may be the shifting of your awareness, thoughts, or perceptions, or it may be a choice to take a different approach or redirect to a new path. The change we are talking about must always be intended to lead to growth and expansion, and it is always about healing and honoring your true self. This is how you begin to become empowered.

I have said that all of our experiences and the consequences thereof are designed to teach us something. And that "something" is how to properly love, support, and honor ourselves. On a higher level, we choose these lessons in order to grow and expand the highest qualities of life. From your analysis you likely determined that some area of your life is bringing suffering or unhappiness. Fully consider the details of your current circumstances within this area of life. What are these experiences showing you about how you could take more ownership (or responsibility) for your own joy and fulfillment? Remember, it is not about another person, it is always about your need to heal, grow, or change within. The outer circumstances (including the challenging teachers in your life) will change to reflect this new inner development.

I am certain that you will recognize the old way of handling unsatisfying circumstances was to blame someone else, whether this person is in our present situation or someone from our past. "If only they would..., then everything would be better

141

for me." If only they really loved, accepted, valued, acknowledged, and appreciated me. What if we let them be who they are, instead of expecting them to be who we want them to be? What if we really loved, accepted, valued, acknowledged, and appreciated ourselves?

If we don't make this shift toward inner healing and personal responsibility we will continue to suffer in our present circumstance until something devastating causes it to end, or we will end this circumstance, only to then find another one that will ultimately reflect the same qualities back to us. Once we do make this inner shift we will no longer be stuck in that unsatisfying circumstance, because we will no longer require it to teach us the need for inner healing. The circumstance will either change to be more favorable and satisfying, or it will end and you will create a new circumstance that is more favorable and satisfying.

Do not wait until your circumstances are unbearable. And don't wait for someone else to decide your fate. Be bold in recognizing the cues that life is giving you. With personal responsibility you are empowered to utilize your wisdom and inner strength to support your choices leading to the external circumstances you wish to experience.

The fact that we are always changing and growing means that you will be required to utilize your awareness (or if unaware, your experiential lessons) in order to continue to heal and evolve on a deeper level. Personal and spiritual growth is a lifelong process; there are always deeper levels of healing and expansion to attain. With this understanding you may now and forever recognize your challenges as *opportunities* instead of problems. This is the road map for turning suffering into joy.

This level of personal responsibility and accountability requires great courage and inner strength. It also requires great awareness and self-love in order to begin to gradually develop this higher presence. Some may think that to live and process in such a way is beyond their ability, and that it is simply human nature to experience drama and suffering due to our selfishness (or that of other people). Or maybe you feel that your past, and therefore your current circumstances are just too much to overcome. The awakened path, which is your true calling, is not complex, but it does take effort and personal accountability.

I think that to some this wisdom appears so simple that they say it can't be real. The truth is that while simple, it is not easy. Easy is continuing to go through life as you always have. This takes little or no effort. But if the results have been in any way unsatisfying, then you are just cheating yourself and others. Easy is blaming other people for the unhappiness you feel in your life. Why put all of this effort into living more consciously, in order to experience greater wellness, peace, love, and fulfillment? Why take the steps to shift the way we think and act in order to reach our highest potential? And why be responsible for your thoughts, words, and actions for the benefit of others? In short, because you deserve to live your highest purpose, your inherent Divinity!

It all goes back to accepting who you *really* are (higher Education is the first step). Overcoming your challenges and transforming into a more conscious, awakened being is your true purpose. This is the expansion and ascension of the soul, and has value beyond this human lifetime. When you begin to shift into this perspective, you will gradually begin to see your circumstances differently. What you now think is too difficult to overcome will become doable, one step at a time. As opposed to being consumed by the totality of your circumstance, you may now consider a new more-empowered approach. Plus, you are no longer incapacitated due to fear and attachment to the past, and this new path will be natural and fully supported by higher Divine forces. In fact, the way that you previously functioned in the world will be glaringly unnecessary, unwise, and unsatisfying.

By walking this path of consciousness you are not putting your faith into those of us who teach this, you are putting your faith in yourself. You are deciding within your being and expressing to the world around you that **"I am worth it."** You are worth this effort to heal and transform, and worth the peace, joy, love, and fulfillment of purpose. You are worth it for you, for your family, for your friends, and for all of humanity. Take a chance on yourself, open your eyes and heart to understand that there is a better, more empowered way for you to live. Accept fully that YOU are the architect of your life.

Personal responsibility asks that you do things for yourself without asking (or demanding) that someone else does it for you. The fun fact is that when you take this approach of serving yourself, but from a place of integrity for all, you will be surprised at how many people are suddenly so willing to support you. The truth is that we are all much more able to lend a hand, or words of encouragement, when someone is willing to do the heavy lifting for themselves. The heavy lifting is always the internal work that brings a level of healing and inner peace so that the external reality is not so overwhelming to you, or burdensome to others. Plus, people who are willing to take appropriate steps to heal and grow are more inspiring to others than those who continually complain about their poor circumstances.

Through the development of our personalities, our life training, societal expectations and standards, we have all created various insecurities and self-defeating beliefs about ourselves. We continue to engage in numerous relationships, whether for personal or work purposes, that will require us to deal with our insecurities. We will encounter many people in our life that will push our buttons, meaning that they will press these sensitive areas and thereby force us to acknowledge the existence of our need for healing.

There are two basic ways to respond to this, one supports growth and healing, the other disempowerment and suffering. Until we begin to awaken to our true power, we will invariably choose the latter. In this scenario we will try to put ourselves in positions to avoid dealing with these issues altogether. But this is impossible because our purpose is to grow and expand, not hide or recede. Like it or not, you will continue to be confronted by people or situations that will challenge you. So now you are forced to face your internal demons. This usually entails the ego stepping in and assuming the battle position. You will defend and attack on the outside, while feeling negative emotions for yourself and others on the inside.

Since accepting personal responsibility for our own healing is often a last resort, we will continue to experience these confrontations that lead to drama and suffering. When you have the expectation that others should treat you in a certain manner, and they are unwilling or unable to do so, you have an issue that only you can settle within yourself. The old way was to use all of your "skill" to debate, manipulate, or coerce them to do what you want them to do, even if all you wanted was for them to treat you with some kindness and respect. The fact that you so strongly require this from them is an indication that you believe that you are lacking these qualities within yourself. And like it or not, this person is a mirror that reflects this truth back to you.

With awareness, which is always the key, you can recognize this truth and realize that you have some inner healing to work on. You also can more objectively evaluate if this person needs to be in your life. A main point of accepting personal responsibility is that you will no longer expect others to give you what you are unwilling to give to yourself. Once you begin to develop the qualities within yourself that are most important to you, which usually involves healing those insecurities and self-limiting beliefs that you contracted earlier in life, you will attract more people who will reflect these higher qualities back to you. You will naturally experience more enjoyable relationships that feed your energy instead of deplete it.

I personally have experienced many relationships from a much disempowered, unawakened position. I did everything that I described earlier, which led to being hurt, insulted, angry, combative, and defensive. This caused great suffering while feeling misunderstood, disrespected, and unappreciated. Like many, I exerted much energy trying to convince others of who I was or was not (based on their accusations). When you honor yourself you will get out of the relationship and not subject yourself to these conditions, otherwise, you will stay in it and gradually lose your power to this person. There is no happy ending when you are unwilling to take responsibility for your own happiness.

I now take a very different approach. I use my awareness to recognize both the energy, and the external qualities in all interpersonal connections. I trust my intuition to tell me where this relationship may be going. Is it supportive in some way, does it add to the light and love that already exists in my life? I have learned to honor my instincts early, before anyone has a chance to undermine my energy and highest knowing. I am not looking for anyone to tell me what is right for me, or to make me whole and complete, because that is my job. I am looking toward other people to assess their expression of energy, then, determine how it fits with my energy. No one is good or bad, worthy or unworthy, it is merely a matter of making a connection that is empowering.

I have conducted too many failed experiments to go down the ego based path again. My life is worth more than that, and so is yours. I have utilized the value of these experiences to their best advantage, and that is to learn what works best for me. I don't need to re-live any past pain and suffering. I don't need to harbor any fear or resentment. With forgiveness in my heart for others and myself, I am at peace with the past, and free to choose to create the best life I can in each present moment.

Personal responsibility that leads to true empowerment does require a spiritual perspective, even if the word spiritual is not in your vocabulary. It requires us to see the higher path of being, both within ourselves and other people. Living in this manner necessitates that we observe our natural ego tendencies, especially when we are fearful, and choose another way to respond within and without. We are more concerned with how we feel, heal, and love in these situations, than how we are thought of by others. We are feeding spirit, and not ego. This is a position of great inner strength and therefore empowerment.

"If you want to reach a state of bliss, then go beyond your ego and the internal dialogue. Make a decision to relinquish the need to control, the need to be approved, and the need to judge."

– **Deepak Chopra**

The Need for Developing Self-Love

As a part of us men taking ownership and personal responsibility for our lives, we need to develop patience and self-love. That may sound like a flowery statement to many, but what I am really saying is that we need to give ourselves a break and stop sabotaging ourselves. We sometimes try to take on too much, too quickly, then when everything doesn't instantly work out as we hope, we fall back onto our false education that has continually brought unsatisfying results. We can doom ourselves to failure before we have ever given ourselves a real chance to improve. Remember, this transformation is not easy, and at times we all will fail. Failing is not the problem, giving up is the problem. Part of what created the challenging circumstances we now face is the fact that we can be so critical of ourselves that we become our own worst enemy. Whenever you stop to criticize yourself you cease to make positive progress, and when you do it often enough you develop self-defeating patterns that can define your life.

I am sure that you have noticed both with yourself and others that the people who are most judgmental toward others are also extremely critical of themselves. Outwardly they may pretend to have great confidence, but if you get to know them better you will see that their inner belief is based in profound insecurity. Being critical of ourselves and others means that we are placing too much emphasis on how we/they look from the outside, it is false judgment. It is fine to have high expectations for yourself and others, but never when it strays away from kindness and supportiveness. If you have not noticed this yet, you will; as you continue to develop inner strength, the people who are the most loving, kind, and accepting of themselves are also the most loving, kind, and accepting of others as well. Again, do you want to serve ego or spirit?

I always suggest you try to serve spirit, but within the context of creating the supportive space that you will require in order to shift and build the life you want, it is imperative. Eventually you will be more comfortable using the word love, and mean it to express a positive supportive energy for yourself and others. Many men fear using that word as it connotes intimacy and commitment. I myself have had to learn and grow to be more comfortable with the word "love", which was not commonly used in my household while growing up. However, I did create a new habit and comfort level by always using that word with my children.

The truth is that "self-love" is an inherent quality that follows us into this life. Once here, it seems to be lost or taken by the world of ego. However, we all must re-learn (remember) this Divine trait. It is the opposite of self-aggrandizement, self-consciousness, self-pity, self-loathing, etc. Self-love puts spirit first, the other self-words put ego first. There is no true personal growth and healing without putting spirit first. The bottom line is that spirit is love. So as we are focusing on inner development as a way to create more satisfying lives, we are actually shifting to a greater connection to spirit.

Self-love not only shifts the way we see and define ourselves, but it also fosters the on-going thoughts, words, and

149

actions that will now create a new more joyful and loving life. Being more loving and patient with yourself means that you are more accepting of who you are, both in the higher sense of your being, and as a human who is in the process of growth and healing. **This is huge!** You can more gently and supportively recognize your weaknesses while at the same time know that you are on a path to reach your highest potential. How could you possibly reach this level by being overly critical and demanding of yourself? The truth is that you won't.

As men, most if not all of us received an early education filled with criticism; from parents, teachers, coaches, other males, and even women. Our egos were trained like marines. Be tough, be competitive, never show or acknowledge weakness, survival of the fittest. We had to protect the image of manhood, plus be smart, successful, physical-athletic, attractive, charismatic, outgoing, or if not, we were labeled losers. As the character Ricky Bobby says in the movie *Talladega Nights: Ballad of Ricky Bobby*, "If you ain't first, you're last!" It's a funny line in a movie (especially when delivered by Will Farrell), but as a way to live your life, it is a path for great unhappiness and suffering.

This destructive misinformation is so engrained into our psyche that it brings inner shame on some level for not being better than someone else at something. This is why, along with focused effort and awareness, the exercising of great patience in pursuit of true values is most necessary for men. Throughout the process of personal and spiritual growth we are re-training the mind to see truth and release our false, self-defeating education.

Developing self-love and patience leading to a greater acceptance of what "is", instead of what you think "should be", places you on a true path for happiness and success. It is for you, and not "society", to define how best to live your life. And with the development of self-love you can now do this from a place of greater strength and empowerment.

"You don't have to be great to start, but you have to start to be great."
– Joe Sabah

Develop a Plan to Support the Transition to the Life You Want

The key take-away of Ownership, is to take responsibility for creating the life you want. Start with an analysis of your current life circumstances, and within all of the areas that matter most to you, determine what it is that you want to create going forward. Then utilize all of the resources available to you to make your plan for realizing these experiences. Remember, your present life was created by the choices and actions of the past; your future life is largely determined by the choices and actions you take from this present moment forward.

It is often said that the definition of insanity is, "continuing to do things the same way and expecting a different result". So as you look at your current life and decide on the things that you want to be different, know that you must make the necessary changes in order to heal, grow, and manifest this new result in your life. While your thoughts and intentions are extremely important to the process, I am not talking about wishful thinking; real inner and outer changes need to occur.

In your quiet, reflective space, utilize a higher connection to inner truth when contemplating your current circumstances and developing the specific goals you wish to realize. Depending on your spiritual practice, this could be meditation, prayer, or just turning inward in a state of complete honesty and respect for the process of personal growth you are undertaking. Take it a step at a time. You may have only one or two areas that you feel are in need of improvement in order to achieve your ideal life experiences. Or, you may feel that you need a complete overhaul. It is the same process, nothing is insurmountable. You just need to shift and grow at a pace that is reasonable and realistic for you. Once you truly commit on this deeper level, the Universe will conspire to support you fully. But it has to start with you!

The plan you create to begin to shift into your new awakened life should be documented and well thought out. You may want to journal or make lists of the things you like or don't like, and why. Be open to the intuitive messages you receive during this process. Consider both the short and long term, but know that it will be wise to maintain flexibility in your plan. In the long term you can consider things that seem well out of reach, maybe things that you have only dreamed about experiencing. Make sure that within your mind it is achievable, even if you presently do not know how to achieve it. For instance, I love major league baseball, but I know that I will never play it. I accept this and move on to the things that are realistic for me. Your short term goals will be steps along the way toward reaching the longer term goals. These should be readily doable with your commitment, belief, and effort.

Personally, I have had the dream of writing for quite some time. This was not in my formal training or background, and I did not know how, when, or exactly what I would write about. Yet, this dream seemed reasonable and within my inner belief of achieving. However, I never forced myself to stare at blank pages until I thought of something creative or interesting to write. Instead, I focused on my own inner development (healing and growth) that would shift me into the position of performing this service as a way of fulfilling my higher purpose. I would now have something of value to say, and be more comfortable speaking and living my truth.

Suddenly when the time and energy was right the words just poured through me. Yet, I was disciplined enough to manage my time, and be as productive as I could (while maintaining a healthy life balance). I was content to live within and utilize this creative process while it existed. I intuitively knew that this writing process was enough for me to focus on. Occasionally my ego mind would bark, "what about all of the other steps necessary to make your manuscript a book, and then to publish, market, promote, etc." I knew that if I allowed myself to be scattered with all of the what if's, and how to's, I would miss the value of staying present and receiving spirit's guidance with the message of the book. I was patient, self-loving, and persistent enough to trust my inner process, and not succumb to fear or doubt.

I trusted that just as I was guided in the writing, the opportunities for support and assistance (including an audience for the book) would come forth in the perfect time and way. After I finished the first few drafts, my energy naturally shifted to focusing on all of the business aspects of publishing a successful book. And now I felt great passion for learning many new tasks and concepts, and working with those who could assist me with their expertise. Had I allowed myself to be consumed by the enormity of this project (having never done this before), I may have been so overwhelmed so as to not even start, or quit early on.

Everyone will be starting from a different place, so there is no one-size-fits-all plan. The first change you will need to make in your life is to prioritize your time and effort towards the things that support you on both the physical and spiritual levels. The physical level may be working, providing income, and meeting your physical needs (food, water, shelter, safety, etc.), as well as those for whom you are responsible. The spiritual level will be the time and effort put toward your inner development, which will also lead to discovering your higher purpose and wisdom.

Start with at least enough focus on inner development that you can connect with your higher knowing for the purposes of beginning your plan and identifying your primary area(s) of emphasis. Then, pick one as your initial starting point. It is not enough to say I want a better job with a higher income, or I want a better partner relationship, or I want to be physically healthier. You have to really contemplate on what exactly you are currently experiencing, what your desire looks like to you in detail, and then begin to visualize how you would experience your ideal circumstance.

Two things are really important here. First, you are opening your heart and energy to higher wisdom, designed to transform and shift your life. This truth cuts through all of the excuses, blame, laziness, and misinformation that has previously left you unsatisfied in areas of your life. And second, you are being asked to be detailed and specific about what you want your future to look like. It is as though you are outside of yourself and observing you in this process, and without judgment, you are simply making choices that are better suited to bring you what you want. I said before that you are a spiritual being having a human experience, and this is a great example of using your head and your heart, your humanity and your spirituality for optimal results.

As you are now formulating your short term plans, and prioritizing your time, you will likely have to make choices that affect your current lifestyle. You may have to pull back from

154

situations and associations that currently occupy your time and energy but are a hindrance or road block to your new objectives. This very thing will stop some people from ever reaching their dreams and living their highest potential. Many of us feel more accountable to others than we do to ourselves, and this manifests in the external experiences we attract. It can take great courage to step up and be accountable for what's best in your life. Perhaps you have some bad habits to break, as part of your healing and transforming process. Answer the following questions: What habits and associations need to change or end in order for me to grow and expand? How can I best alter or eliminate these things in my current life?

Eliminating the external obstacles (that can and should be eliminated) now allows you to focus your mind and inner light on visualizing your goals and completing the steps that you can now take. Utilize your mindfulness and awareness to shift your thoughts, words, and actions to inner development and peace. See your plan coming to fruition, and always in a way that adds love and light to your life as a whole, and to all others as well. This cannot be overstated: always look to experience joy in this process. You are doing amazing things just by loving yourself enough to take responsibility for changing and growing in this way, so have fun with it and don't be too hard on yourself.

Now you have the initial plan to create the life you want to live. You have determined the major areas of emphasis for improvement, and you have detailed what you want this part of your life to ultimately look like. You have identified the initial external hindrances to the successful achievement of your goals, and you are beginning to visualize and focus your attention and awareness on completing the steps in your plan in a joyful manner. Congratulations, you are on the path of transformation and transcendence!

"The secret of success in life is for a man to be ready for his opportunity when it comes."
- Benjamin Disraeli

Taking Ownership when Attracting a Partner

In deciding what you want to experience in your life, and creating a plan to get there, you need to think of yourself as the main character in the movie of your life. I am writing this on the level of empowerment, not selfishness. You can never be your best for someone else until you are the best to and for yourself first. Everyone else that you connect with along your path is a supporting character (just as you are a supporting character to them). Some will have bigger roles than others. Take ownership in recognizing your own wellbeing while determining what works best in your life; what kind of lifestyle, circumstances, and experiences bring you the most fulfillment, love, peace, and joy. Meditate on this and write it down in your plan.

When we are disconnected from spirit (and our own empowerment) we often attract a partner according to various ego based reasons, then we compromise who we are, and defer so much of what we really need in order to be compliant and stay in the relationship. It's as if we take on a supporting role in our own movie (life). This is because our ego leads us to make choices which are based in fear and lack. This relationship is valuable as a learning tool (teaching us to love and honor ourselves more), but it is a very poor way to experience joy and satisfaction in the partnership. Predictably, we combine our lives with this person and then spend every day trying to persuade the other to be more like us so that we can live more of who we are (or want to be). This never works out well, and yet most everyone does this.

The way of creating that I am advocating, which again does require you to be connected to spirit more than ego, is to first determine what you want and need in a relationship, then find/attract the person that fits. Wow, isn't that logical? We attract that which we project from within. The basis of this plan is that you are whole, valuable, capable, and worthy all by yourself. You can have this more satisfying relationship only when you decide that what you desire will **ADD** to your already happy, healthy life. To desire to attract a partnership for any other reason is telling the Universe that you are ready for another partner to teach you challenging lessons; and if this is where you are, that is fine, we always receive exactly what we need, but it likely will not bring you the higher qualities you desire in your life.

It is not about being obsessively picky or critical about every quality of a person you want to attract, it is more about understanding the key qualities and characteristics that work best with you. Beauty is in the eye of the beholder, and for the awakened person, what is recognized as beautiful takes on a wide range of qualities and characteristics. You will know if you are attracted to each other for intimacy, so that is a given, though you can decide how important that is to you in relation to other criteria.

The primary issues for long-term healthy relationships are as follows: compatibility of desired lifestyle and life goals; personalities that are equipped for cooperation, support, and joy; evidence of sufficient inner healing; and a strong sense that you will be able to grow together. Since you are coming from a place of significant inner healing, and complete self-honesty, these issues are very relevant to the ongoing love and joy of the relationship. We are already past the point of considering a partnership with someone who is clearly filled with ego, without any intention or awareness for the need of their own inner healing. It is a given that this person will **NOT** add to your joyful life, and the potential will exist for a major fall.

Some of these compatibility issues (or lack thereof) will be evident in your initial interactions, and others will take more time and investigation to determine. Since this is an important decision for both of you, be as patient and thorough as possible. It is not a matter of expediency; instead it is about making the most empowering, conscious choices for you (the main character in your life). Never let anyone rush, pressure, or manipulate you into this decision. In fact, by acting this way they are telling you that they are not sufficiently focused on your well-being. Be completely honest with yourself and in your communication with each other, and you will know the truth. After that it is a matter of trusting your higher knowing, which will take great inner strength.

You may think that it is not possible to be so wise and analytical about love, but the truth is that the typically dysfunctional relationships that we so often get into have little to do with true love. There may be some compatibility while alleviating loneliness, lustful attraction, financial reliance, etc., but very little love. The true highest love needs to be within yourself first, in order to be shared, and this will support your love for all people. However, you are not planning to share your daily existence with all people, so you need to utilize your spirit, heart, and head if you want a chance at a successful loving relationship, and a balanced, healthy, joyful, and fulfilling life. Once you recognize your partner as the right match, then be as open-hearted, loving, romantic, and caring as you can be!

If you feel that it is more important right now to have a partner just as you are, without further development of your inner love, peace, strength, and wisdom, that is always your choice.

Relationship is one way in which we can learn about ourselves for the purpose of growth and healing. However, the actual healing and growth is done by you alone, and is more difficult to do while co-existing with someone else (who is likely in need of *their* own healing). Typically, someone who is choosing a relationship from ego is either unaware of their need for healing or unwilling to take ownership of their own healing and happiness. In any case, always use your highest awareness in order to choose the most empowering path.

If you are not involved in a committed partner relationship at this time in your life, your best strategy for attracting the healthiest connection is to focus on your own healing and self-love. When you know at least the basics of what you want to experience in your life within the realm of relationship, you may now choose to live your highest potential for a loving, happy life, while growing and sharing your best qualities with your partner. You will still learn from each other, and you will have times of lower energy that will be less supportive than other times. But you will each have the tools to support your own healing, peace, and balance, without diminishing your self-love or love for each other. This is the highest form of partnership. It is about two healthy, awakened people taking ownership for creating their highest life, and choosing to do that together.

The truth about being single

Contrary to popular opinion, being single is not a curse or a devaluation of your status as a human being. You can be awakened and healthy, or disconnected and unhealthy, and be either single or in a relationship. So many messages from endless sources seem to indicate that you can only be happy and fulfilled with a partner. The best false statement comes from the movie, *Jerry McGuire*, when Tom Cruise says, "You complete me." This seems innocent enough, and romantic when coming from a movie star, yet it is one of the most disempowering and incorrect beliefs we can have. You are ENOUGH; you do not need anyone else to complete you. When you truly know who you are, you are everything you need. Sharing your life with a partner is a choice.

You are on your path for your own spiritual purpose. You have every opportunity to heal, grow, and develop within a life of great meaning, with or without a spouse, or significant other. You may very likely decide to have this experience, but do this because it adds to your already healthy, happy life, not because you judge yourself harshly without it. The sad truth is that many people that are in an intimate relationship are simply sharing the misery of their unawakened, unsatisfying lives. So, instead of jumping into that boat with someone, appreciate the opportunity to create your own satisfying life. Use the time you have while single to focus on your personal and spiritual growth.

I have personally been single (not in a long-term committed relationship) for the past few years. During this time I have made the most significant progress of my life toward inner healing and transformative growth. Yet, during this time I have come across many people that seem very interested to know if I am in a relationship. I often sensed a curious energy of disappointment in them when I said no, as if to say, "why not, you're a great guy, you should be". And since it pressed a sensitive point within me, I sometimes felt the need to explain with words of justification. Now that I am living from a more empowered place, people rarely ask, and I don't feel defensive. I know that a higher force is at play, and that my ascension needed my full focus during this time. Later, when the energy shifts and the right woman steps onto my path, I am open for the connection.

160

One thing that I learned personally during this time of awakening is that we can find great growth, joy, and fulfillment from our other relationships as well. I have created more amazing friendships in the past few years than ever before. Plus I have been more available to enjoy valuable time with my adult children. It is interesting to see how much we have to offer to so many other people, when our primary focus is not only on one person. So honor yourself and your potential for love, joy, and fulfillment in all of your relationships. You will naturally associate with many other people in your life from which to learn many valuable lessons. Utilize this for your own benefit first. Develop such an inner strength, love, and peace, that you begin to live your life with complete enjoyment and fulfillment. Know that this is possible! Don't be pressured to think like the herd.

When you can do this, you will elevate your energetic vibration to a level that most assuredly would place you in a space of attracting a partner that is a healthy and positive influence in your life. If we do not take this approach of enjoying our own healthy life first, we risk attracting and attaching to a person for the wrong reasons. First, we might be looking for someone to simply make us feel better about ourselves, without any real loving connection. This is a recipe for disaster, and a burden that should not be placed upon someone else. It means that we desire someone whom the world (ego) decides is valuable, which usually means physical appearance or wealth. We want companionship, sex, and to be admired by others. We want to be included with those who are in relationship, so that we don't feel left out and isolated. Most of all we don't want to be alone with ourselves, because we have not really learned to love and appreciate who we really are.

We want to be with someone, even if they will bring us more lessons through suffering. If we need to continue to learn this way, than that is what we will choose; but if we think that we can find someone else to take away our need for personal healing and shift us from ego to love (spirit), when we have not begun to do this work for ourselves, we are sadly mistaken. You will experience much frustration (or worse) while wanting this other person to be who you need them to be. The only way that any relationship will work in true love, peace, and harmony, is for you to develop yourself to the point of living your true divine qualities and gifts, then connect with someone else, and accept them as they are.

Make the empowering choice to honor yourself within your status of "single". Develop yourself with wellness, including balance, physical health, and a spiritual practice. Pursue the things that are most fulfilling and enjoyable, within your work, friendships, hobbies, etc. Then from a position of true power, if you desire to share your life with someone else, determine the higher qualities that would be best suited from a partner in your life. Note that you choose the qualities that are most conducive to your wellbeing before you meet, and not after. You never want to try to change anyone. Manifest this person into your physical life through your intentions, and be open for the connection.

"There are two primary choices in life: to accept conditions as they exist, or accept the responsibility for changing them."
– Denis Waitley

Creating Empowerment in Your Current Relationships

If you are currently in a committed partner relationship, your path for personal and spiritual growth is very similar to someone who is single. You are still the one who must take ownership of your life. The first step is still to evaluate your life in order to truly and honestly determine what it is that you need in order to heal and grow. At this point it is not about your partner, and in reality, they will need to do the same thing for themselves. Your highest form of relationship will involve the two of you choosing to be together as a way of adding love, joy, peace, and light into your lives. This always means that you are the one responsible for healing yourself. You cannot heal each other, you can only support or hinder each other's personal healing process.

If you feel that as a couple there is genuine love and an opportunity for inner healing that supports each of you individually, while aligning you on a higher path, then you may begin to take the appropriate steps for growth, healing, and connection. As always, this must be done with complete openness and honesty. You must work to develop your inner and then outer love, in order for each of you to develop your highest potential as a partner.

The primary goal is to heal and take ownership for your life; the secondary goal is to stay together. I know that for most people, this goes against their beliefs and early education from society. You are spiritual beings capable of great love, joy, peace, wisdom, and abundance, but only when you consciously choose this higher path. Either build a relationship that supports these qualities together, or release each other in love so that you both may have the opportunity to create your own empowering, happy lives' apart.

Some of you may recognize that your current relationship is very dysfunctional and fosters great anger, frustration, and unhappiness. It is possible that it may have started out as something very enjoyable. Either way, the truth is that you came together for a very specific teaching experience. Your attraction was no accident, as you were each a vibrational match to the other energetically. Regardless of the current circumstances, you needed each other in order to recognize the need to grow and heal. The problem now may be that you have stayed connected beyond the period of time in which the experience was designed to bring value or benefit to each of you.

Perhaps this was intended to be a short-term connection. Sometimes the lesson is to share love and support with someone for a specific length of time, which then may lift us to another level of personal healing and growth, in order to move along our higher path. But we refuse to let go, we become comfortable and attached even beyond the blessing that previously existed. At this point we recede back toward ego and forfeit the gain that was achieved. What was once a beautiful and beneficially supportive connection may now turn ugly and difficult. In addition to taking ownership and utilizing higher awareness in order to experience your highest value in a relationship, you must stay present and connected to spirit. Feel the energetic flow between you and your partner, and assess the impact this has on your personal and spiritual growth.

Relationships are opportunities to learn, and grow spiritually, while experiencing life in human form. When we cut out the spiritual aspect and are left with only the human experience, we are more susceptible to the chaotic whims of our ego nature. We are always working on our own healing, and in fact learning to become more empowered through the experience of relationship. When we consider the truth of our spiritual nature in this process we will be working with a higher wisdom that may assist us greatly. This is deeper spiritual work, whether or not people want to use this term. However, the extent to which your life is controlled by ego will determine your external interactions and expressions of energy (thoughts, words, and actions), and likely the ease in which you learn your lessons.

This can manifest in your partner relationship as mild displeasure, in which case you may be able to make the adjustments to shift to greater awareness and internal healing rather easily, as a way to find more joy, peace, and fulfillment in your life. On the opposite side of the spectrum, you may be experiencing tremendous internal pain and suffering, that is manifesting as a bitter, angry, and divisive connection. In this case, you are no longer serving each other in any beneficial way from the standpoint of spirit, and likely you will continue down a path of self-destruction from which you may not return. This is the epitome of two people unwilling to take responsibility for their own lives.

Even if there are extenuating circumstances (and there often are) that make a dissolution challenging, you must take the steps necessary in order to regain your life and have any chance of fulfilling your highest potential. Utilize whatever outside support you need in order to see the situation more objectively, and if appropriate, find the courage and strength to transition out. A relationship need not be a death sentence. You always deserve a quality of life that affirms personal empowerment and the opportunity to live your highest purpose. No matter what choices you have made that have led to this place, forgive yourself and know that you can always make new choices that honor and support you. Most important, know that this is about you, and not your partner. This is about your healing, which now requires your strict attention.

Of course, most relationships will fall between these two extremes. Again, you mutually decided to come together to fulfill some higher purpose, and to learn, grow, and experience your individual path in this relationship. If you are looking to elevate your life and your relationship, you need to continue to grow and heal both individually and as a couple. We are here to expand, and transform to higher levels of consciousness. We are not here to flat-line and merely exist. So, even healthy relationships must continue to evolve.

As you define what it is that you want in your relationship, and your partner does the same, you have the opportunity to address these things with each other. Understand that most of the qualities you are looking for from them, you rightfully must recognize within yourself, and be willing to express to your partner. If you want more love, affection, trust, peace, joy, support, appreciation, encouragement, respect, or independence, for example, you must be willing to develop a level of inner healing that supports you in recognizing these qualities within yourself. Once you start to do this, you will naturally and authentically offer these qualities to your partner within the relationship. If the positive changes that you most desire do not support or strengthen your connection together, or if you and your partner desire qualities that are in opposition to each other, you will have to face whether or not this relationship is going to fulfill your highest purpose going forward. At least you now have the basis of a real meaningful and responsible dialogue whereby you each are empowered to choose your higher path. This is a truly unconditionally loving space.

We can apply the steps of personal and spiritual growth as a very supportive continuation, and ascension of our relationship. It does take two, however. It also takes honesty within us, open communication, and the pure intent to love and honor ourselves and each other. If you are so inclined to experience the highest fulfillment within this human life, then utilize your highest capabilities for inner healing and expansion. This always involves change/growth. So either we change individually and outgrow the need for or benefit of our relationship, or we find new ways to recognize purpose and meaning within our own life that may be supported within the partnership.

While personal and spiritual growth is an individual process that requires that we take ownership of our lives, it does not eliminate the desire for or value of a partner. In fact, two healthy people working together and supporting each other with the highest love, peace, and joy that they have within themselves is a true blessing. It is not our only purpose and service on the planet, but it can be a great factor in a wonderful, balanced life, but you as a separate being have to come first, before the relationship. It cannot be all sacrifice of your own needs, or the neglect of your own healing. You will only be deceiving yourself into thinking that this is your highest path. You love each other and compromise because that is your nature, which has been developed from your own personal growth, healing, and inner strength. Now you are free to give love unconditionally.

"The golden opportunity you are seeking is in yourself. It is not in your environment; it is not in luck or chance, or the help of others; it is in yourself alone."
— **Orison Sweet Marden**

Taking Ownership in your Career

As men we have often defined our career not as our service to the world, but as our very identity and source of self-worth. This is where the majority of our time and attention has been focused, and it is how we have received our financial sustenance. Our jobs provide support for our material needs as well as many of our ego needs. The ego is insatiable and always wants more - income, prestige, respect, power, control, and recognition. Therefore, we often use our jobs and careers to feed this ego monster. Then of course we want to compare our jobs with those of other men, as a way to elicit false power and control.

From a higher perspective, our work should be the external expression of our highest purpose, passion, gifts, and talents, offered in service to others. We are all uniquely created with interests and abilities that could fully support the needs of society as a whole. In what sounds, in this day and age, like a purely utopian fantasy, it is truly what would occur if we worked (served) with each other from a higher knowing of who we really are, and what we are capable of accomplishing.

One of the evolutionary shifts that has occurred is women gaining more prominence in the work force. While this is, of course, a very good thing for society, it has had the effect of eroding the confidence and self-esteem of many men. Many jobs historically held by men are far scarcer. Any man who has experienced being unemployed for any length of time can attest that it takes a toll on our pride. As long as we continue to define our self-worth according to our employment status, we will remain unbalanced and falsely aligned with ego.

The truth is that, as a group, women have been much more active and accountable for their own inner healing, and consequently have made the greatest strides in balancing their energies and, therefore, offer the greatest service to others. Personal and spiritual growth is a mandate for modern man as a way of truly finding their highest power and supporting a more enlightened age on the planet. In the end the jobs will go to those who have the most to give (offer to others) and not just to those who feel entitled. With growth, healing, and inner strength, men will develop themselves to contribute more value with their service to the world.

While the circumstances and readily available opportunities for employment vary widely from person to person, it is crucial for each of us to take ownership in our own growth and healing in order to find true fulfillment and purposeful service from our careers. As a society of humans, there are countless needs, opportunities to serve (fill those needs), skillsets, interests, abilities, and potential for success. Like any other aspect of personal growth, in order to take ownership of your career, you must start from where you are in this present moment.

As always, this requires an honest personal assessment of your needs, desires, interests, and abilities. In the short term, you must be able to support your basic material needs. If you can remove your ego as much as possible, and refrain from judging or comparing yourself to someone else, you will find that these needs are relatively minimal. While supporting yourself, in whatever job is available, you have the opportunity to evaluate your true dreams for serving and expressing your unique gifts to the world.

169

Everything is process, and there are many steps along the path. Focus on meeting each step with your highest awareness, passion, and intention. You may temporarily serve in a job that meets your material needs, but is not the highest fulfillment of your purpose. That's okay; you are in the process of developing the skillset, inner healing, empowerment, and opportunities necessary to participate in the career that does offer your highest fulfillment. You are now reaching and expanding to live your highest potential for a joyful, loving, peaceful, empowering life, therefore more ownership is required of you than you likely have given before. Your goal is not money, respect, prestige, power, etc.; you are transforming and growing in a way that will bring lasting benefit and higher rewards. This requires not only your best effort and higher focus, but patience, self-belief, courage, wellness, and wisdom.

Everything in your life must come from this higher perspective. When you stumble or doubt yourself, you can move to a healing space and re-connect to spirit, and continue on your path with an even greater knowing that you are on purpose. In order for our careers to be fulfilling and rewarding, there must be meaning. Often we start down the usual path of trying to find success in our worldly accomplishments and accumulation of material gain. Eventually, if we are honest, we recognize that this stressful way of living, of always trying to keep up with a competitive world that offers no lasting peace or happiness, is not fulfilling our highest objectives.

We were told that we just need to be tough, buckle down, work hard, and be grateful for whatever you get in life (after all, someone somewhere always has less). This may make sense to the generation that lived through the great depression, and have since fostered the belief in lack and poverty consciousness. Again, this has nothing to do with making money and having lots of things, this has to do with creating a fulfilling, abundant life. We create our external reality from our expression of energy (thoughts, words, and actions), so let's shift our perspective, and insert an awareness, appreciation, and utilization of our Divine nature in order to reach our highest potential.

Sometimes we can't see it from where we are now. Your highest dreams for serving may feel impossible today. Still, flow in the intention that you are fully capable of living and expressing to the world the greatness that most resonates within you. Stay within your integrity and take the steps to develop your authentic self. A quote from Henry David Thoreau proclaims, "If one advances confidently in the direction of his dreams, and endeavors to live the life which he has imagined, he will meet with success unexpected in common hours." Trust in your higher power, and steadily advance toward your goals. You will be amazed at the support, assistance, and encouragement you will receive that will show up at the perfect time. The synchronicity of events that will transpire will astound you. So focus on the step at hand and allow the Universe to guide and protect you on this journey.

In his book, *The Shift*, Dr. Wayne Dyer says, "Don't ask what the world needs; don't ask what others think you should be doing with your life. Instead, ask yourself what makes you come alive – because, more than anything else, what the world truly needs are men and women who have come alive."[3] We need to be sincere in living our true passion. My favorite mantra is simply, **"How may I serve?"** Spirit knows your highest purpose, gifts, and talents, and it knows where and how you may offer these qualities for the highest benefit for all. So trust this higher power within yourself, take ownership of creating your opportunities by

---

[3] The Shift, by Dr. Wayne D. Dyer, excerpt from page 95.

shifting your connection from ego to spirit, where you are then aligned with the Source of all that is.

This shift to spiritual alignment, along with the inner reflection and determination to live your higher purpose ("that which makes you come alive"), will start you down a new path of serving that brings true meaning. Your best opportunity for success in all areas will come from this service that utilizes your highest skills, gifts, and passion. You will emit an energy that is positively charged to attract you to your highest good.

Your personal and spiritual growth and healing process will also serve you in any job you may currently have that has been less than satisfying. Chances are that you have created the circumstance of giving away and not owning your own empowerment. In our jobs we work with people. These people are functioning at varying levels of consciousness and need for inner healing. Therefore, it is up to us to develop the inner strength that protects us from being negatively affected and reacting from ego. Like all personal growth, this is not easy. Some people will really push your buttons. Utilize your best efforts to apply the wisdom talked about in this book, in order to function from your place of inner peace. Creating this space for yourself will provide the best atmosphere for you to then do your job to the best of your ability and satisfaction.

Always work from the premise that you are in control of you. You always have options, so you need to make choices from the place of inner strength and empowerment. Some situations will manifest which lead you to make the choice to honor yourself enough to leave. Others will guide you to the inner development that will support your growth without the need to leave before you have created the next best opportunity. When you are doing your inner work and healing, you will know what truth is for you.

Don't be endlessly tied to a job or any circumstance out of fear. Trust your inner knowing and be courageous in pursuit of your highest path.

A related and extremely important topic is ENTITLEMENT. While each of us is in different circumstance from which to care for ourselves and serve others, it is imperative that we do our best to live in our highest integrity. From a place of pure ego, many people feel that they do not have to contribute, and that, in fact, others are responsible for fulfilling their needs (materially speaking). We are all responsible for our lives and expressions of energy. No one can be fulfilled or empowered if they choose not to contribute. It is no crime to ask for help, but it is an error in virtue to expect help with no intention of supporting the whole dynamic in any way.

This is another way of the ego putting our own selfish desires ahead of anyone else's needs. It fosters separation and ill-will from those who are contributing. As we each apply and practice personal and spiritual growth, we experience the inner healing that encourages us to be empowered and to do our best with purpose and meaning. If we are existing off of the generosity or forced assistance from society we will surely experience very little meaning or purpose. So in the long run this is detrimental to your wellbeing and that of others.

On the other side of the coin, the ego of those with the highest wealth can be very strong indeed. Yet, it is my hope that they would find the higher joy and fulfillment in support to humanity, rather than hoarding their lavish riches. Whether we have created conditions of great wealth, worldly achievement, and acclaim, or we live with much lessor financial means and relative obscurity, ego control will bring suffering. No matter which part of the spectrum you are functioning within, choosing to serve spirit will improve your inner life in the most meaningful ways. And it will also be the most supportive to all others with whom we are connected on the level of spirit.

As we all develop the higher consciousness that connects us to spirit and each other, we will have an opportunity to serve and heal the planet and its inhabitants. However, we all must take ownership of our own lives, as a way to reach our highest potential and bring benefit to others. There is no easy way out; it will take everyone choosing to recognize and pursue their higher spiritual purpose above the demands of ego. We are in this together, so let's all do our part.

"Strong lives are motivated by dynamic purposes."
— **Kenneth Hildebrand**

Shifting to a Higher Purpose

On the path to personal and spiritual growth, ownership and accountability are synonymous. Within the step of **ownership** you understand that you (and really only you) are responsible for developing the inner strength and healing that feeds your higher awareness in support of creating a more empowered life. You are now able to utilize greater freedom from the past by releasing the false, limiting beliefs you have held about yourself. While these thoughts and feelings will continue to arise, you are now in a stronger position to realize what is happening; your ego is trying to get back in and regain control. As you can observe yourself and these thoughts without the immediate need to fall into old unconscious patterns, you are now developing the patience and self-love that will lead you to a peaceful solution of any present issue.

As you understand the need for taking ownership of your life in order to effect or manifest the changes you desire, it is necessary for you to shift your focus to a fulfilling life that supports the higher purpose you came here to experience. Even people who are functioning fully within the clutches of ego can learn to take charge (or ownership) of their lives, but their goals and focus are mostly intended to serve this lower nature. When shifting to a higher perspective, taking ownership of your life is an empowering force for growth, especially for someone who has hidden in the shadows of others, and never really ventured out of their comfort zone to find the light of their own truth.

One of the benefits of creating a formal plan to support this process of claiming ownership is in facilitating our transition on the path. If we have been stuck in self-defeating patterns leading to areas of great dissatisfaction, then we need a process that is relatable and logical to our thinking mind that serves to objectively analyze our current situation and detail how we may move forward. We are utilizing the power of our logic with integrity, to support our spiritual purpose.

As we gain experience with this practice of finding our power, and living the truth that we *Matter*, we need to always be conscious of what we desire and create, and how this impacts others. For some people a little power can light a fire under the ego, sending them in the wrong direction. Ego exists when we tell ourselves that "we are not good enough to...", or "we don't deserve that because..." This is the voice of ego that led you down the self-defeating path of suffering. However, it also says, "Look how strong I am now, I can take advantage of someone who is weak, like I once was." Therefore be vigilant to this deceiver of humans. This was well expressed in the famous line from *Spider Man*, "With great power comes great responsibility."

We must continue to shift into a spiritual perspective in all we do; this is our true nature, and the only thing that brings lasting love, joy, and peace. We are not just changing, but growing, ascending, and returning to our higher form. We are shifting to a state of being that leads to the fulfillment of our highest purpose in this life. So as you gain power due to this "remembering" of your true identity, you must use your awareness to guard against the ego that has been so destructive and engrained into your psyche.

I find that humility is a great separator of those who reside in spiritual power vs. ego control. This is the difference between one who has true inner strength and the one who merely gives the appearance or impression of strength. When the Bible says that "the meek will inherit the Earth", it is talking about this inner strength that needs no boasting or approval, and leads to true empowerment. True inner development is a process of falling and rising, but ultimately of growing. Always be completely honest with yourself in order to continue to heal and transform. It serves no purpose to try to deceive spirit, it can't be done, and you will only be delaying your progress.

So the plan we design, and the steps we take to transform our present life into one that more closely resembles our highest ideals, involves more than just changing our circumstances away from suffering and drama. Our goal is not an easier life, with less pain and more comforts. We are to shift to a higher perspective and a higher purpose. We are overcoming all of the false identity that we accepted as truth throughout our life, for the purpose of experiencing life from a place of conscious connection to our

Divine Source. We are taking ownership of transforming to live our higher purpose.

We recognize that, as spirit, we are all connected to each other and to the energy that created us and all things. Therefore, we are taking ownership or responsibility for minimizing the part of ourselves that was striving to remain disconnected from our true identity and purpose. As we make this shift we make choices that support us within a framework of higher potential, and not only us, but all others as well. As more people on the planet make this shift toward wholeness and unity, our opportunity to function in this higher capacity increases.

As it stands now, the reason that this is not an easy path is because most people are still living in the old ego-based mindset. It promotes the concept that all we are is what we have, what we do, and what we can detect with our physical senses. It also says that, "We are all here on this planet for a short time, and resources are limited, so you better get yours while you can. Once I get everything I need/want then I will think about your needs". Of course one of the problems is that to ego, enough is never enough, you always want more.

So, in order to shift to this "higher perspective and purpose" what do we need to sacrifice, in other words, what's the catch? Do I first need to heal my addictions, my inner pain, my anger, my fear and mistrust of others, my sadness and loneliness, my self-judgment and guilt, my stress, my perceived lack of meaning, and my feeling of inner and material lack? You must only be willing to begin the process, from wherever you are in this present moment. Be willing to recognize a sincere inner desire to heal and grow as a way to create a better life. Be willing to start to take ownership of your life. And open your mind and heart to new empowering possibilities.

The truth is that all of us have lived with one or many of these unnecessary afflictions for so long that we don't know who we are without them. Additionally, we have little or no way to heal these things without living an approach that deals with inner healing and a profound shift away from how we have thought of ourselves and others. We are in need of a radical realignment of our understanding of the Divinity that defines who we really are, and therefore the higher ideals we came here to live and experience.

What about jobs, family life, friends, intimate relationships, hobbies, social activities and entertainment? Does a shift to a spiritual perspective mean that I am limited in working my job, making money to support myself, raising my family, dating, going out with friends, etc.? No, of course not. It does, however, support you in finding work or service that is most fulfilling and in alignment with your true interests and skillset, because now your purpose for working is more than just to make money. When you are working at something you enjoy it is more rewarding, you will be more successful, and in the end, these things usually lead to more income.

You will have greater appreciation of your time with your family because you will foster greater cooperation without the usual battle of the egos. You will see your children and spouse as a blessing that adds to the wholeness and fulfillment you already feel within yourself. Instead of looking for them to be or do something for you, you will now focus more easily on how you can help each other. Your other relationships will be more enjoyable and rewarding since the greater self-love and acceptance you have for yourself now brings greater love and acceptance of others.

You will honor yourself now by associating with those individuals who add to your life, instead of hanging around people who use you or take away your energy. You will appreciate these associations with people where you have mutual trust, support, kindness, generosity, and compatibility. To help balance your life you can have as much time with hobbies, exercise, outdoor activities, reading, TV and movies, meditation or personal reflection and relaxation time, etc., as your schedule permits.

Not only will you have a greater personal space of inner peace and joy from which to experience a full balanced life, but you actually will have more time to enjoy your life lived on purpose, without so many missteps that generate the drama and suffering that has consumed too much of your life already. When we live in this way of honoring our higher authenticity, we share our light with those in our circle of relationships. We also support a shift in the vibrational frequency of all beings on this planet. So how important, relevant, and consequential do you think it is for you to begin to take ownership of your life, choices, and inner healing? Your fellow humans are counting on it!

"Let him who would move the world, first move himself."
- **Socrates**

Ownership to Leadership

As we are now learning to take ownership or responsibility for our own whole and balanced lives, we are creating the experiences and opportunities to be positive examples for other men as well. True leadership starts within us first. When we heal

179

and develop great inner strength, joy, and peace, we begin to shift to a more empowered way of handling any situation that arises in our life. We emerge with an expanded view of all challenges. Our ongoing work or path is to utilize our higher awareness to recognize things as they truly are, instead of how other people will interpret them from a position of ego.

The development of personal and spiritual growth will not eliminate unpleasant circumstances or experiences (from a human perspective) in your life. From the standpoint of spirit all things happen in a way and time according to Universal Law. As all of our lives intersect in this human world, each with their own expressions of energy, levels of consciousness (connection to spirit), and higher purpose, consequences will arise that create every kind of experience. **We** are creating these experiences through choices we make that support either our spirit or our ego. These experiences are not created by "God", or by some other person, and then forced upon us as a blessing or curse. So if we have the ability to create our experiences, better to do this consciously rather than unconsciously.

By taking ownership of your life, and thereby your choices, experiences, and consequences, you will participate fully in understanding the lesson for growth and healing, as well as the best way to move along your path in a positive way. This is how we are meant to function. You will certainly face situations that bring out emotion, attachment, and judgment at times. Some experiences will generate a minor disturbance, and others will create a shift that will feel very challenging, while redirecting your path in a significant way. Maintaining your perception that all things are leading to a higher path will serve you and others greatly. Use your energy and effort more wisely toward finding this higher message and path, instead of wasting effort on "why" something happened and judging it as bad or good. Be solution oriented.

Sometimes experiences are primary to someone else and secondary to us. Yet our ego wants to make everything about how WE are affected. Choose to work within situations that you can control, with an eye toward spiritual truth, and for the things that happen outside of your control, work to release it and flow with whatever impact it has on you. Chances are that the experience was primarily for the benefit of someone else (even if the thing that happened seemed tragic or negative in human terms), and less about you. In this case, what is actually in your control is how you respond to how this experience has impacted your life. A primary example of this is when we lose something that we are attached to, like a relationship, a job, or someone close to us transitioning out of human form, etc. Many times these things are outside of our control, and for the personal/spiritual evolution of another person. Yet we become angry, distraught, and resentful because of how this peripherally affected our lives.

Let's take the most devastating of human experiences, someone close to us passes away. This has the potential to bring great suffering. We may have a sense of sadness and disappointment for this person, we may experience a void left by them from the standpoint of memories and current interaction, you may be fearful or unsettled by how their human life ended, and you may be forced to look at your own life and mortality. This can be difficult for any human regardless of their level of consciousness.

However, with a spiritual perspective you will understand that the person's passing was a transition for them, and was far less about you. You will also know that they, like you, are spirit first, and that they are merely returning to their true home before you do. You or they were not punished, and "God" did not do this. They, at a spiritual level, made this choice. Soon enough we will make a similar journey. So the real issue becomes how to fill the void in our lives. This is the one place in this scenario that we have primary control over.

If we have circumvented our own fulfillment in life in favor of supporting the person that passed away, then we are going to feel lost, and as though a big part of us died. As a person that has taken ownership in their personal and spiritual development, you may likely and reasonably have a period of sadness for the human connection that you lost, but this will not diminish your love for them (or your self-love). Additionally, you will have a full and balanced life from which to regain your loving focus on your own path; and your strength and love will be available to assist others who are in need.

This is the inner strength that our transformational work has been leading to. When I talk about achieving our highest personal and spiritual potential you can see the very practical (human) application and relevance, as well as a higher (spiritual) perspective that confirms our true identity and purpose. We are not only creating new opportunities to move into a future that more fully supports our highest ideals; we are also developing the qualities whereby we may continue to evolve individually and collectively. We are now "remembering" who we truly are and what we came here to do and be in this short span of time. As we gradually release the false education led by the collective ego of humanity, and embrace our empowering spiritual truth, we will lead ourselves and support others with love, encouragement, and cooperation.

Chapter 4 Exercises

Exercise 1:

Develop a plan to support the transition to the life you want to live going forward. Look at the various areas of your life (career, relationship, family, health, leisure, etc.) and document your current level of satisfaction in each area. You can quantify this by assigning a number from 1 to 10 (10 being the highest amount of satisfaction possible) for each classification.

Next, determine a priority for the areas in your life where you want to emphasize growth and healing. Within your internal meditative process consider the qualities that most resemble your ideal life. Document the specific events or outcomes that you want to create in order to experience these higher qualities. Document any fear or resistance that comes to mind that might challenge you in attracting or manifesting these outcomes. These are the areas that are in need of healing and re-education in order to experience the growth you desire. Identifying these issues is a very significant first step in the process of personal and spiritual growth.

Everything that you want to attract can be broken down into smaller steps. In fact, this is the only way to affect significant growth and healing; this is the journey or process. So pick one or two areas that are your highest priority and document an initial plan of the steps you can take now in order to start you on this journey of achieving your desires.

Exercise 2:

Evaluate your current career; document the skills you utilize in performing the duties that are required of you. Reflect on how you truly feel with respect to these requirements: duties, job conditions, relationship with co-workers, the objectives of the company, etc. Are they primarily in or out of alignment with your inner (higher) truth?

In your meditative process consider your true interests, skills, gifts, and passion. Your greatest satisfaction, contribution, and reward come when your work is in alignment with your higher purpose. **If in reflecting on your own unique plan and purpose, you feel that a shift in career is necessary, document your optimal career in as much detail as you can. Now begin to consider a plan for shifting your perspective and taking the initial steps to create your highest desire.** This is not meant to be an impetuous career change; instead this is the beginning of an INTERNAL process of taking the steps to come into alignment with your highest truth.

Look at your career potential from the standpoint of fulfilling your unique purpose, which brings true satisfaction. At this point you are not focusing on more money or accolades from others. If your highest priority is the money, don't be surprised at a lack of overall satisfaction and fulfillment; your highest priority should always be giving value that is in alignment with your higher purpose. This is a spiritual perspective instead of an ego perspective. If you are currently unsatisfied with your career, it is likely that your choices came from ego; you are either chasing the wrong values, or you are stuck in a self-defeating perspective that is limiting the achievement of your true potential.

CHAPTER 5:
WELLNESS

"Within each of us, nature has provided all the pieces necessary to achieve exceptional health and wellness, and then left it up to us to put them all together."
- Diane McLaren

What is Holistic Health?

When I talk about Wellness I am speaking of holistic health. This is an awareness and approach to optimizing our wellbeing on all levels. It is a shift in perspective that supports and facilitates our highest state of being, and the fulfillment of our personal and spiritual growth and healing. It is a process of balancing our energies and activities, and combining the philosophies of both eastern and western medicine.

According to the book, *The Gnosis and the Law*, "The human organism, as we know it is composed of seven distinct bodies, all invisible except the physical. These 'bodies' are divided into two parts; the first three represent what is higher spiritually in man, while the lower four, being of the world of form, are connected while man lives in physical form. ... and makes man able to come in contact with the lower kingdom of nature as well as the higher spiritual values."[4] According to this book, the Higher Triad consists of the Monadic, Spiritual, and Intuitional; while the Lower Tetrad contains the Mental, Emotional, Etheric, and Physical.

In addition to these various energy bodies, we have a system of seven major energy centers called chakras. "These "seven centers" are not to be found "in" the physical body, but are close to the same region where the seven major glands (endocrine system) are located, and each center of force provides the power and the life of the corresponding gland which is, in fact, its externalization."[5] The Chakras, area of the body, and the glands which correspond to their force are as follows: 1st Chakra – Spinal (base of the spine) – Adrenal; 2nd Chakra – Spleen – The Gonads; 3rd Chakra – Solar Plexus – Pancreas; 4th Chakra – The Heart – Thymus; 5th Chakra – The Throat – Thyroid; 6th Chakra – Between the Eyes (third eye) – Pituitary; and 7th Chakra – Top of the Head (crown) – Pineal. In addition to the chakra energy centers, there are energy meridians and *nadi's* that connect throughout the physical body. Whether or not this specific information resonates with you as valid, interesting, or useful is up to you. The point is that there is possibly a greater interconnection between our human and spiritual essence that supports the intricacy and activity within the design and flow of our body system than you may have been aware of.

The foundations of the eastern healing philosophies are focused on healing and balancing these various energy pathways and vortices. It is said that by working to maintain the health of our energy systems we are able to prevent or heal many of our

---

[4] The Gnosis and the Law, By Tellis S. Papastavro, excerpt from page 60.
[5] The Gnosis and the Law, by Tellis S. Papastavro, excerpt from page 85.

common ailments. Many now believe that our illnesses and diseases are the physical body's way of healing from an imbalance, disconnection, or trauma to our energy body. So the significance of focusing on inner healing, including the release of past emotional blockages, cannot be overstated. I believe that both eastern and western philosophies hold a legitimate stake in serving a valuable purpose toward a comprehensive understanding of our wellbeing on a holistic level. I am not advocating for one over the other, just know that alternative treatments exist, and do your best to research and discern what may be most appropriate for you.

I do however believe that a holistic approach, whereby we focus on living from a place of healthy connection to Source, is critical to our wellness. With respect to our quality of life as it relates to wellness, we certainly would benefit from shifting away from our inclination toward ego. Through our personal and spiritual growth we are developing inner peace, which supports the letting go of suffering on the mental and emotional levels. As will be elaborated upon later, an appropriate life balance allows you to eliminate great stress by necessitating that you focus on all of your needs, and not be overburdened in any one area of life. The development of our connection to Source, as promoted in our spiritual practice will open us to inner healing and the development of greater awareness regarding all body systems in order to take positive steps for healing before we are in crisis.

"Nothing can dim the light that shines from within."
– Maya Angelou

Balancing and Monitoring your Energy

Like all things, we are made up of energy. What feels and looks solid is filled with space on the level of quantum physics. Energy runs the Universe and all of creation, including us. Therefore, it is certainly worthwhile to consider the vibrational characteristics of the energy that flow in and around your life. When we are connected to our spiritual truth and nature we are said to vibrate at a higher, faster rate. Within this capacity we are more closely connected to the Divine realms and beings of light that reside solely in spirit form, such as Arch Angels, Angels, Ascended Masters, and Spirit Guides. As we develop a greater awareness and association with this aspect of ourselves, we are more readily open and available to receiving the Divine support and assistance available to each of us.

Our consciousness now resonates with a higher love, light, peace, and joy, as we have awakened to our connection with these Universal energies. We know that in spite of the perceived separation due to our individual physical forms, we are all one. As a goal for living your true purpose, for the highest fulfillment of your human life, and for shifting the consciousness on the planet into a New Age of enlightenment, this level of awakening is what we are moving toward.

Contrast the description of higher energy above to what we have primarily experienced in our past and present ego-driven world. We have been led to think that this higher energy vibration is not available to humans. Surely we have had numerous interventions of inspiration onto this planet, by enlightened teachers, that have sporadically contributed to advancements and evolution to some degree. This world is not completely dark. However, there still exists a great need for each of us to shift toward a greater awareness and acceptance of our Universal life force energy.

We reside in lower and slower vibrational frequencies when we: 1) need to be "right" and are critical of others instead of being kind, supportive, and compassionate; 2) hate, dislike, or disapprove of someone because they look or think differently than we do; 3) choose to dishonor ourselves and hide our light, because we believe we are unworthy; and 4) manipulate and abuse others for our own gain. This usage of energy keeps us stuck in the false education of ego, and it creates separation from Source and the light of creation. In our state of disconnection or unconsciousness we are not only greatly limiting our potential for love, joy, peace, wisdom, and abundance, we are also draining and darkening the collective consciousness for all beings on this planet. Clearly this has a detrimental effect on our wellness.

Personal and spiritual growth is absolutely required in order to shift your energy to the higher path. I am very specifically stressing the word *growth* here. We are all in the process of living our human life with the potential for growth. This implies transformation and ascension to a higher and faster vibrational frequency; one that is more connected to Source. No one person is functioning solely from ego or solely from spirit. We are all in various stages of living within the awareness of our higher consciousness. This is the relevance of the sub-title to this book, **"A Guide to More Conscious Living."** When our attention is placed upon our true ability to elevate the quality of our energy, we are capable of great shifts in all that we manifest and contribute to the world.

189

Balance your masculine and feminine energy

This may be an entirely new concept to you; that the energy that comes from Divine Source contains either masculine or feminine qualities. However, this is a significant and pertinent issue for all people, but especially for men. These energies are not to be confused with any physical gender association. This is purely about energy. Contrary to some religious teaching, "God" is not a wise old man in the sky or in "heaven". Divine Source is pure energy, and this energy encompasses the duality of both masculine and feminine qualities.

With an historic view of a "Father-figure" God, humanity has developed the definition of power to reside almost exclusively in masculine qualities. This God was thought by some to be domineering, jealous, ruthless, violent, petty, and vengeful. As you can see, we made God in our image. The truth is that we were created in the image (energy) of Divine Source, which includes the higher qualities as stated often in this book.

The predominant spiritual thinking of today gives credence to the rise of the Divine feminine. While many women have taken strength in this, due to their previous status and subservient relegation, it really is not a woman's issue. To me, it is about honoring the value of feminine energy in each of us. From a balancing standpoint, this is especially relevant for men, as this adds to our empowerment.

Masculine energy is said to be focused on action-doing, mental-thinking, and mind-centeredness – essential for logic, planning, building, and outer strength. Feminine energy is more about receiving-being, intuition-creating, and heart-centeredness – which supports cooperation, compassion, communications, and inner strength. If you take away the connotations of masculine/feminine that come from our ego-based thinking, would you not recognize that we all would function at a higher level when balancing all of these qualities?

These are all Divine energetic qualities that come from the Source of all that is, hence the duality of energy of Universal Intelligence. It is truthfully said that we were created in God's image, not as a male or female (God does not have a physical form), but as the embodiment of the energetic qualities of our Creator. Interesting how there are nuggets of truth in some of our religious teachings when we see them from the standpoint of spirit instead of interpreted through ego.

The truth is that we have within us the same Divine characteristics as Source, available to each of us if and when we decide to utilize them. This is why it is possible for us to create/manifest our experience, love others as ourselves (as Source loves us - unconditionally), and connect with Source for higher guidance and support. You can see that when we deny our spiritual truth, we are eliminating so much of our true power and purpose. So the ultimate goal in balancing our Divine energies is to develop toward the attainment of our highest personal and spiritual potential.

The emphasis of this book is geared toward the empowerment of men, so let's focus on that. We must truly begin to evolve in our education and thinking about how we define strength and weakness, and how we define ourselves and others. First of all any attempt to define something merely limits that thing. I am well aware that any attempt I make with my words to define the Source of all that is, will be woefully inadequate. I am merely trying to relate Universal wisdom in terms that may be useful in developing us toward a life of higher consciousness.

Throughout history man has defined men as strong, women as weak; intelligence as strong, spirituality as weak; aggression as strong, compassion as weak, etc. Much in the way we have erroneously defined God, we have been led down a false and deceptive trail. The old ego-based education pitted us against each other for the sake of survival. The new spirit-directed truth opens up a path for living our highest human and spirit potential.

This is not to say that the feminine qualities are better than the masculine ones. However, when talking about men (as a group), we have pushed the goodness of the masculine qualities to a place of destructive weakness. As for developing the balancing effect of the feminine energy, we have a long way to go. It starts with our recognition of our imbalance. The ability for us to shift to a whole and healthier position requires our attention and intention of shifting from ego to spirit, and from head to heart. We will more naturally utilize our amazing masculine energetic qualities to build instead of tear down; our powerful minds will find solutions to humanitarian problems instead of the insane quest toward greed and dominance. We will now introduce humility and gratitude alongside our achievements, as well as compassion and cooperation as a way to lift others toward their highest potential.

Accountability for our personal and spiritual growth is a must. We have to be able to look at ourselves and know that we did this, we created this situation, and we are each responsible for changing and growing. You cannot blame anyone else for anything that is not going right in your life, if you want to see positive change. I have routinely met men who are unhappy with their lives, but few who will understand the value of talking to a life coach or counselor. A lot of this comes from the false perception of weakness in admitting that you need to change and grow – that you need help. Our lack of humility and stubbornness has done a great disservice to our wellbeing. Another part of the problem is indifference. Too many men are looking for the quick and easy fix. This all needs to change in order for men to evolve.

For so long men have had the easier path, compared to women, that's the way we stacked the deck. However, like it or not, the world is changing and we need to evolve just to keep up. By ignoring our ability and responsibility we are blocking the very healing we need in order for us to create the happiness we so desire, and to find true fulfillment and purpose in our lives. I have seen tremendous growth and healing of women, who are much more likely to recognize their responsibility for their own happiness and then take positive steps to grow. There are many women who are disappointed in men for seemingly being disinterested in their own growth and evolution. This book is a call to men to wake up and grow up, from the standpoint of consciousness. The mere fact that you are reading this book indicates that you resonate with the energy of growth and evolution, and the creation of a better life. We have every capability, as one created in the like-ness of Source, to create lives of meaning, joy, love, peace, and abundance. Creating balance within your own life is reflected out into the world and assists both personal and planetary healing and transformation.

"I have just three things to teach, simplicity, patience, compassion. These three are your greatest treasures."
– Lao Tzu

Creating Life Balance

It's not always that men aren't doing enough in their life; it's that we are not doing enough of the right things (and sometimes too much of the wrong things). Often it is too much of one thing, and not enough of several other things. **Balance is a key to Wellness!** We have been really focused on work and money, and not just because we want to serve others by using our skills or because we need a certain amount of money in order to support ourselves. These things are important of course, but when we are ego dominated, we assign a measure of our identity and a level of importance to our job and income that is completely incompatible with living in higher awareness or consciousness.

With the majority of my work background in accounting, the concept of balance is very obvious and natural for me. Balance was the guiding principle and without it your work was erroneous, incomplete, and unreliable. This is just as true for the human life that is attempting to function without sufficient balance. We are living in error, we are incomplete, and we are less reliable to ourselves and others. We know that as life flows, certain circumstances and activities take priority. Of course, you must address that which is required and most critical. The problem arises when one area of our life is always the priority. By necessity other parts of your life are ignored and begin to atrophy, and ultimately this imbalance creates dysfunction and disharmony. In many cases this leads directly to a physical illness, injury, or relationship trouble, which then forcibly brings us back to balance for the sake of healing.

Developing and fostering spiritual awareness implies that you are present in your recognition of the quality of your life as a whole. Your growing conscious connection to spirit is beginning to be reflected in your understanding of the importance of wellness, and nothing contributes more to overall wellness than balance. The key to balance is in recognizing energetically when you are out of balance in any particular area. Then with this awareness, taking the steps you have learned in order to make the necessary corrections to a healthy balance, before your life force has to "correct" you.

If you feel that you are not in balance: 1) choose to honor yourself fully, and know that you are worthy and capable of living in balance. Appreciate the awareness you have developed that now is present enough to recognize this truth; 2) assess the situation that is causing the imbalance. Is this temporary, what is the estimated timeline? Is this highlighting a needed change (large or small)? 3) Develop a plan from which to take corrective action. Is the imbalance related to physical health, to your work or income, to your spiritual development, or to the needs of someone else?

Allow yourself to release some of the fear that is causing you to focus so much time and energy in one particular area of life. Step aside and do something healthy and unrelated. Open up to higher guidance, a solution always exists. Maybe not immediately, but with awareness and the willingness to take the appropriate steps, you can eventually find the place of peace and balance. The bigger problem is not that we cannot create balance; it is often that we are unwilling to change and grow. Many of us have functioned in such a chaotic and dysfunctional way our whole lives that we cannot imagine any other way. We are more comfortable with the "known" suffering, than the "unknown" peace.

In the end we are all responsible for what we create in our lives, so the choice is always ours. If you recognize an imbalance that is bringing suffering, but you need encouragement and ideas for solutions, consider hiring a coach. A coach with real-world experience, along with an understanding of spiritual principles, can bring an objective, solution-oriented approach.

So, we have this one human life, and in it we may be asked to somehow balance work, family, friends, health, spiritual practice, and restful downtime. This can be challenging for those with the greatest consciousness, and for those who are controlled by ego it is even more difficult to find a healthy balance. Your goal is to prioritize from a place of your greatest empowerment, in other words with your highest awareness, self-discipline, and wellbeing.

Use your integrity and do the best you can, while finding peace and acceptance within yourself. You will not please everyone all the time, and in fact, the pursuit of attempting this is likely a significant cause for the imbalance. Part of taking ownership for our wellness is in understanding the need to setup healthy parameters and expectations. We must be able to offer a polite "no" when necessary. Use your highest discernment, and evaluate a situation or opportunity thoroughly before you say yes, in order to determine if this supports your overall health, joy, and success. Only you can truly care for you; and the best you is better to those around you than the stressed and "buried" you. So protect your energy, and choose your commitments consciously.

We have all heard it said that, "On their death bed, no one wishes they would have spent more time working." So while you are attending to the "priorities" (or perceived crisis) of the moment, try to develop an overall plan that takes into account the things that are truly most special and rewarding in your life. Eventually, everything in our human life is fleeting and temporary. Spend sufficient time with your loved ones – children, spouse, family, etc. Be present with each other as often as possible, and learn to give them your best qualities. In other words, focus your mind and heart on this connection. Set aside other more trivial issues and concerns. This will not only bring more fulfillment to your life, but will have an amazingly positive impact on those around you.

"Inward calm cannot be maintained unless physical strength is constantly and intelligently replenished."
- Buddha

The Truth about our Physical Body

I have already discussed the fact that everything is made up of energy. We are spirit, which came (from the unmanifest world) to incarnate into a physical form in order to experience a human life (in the manifest world); and finally, when this form expires, we will return to the unmanifest world. Our physical form is still energy, but is much denser, so as to give appearance of being solid. Our body allows us to function within the manifest world where all other objects also seem to take on a form that is solid.

Like all physical matter, our bodies change over time, according to our DNA, the activation of our Divine Blueprint. Moment by moment trillions of cells are constantly growing,

197

dying, and regenerating, and all of this happens on a level that is completely outside of our doing, it is a part of our being. Due to our constant state of change, we will have countless bodies over this lifetime. You cannot hold onto or re-create any of them. For example, can you find your 3, 15, or 21 year old bodies? Yet don't we so thoroughly identify with our "body"? It is said, "That is real, which never changes." So between your body and your spirit, guess which one is real.

Our body is really here just to serve a spiritual purpose. How sexy is that? Yet to the ego, which only exists in this body/personality, it is everything. This is because when the body dies, the ego dies. However, this body and physical lifetime, which seem so substantial to us, are but a parenthesis in time. Making it all the more ironic that we devote so much time and effort to our physical appearance, and so little to our spiritual development.

However, because of the irreplaceable role your body plays in your human experience, it is worthy of being cared for and appreciated, and the best way to do this is by attending to its wellness. We know that our bodies are made up of muscles, bones, organs, joints, arteries, skin, and more. For the most part, these components function independent of your conscious intention (for example you don't have to tell your heart to beat or your lungs to breath). However, in order to function better and last longer, you will want to pay attention to the indications your body is giving you; stop doing things that are damaging it, and do enough of the things that are supportive to its optimal health.

5 Basics: exercise, breathing, nutrition, water, and rest.

I think that we all know that a proper balance of these things is important and helpful in supporting the wellness of our physical body, but perhaps they are each more significant to your health than you realize. The goal of wellness is to support your spirit journey in this human form. We can strive to assist our body's functioning in a normal healthy state, or if you have goals and activities that require your body to function on a higher level you can pursue that too. There are many specialized programs that support this achievement, but my primary concern here is the optimal level of health for normal everyday functioning.

Exercise is a must. With the advancement of automation and technology most of us have moved into a more sedentary lifestyle. In fact, many schools have now eliminated physical education (P.E.) from our children's required curriculum! So, the act of movement and physical exertion of the body now seems to be a conscious and intentional effort and plan for each person. Whether you go to the gym, work or play outdoors, participate in sports, go for walks, use the stairs, or just jump up and down for a few minutes, make an effort to move your body. Do your best to have a regular time of physical activity. If you can't always find the time for a full workout, do the little things that you can do to move around. This gets the blood flowing, supports cardio and pulmonary functioning, increases endorphins, manipulates muscles, joints, lymph nodes, and strengthens bones. In short, it assists the physical body in maintaining homeostasis.

If you are interested and able to participate in a more active exercise routine, then do so. Work within your physical limits, and progress gradually according to your ability and fitness level. Exercise is good and valuable, but more is not necessarily better. Do not overdo it, or try to compete in a way that is dangerous to your health. If you are inexperienced or returning to an exercise program after significant time off, it would be wise to consult with a trainer. Remember, we are talking about wellness, which is of the spirit. It has nothing to do with ego, so always stay within your awareness and use discernment when maintaining a fitness plan. However, a proper fitness program or athletic activity can be great fun and add to your overall life balance.

During a particularly challenging time in my life, I was very stuck in my circumstances and filled with grief. Not yet able to see my experience for the advanced learning opportunity that it is was, I instead was consumed by depression. I decided to get some counseling to work through my situation, I even considered medication to help me cope. The Psychiatrist asked if I was exercising. Now, I have worked out off and on my whole life, but during this period I was not really taking care of myself. I told her that I was not. She suggested that I start working out again, as opposed to prescribing any medication. So I joined a gym and began exercising regularly. Before long I was feeling better, and I had more energy. I once again had a healthy activity to focus on, instead of constantly reliving the dream I was stuck in. In truth it was a tool to help me transform from my ego attachment to beginning the steps to wellness. And I never did have to use medication.

The value of breathwork. Breathing, what could be simpler, right? After all, we do it automatically, and without it we only last a few minutes. In an excerpt from his website, Dr. Andrew Weil, explains the following: "Breathing is special in several respects: it is the only function you can perform consciously as well as unconsciously, and it can be a completely voluntary act or a completely involuntary act, as it is controlled by two sets of nerves, one belonging to the voluntary nervous system, the other to the involuntary (autonomic) system. Breath is the bridge between these two systems."[6] For the sake of wellness, breathing can and should be a more conscious activity, while very simple, breathwork is powerfully impactful as a daily practice to further your health and wellbeing.

Dr. Weil goes on to explain: "Most people do not know how to breathe so as to take full advantage of the nourishing, health-giving properties of the act of breathing. Knowing how to perform simple breathing techniques can help lower your blood pressure, calm a racing heart, or help your digestive system without taking drugs. Breathing has direct connections to emotional states and moods - observe someone who is angry, afraid or otherwise upset, and you will see a person breathing rapidly, shallowly, noisily and irregularly. You cannot be upset if your breathing is slow, deep, quiet and regular. You cannot always center yourself emotionally by an act of will, but you can use your voluntary nerves to make your breathing slow, deep, quiet and regular, and the rest will follow." Dr. Weil and many others offer valuable insights and techniques for more conscious breathing, whether as a specific practice or for everyday functioning. I suggest that you research this topic further, and begin to incorporate breathwork into your Wellness program.

Nutrition Matters. Nutrition is a very broad topic, with many varied opinions. The good news is that you will have much available information from which to research on your own, in order to find a diet that best supports your needs, desires, and preferences. Shift your focus to health and the highest nutritional value of your food. The not-so-good news is that many opinions are contradictory and supported by special interests that are more

---

[6] Dr. Andrew Weil – http://www.drweil.com/drw/u/ART00519/An-Introduction-to-Breathing.html

concerned with making a profit than your health, so use your best discernment in order to decide for yourself a philosophy or program that will bring the desired benefits.

Recently, I have changed my diet to one that involves a greater balance of whole-food plant based foods. While not a new concept, more and more people are accepting the research that claims there are significant health risks associated with a diet consisting largely of animal products. Studies suggest that meat and dairy products are a leading cause of heart disease, cancer, and diabetes (among other problems). Heart disease is the leading cause of death in the U.S. The other significant problem with the typical American diet is that it is loaded with sugar, salt, and fat. Consequently, disease is on the rise and obesity is rampant. I recommend the movie (or book), *Forks over Knifes – The Plant Based Way to Health*, as a resource for the research substantiating the health concerns stated above.

We often eat for convenience, and for taste, based upon what our mind has been convinced is pleasurable. Food is the sustenance that supports our body and energy systems. We need to think of food as more than just a way to feel full or receive pleasure. We are consuming the greatest number of empty or destructive calories than ever before in the history of mankind. This food is wrecking our health and our quality of life. It also has a detrimental impact on our financial resources due to the ever increasing cost of health care.

We need to begin to think of nutritional value first! We can retrain our minds to find the pleasure and satisfying taste in healthy food. Your life is all about choices. Every choice you make adds or subtracts from your wellness, and the opportunity for living your highest potential. ***The Empower Model for Men*** is about living More Consciously, and this is certainly very applicable to what you ingest into your body.

So take ownership for understanding what you are consuming and the effect it has on your wellness. Additionally, be an example and support for those in your circle of family or friends who are interested in improving their health. You do not need to count calories when you are eating healthy food. You will get the nutritional value you need and will know when you are full, without fighting the addictive qualities that resides in many of the foods marketed to us today.

If you are serious about living the healthiest lifestyle, one that minimizes or eliminates disease in the body, one that gives you the greatest energy and mental clarity, you might want to try a whole-food plant based diet. Do the research and just see for yourself how it makes you feel. There are many resources for information and recipes that will support this dietary lifestyle. Whether or not you are currently experiencing health problems, your body will thank you.

The necessity of water. Another vitally key ingredient to our health and wellness is the consumption of water. Experts say that water is second only to oxygen as essential for life. According to online research: "The human body is a water machine, designed primarily to run on water and minerals. Every life-giving and healing process that happens inside our body... happens with water. In just the last decade medical science has begun to focus more on the tremendous healing ability our body has and how much that ability depends on water. Our body instinctively knows how and strives to sustain youthful longevity, and in its every effort... water is the key. The human body is made up of over 70% water. Our blood is more than 80%, our brain ... over 75%, and the human liver is an amazing 96% water!" [7]

The website goes on to say: "Our energy level is greatly affected by the amount of water we drink. It has been medically proven that just a 5% drop in body fluids will cause a 25% to 30% loss of energy in the average person... a 15% drop in body fluids causing death! Water is what our liver uses to metabolize fat into useable energy. It is estimated that over 80% of our population suffers energy loss due to minor dehydration."

How much water is enough? According to the same website mentioned above: "A non-active person needs a half ounce of water per pound of body weight per day. That is ten 8 ounce glasses a day if your weight is 160 pounds. For every 25 pounds you exceed your ideal weight, increase it by one 8 ounce glass. An active, athletic person needs 2/3 ounce per pound which is 13-14 8 ounce glasses a day if you're 160 pounds. The more you exercise the more water you need. Spread out your water intake throughout the day. Do not drink more than 4 glasses within any given hour. After a few weeks your bladder calms down & you will urinate less frequently, but in larger amounts."

The power of sleep. Many of us try to sleep as little as possible. There are so many things that seem more interesting or important than getting a few more hours of sleep, but just as exercise and nutrition are essential for optimal health and happiness, so is sleep. The quality of your sleep directly affects the quality of your waking life, including your mental sharpness, productivity, emotional balance, creativity, physical vitality, and even your weight. No other activity delivers so many benefits with so little effort!

---

[7] www.dorchesterhealth.org/water.html

According to the website, Helpguide.org, "Sleep isn't exactly a time when your body and brain shut off. While you rest, your brain stays busy, overseeing a wide variety of biological maintenance that keeps your body running in top condition, preparing you for the day ahead. Without enough hours of restorative sleep, you won't be able to work, learn, create, and communicate at a level even close to your true potential. Regularly skimp on "service" and you're headed for a major mental and physical breakdown." [8]

How much sleep do you need? According to the National Institute of Health,[9] the average adult sleeps less than seven hours per night. In today's fast-paced society, six or seven hours of sleep may sound pretty good. In reality, though, it's a recipe for chronic sleep deprivation. There is a big difference between the amount of sleep you can get by on and the amount you need to function optimally. Just because you're able to operate on seven hours of sleep doesn't mean you wouldn't feel a lot better and get more done if you spent an extra hour or two in bed.

While sleep requirements vary slightly from person to person, most healthy adults need between seven and a half to nine hours of sleep per night to function at their best (children and teens need even more). And despite the notion that our sleep needs decrease with age, older people still need at least seven and a half to eight hours of sleep. Since older adults often have trouble sleeping this long at night, daytime naps can help fill in the gap.

Aside from maintaining the 5 basics described above, use your awareness to notice when something physically or energetically may feel wrong, and if appropriate, seek medical

---

[8] www.helpguide.org/life/sleeping.html
[9] http://www.nhlbi.nih.gov/health/health-topics/topics/sdd/howmuch.html

attention. Setup an ongoing routine of physical checkups, including dental, and at a bare minimum, tend to your hygiene needs. We are honoring and respecting our body as part of an overall program of growth and healing, and we are representing the Divine to others. We are fulfilling our unique plan and purpose in service to the world, the wellness of our body is a valuable tool to support us on our journey.

"Religion is belief in someone else's experience.
Spirituality is having your own experience."
– Deepak Chopra

Developing a Spiritual Practice

Do I really need a spiritual practice, and if so, why? Yes, it is essential that we develop both our human and spiritual natures in order to fully function in physical form, while reflecting the higher aspects that lead to fulfilling our true purpose. This supports the best possible life for us and others. You cannot ignore your spiritual nature and achieve the same thing. Maintaining a spiritual practice is essential to the development and application of our spiritual gifts.

A very common mental position that people take, comes straight from the voice of ego. They say, "Why do I need this spiritual stuff? I live a good life, I'm a good person, I'm a hard worker and I provide for myself (and family), so I'm doing ok, thank you very much!" First of all, most people who say this are confusing spirituality with religion. I believe that I already addressed the vast differences in the Educate chapter.

However, beyond misunderstanding the terminology, many people judge their lives by the outer manifestations without fully considering the inner qualities of their life, which are often quite unsatisfying or unfulfilling. In most cases if they were to honestly examine their lives, they might recognize the following translation: "I live a good life" - I have more material things than many other people, I live relatively comfortably, therefore my life is good; "I'm a good person" - I am usually nice to the people that I like, especially those who have something to offer me; "I'm a hard worker and I provide for myself (and family)" - through my own exhaustive efforts, focus, intelligence, and good fortune, I have an important job title, and I make more money than many other people, therefore I can pay for my family's basic physical needs and luxuries.

Relatively speaking, this person is successfully surviving on a human level. They may have fewer challenges than most, and provide for themselves in a comfortable way, with at least the perception of security. They have worked hard to insulate themselves, which separates, and in their minds, distinguishes them from many other people. This is an example of ego success, which often falls short of the achievement, fulfillment, and contribution available with the inclusion of their spiritual gifts.

You may develop a higher standard of living materially, but are you really finding great meaning and purpose in your life? How directly are you offering your gifts and light to others (and not just to your family and close associations)? If we do not recognize and acknowledge the truth that as Divine beings we are all connected (having come from the same Source), our only real choice is to believe that we are all separate. In which case everything revolves around meeting our own needs and desires; compassion, peace, kindness, cooperation, and unity are often mere intellectual concepts. I love this quote by Albert Schweitzer that says, "The one possible way of giving meaning to (man's) existence is that of raising his natural relation to the world to a spiritual one."

It's not necessarily that we don't want good things for other people (we usually believe in virtue, so long as it does not infringe on us); it's just that the all-consuming concern of ego is to take care of itself. It is often such a struggle to "get on top", and stay on top, that our priority becomes to hang on to what we got. Plus, the ego always wants more, so we usually never quite get around to really serving the needs of others. Living this kind of life is comparatively shallow and ultimately unfulfilling. In many practical and energetic ways they are not fully offering the gifts they came here to express and share. They are not really adding their light into the world, and we all need everyone's light. In the end, they die with their possessions and money, and they likely believe that their existence has been terminated; or they may suddenly awaken to a realization that they have missed the opportunity to serve, grow, evolve, and experience their true higher purpose.

Is this really the highest potential that we humans are here to experience? What if in order to exist in this "higher" standard of living, we traded our inner peace for a "good life", that routinely encountered confrontation, anger, sadness, and drama? What if we were only really a "good person" to those who supported our ego in some way? What if our "hard work" has led to great stress, imbalance, and poor health that adversely affect the quality or span of our life? What if we focused so much on providing "things" that our family never really felt loved, honored, and appreciated? What if we spent our lives accumulating material wealth without ever realizing our true higher purpose and connection to Source? Finally, what if we completely misjudged the meaning of a life of value, and instead of contributing to humanity we actually weakened its evolution?

The human life is about doing, and some people are really good at that. The most valuable lives, however, combine doing with *being*. Be peace, be kind, be love, be support, be compassion, be joy, be present, etc., and in order to be this you must be connected to your higher Source. Ultimately our *being* will support our *doing*. What we *do* is an outer reflection of who we are. When we are connected to spirit we will reflect the qualities of love, peace, joy, wisdom, beauty, unity, etc. When we are disconnected from spirit, and attached to ego, we reflect the lower vibrational qualities of fear, doubt, hate, anxiety, judgment, and separation. In the end we can only authentically give what we are inside. We can fake it for a while, in order to get what we want, but our truth always comes out. If you want to *do* (give - external) love, you have to *be* (internal) love; same for peace, joy, compassion, wisdom, beauty, etc.

What is a spiritual practice? Your spiritual practice is the way in which you develop a connection to your Higher Source. This may start out in one way or form initially, and then shift to a different level and expression as you awaken to your truth. By this I mean that our spiritual practice usually starts out as something we do, and then becomes more of who we are. To get started, I recommend creating the methods, space, and practice that is most comfortable for you. Initially at least, it will be useful to make a commitment to your practice by establishing regular times and duration. This also needs to be on your new healthier list of priorities. Spiritual practice is a healthy habit, and therefore requires your attention and intention in order to establish it as part of your life.

You can participate in your spiritual practice in a variety of ways. The essential thing to keep in mind is that this must be an activity that in some way shifts you from ego to an inner spiritual connection. Meditation and prayer are the most effective practices, but in addition to this, some people find this connection and peace in the following activities: 1) being outdoors in nature (hiking, camping, boating, etc.); 2) creative expression (art, writing, photography, etc.); 3) hobbies (woodwork, gardening, sewing, etc.). Spending time in these activities will create space, away from the chatter and noise of your thinking mind and other people, and thereby, enhance your spiritual connection. While doing these activities, the key is to feel and connect with your present moment energy. Breathe slowly and deeply, and pay attention to the guidance and messages you may receive.

If you were only initially going to practice one method, I would recommend meditation, combined with prayer. Meditation/Prayer is specifically designed to open the channel to the Divine. Here are some of the steps you may take: 1) you will want to be alone or at least in a quiet space where you are uninterrupted. The first goal is to be present, and quiet your thinking mind (as much as possible); begin to eliminate the incessant inner chatter. This may not be easy at first, but stay with it, it will get better. 2) Create the space and intention of connecting to/with your spirit and Higher Source. You are doing this for your inner development and growth, so make it personal and relatable for you. If there are traditions, gurus, or symbols that resonate with you as sacred, utilize them in your space. You are not doing this for anyone else's approval, so begin to remove your ego and be bold by claiming your spiritual practice as your own.

3) As best you can, reside in a state of pure gratitude. This is a process that is designed to assist you in awakening to your

spiritual nature. There are countless beings of light that surround each of us, who have been simply waiting for us to create the space whereby we may connect to receive their love, support, guidance, and protection. Express your gratitude and love for all they do, and in reverence for the Divinity within, open your heart to receive inspiration; 4) Personally, I like to start with prayer, giving thanks for the many blessings in my life. Then, for myself and others I might ask for clarity, guidance, healing, or support of some kind. Finally, I try to find silence in order to hear or feel any response, message, inspiration, or peace.

I recommend doing this practice once or twice a day, for at least 15-30 minutes at a time. You may prefer morning and/or evening, but as a way of developing a habit, try to be consistent in whatever works best for you. There are many different methods of meditation that you may enjoy. If you are interested you can research this for yourself. Many people find it difficult to slow down their thinking mind, and still their bodies long enough to meditate. This is the very reason why we should develop this practice in our lives. The challenge here is not the act of meditation; it is the uncontrolled mind that detracts from our peace and presence. Until we learn to focus within, it is always planning, scheming, manipulating, calculating, and preparing us to DO. The power of our higher awareness allows us to be focused in the present moment, where you are most connected to your higher truth. We cannot change the past, yet our mind is flooded with memories. We cannot experience the future, yet we are preoccupied with all of the "what if" scenarios. So find your true power in the present!

Spiritual practice is just that – practice. It is teaching us how to connect to our heart and spirit, while clearing our mind to be more focused on the present moment. When connected to our heart and spirit we are more conscious of expressing our energy (thoughts, words, and actions) on a higher level, one that is more supportive of us and others. Developing the habit of being more mentally present allows for greater observation and focus of our current energetic state. This observation supports us in detaching from unproductive mental energy and becoming more empowered, as opposed to being caught up in emotional or ego attachment.

Your spiritual practice should include your highest truth and integrity. In prayer or meditation always be honest, even if you are relatively unhappy in that moment. You are connecting your spirit with Source, and sometimes we are experiencing things that are difficult and we really need higher assistance. Even if you need to vent, better to express your pain in this atmosphere of love. Speak your mind (figuratively), and ask for the understanding, clarity, strength, and wisdom to heal and overcome your situation. You are now relying on your higher Source for answers and not your ego, which opens you to unlimited possibilities. By asking for these higher qualities and guidance you are confirming your power to co-create your life with Source. This is very empowering!

Spiritual practice supports the development and maintenance of our own empowerment. As you gain a greater connection to spirit from your daily practice (meditation or otherwise), you will begin to notice that your entire life is a spiritual practice. You will recognize all of your experiences and the people you interact with as teachers. With your presence you will decide whether to react from ego or spirit, and in either case, recognize the benefit of further reflection for the purposes of healing, growth, and expansion. Then, when you return to the meditation cushion you may seek clarity or wisdom from your Higher Source. This is the ongoing practice of spiritual growth.

"We are what we repeatedly do. Excellence, therefor, is not an act but a habit."

- Aristotle

Shifting to Healthier Habits

We have had all of our years up until now to create the habits that make up our current lifestyle and outlook. As always, our growth and healing starts with awareness, then, in order to shift toward healthy habits we will add in a little (or a lot) of inner strength, ownership, and wisdom. So in consideration of your level of overall holistic health, make an assessment of your current condition. For this process, utilize both your head (mind) and your heart (spirit). Be completely honest with yourself from the standpoint of this evaluation. There is no one to fool, con, or manipulate, and there is no right or wrong. There just is the truth in the present moment as you see it.

Next, once you have determined any areas of your wellness that might be enhanced, you can begin to determine some of the possible steps you may take. The first key is to create a plan that supports your ascension to a higher consciousness and personal accountability; it is of little use to try to do this to please someone else, or to emulate anyone else. Your plan for growth and healing must be suited to your highest interest, passion, energy level, integrity, and purpose. Whether you want to eliminate an unhealthy habit or add a healthy one into your lifestyle, you have to REALLY want this for your growth, transformation, and wellness.

You are accountable to yourself first. Then, once you are growing and healing personally and spiritually, you will be a positive, supportive influence on others, but it must start with

213

you. You notice that I do not start the ***Empower Model*** with **Wellness**. That is because it is important to first consider several other steps of development before you jump into wellness; such as knowing your true identity, developing inner strength and peace, and understanding your responsibility to take ownership of your life.

If we start from a current place of ego-control and disconnection to spirit, we are severely hampered in any efforts to change our engrained unhealthy habits or lifestyle. I am not saying it is impossible, but it can be dicey. It can be like, "taking a knife to a gun fight", as the saying goes. You created these habits from ego, and so now you want to eliminate them while still controlled by ego? What usually happens in this case is that we decide to change something we don't like about ourselves for the sake of superficiality and the desire for positive recognition (approval) from others. While this can be a motivator, it does not fully contribute to your holistic wellbeing. At best you may have traded one unhealthy habit for another, but remain under the delusion of ego.

The second key is to take the steps that are best suited for you. If you need to take gradual steps in order to incrementally shift your habits, this is perfectly fine, and often preferred as a way to develop consistency. If whatever you are attempting to change works best for you to jump in and instantly shift, then do that. Your goal is to integrate these new habits into your daily life. Use your higher awareness to determine what is best for you. Also, always utilize your patience and self-love throughout the process. You are taking ownership of your life in order to establish greater wellness on your path to personal and spiritual growth. This is huge and you are to be commended!

Appreciate the courage, discipline, and higher intention you are exhibiting within yourself along this journey. The goal is always out there and always a moving target. So focus on the daily process more than some arbitrary result. There is an initial goal of starting or ending a habit; then the goal may become the achievement of some objective criteria (for instance reducing to a specific body weight); and finally, the goal becomes maintenance. So there is always something to achieve, and you can only get there a step (day) at a time. Therefore, honor yourself each day for the accomplishment of that step. If in that day you are not as successful as you had hoped, honor yourself for maintaining the awareness about the misstep. Love yourself anyway, because tomorrow is a new day to make progress along your higher path!

How or if you choose to express your process to anyone else is your business. The goal is to successfully transform your life to greater health and wellness. This is primarily an internal process. You are shifting your inner beliefs and mental patterns as much as your external activities. As you honor yourself in this process of shifting, use your highest discernment when discussing your objectives with others. Make certain that you are attracting support and encouragement, and not negative critiques and judgments. Someone who is working within a sufficient level of consciousness within themselves will understand, support, and appreciate your inner transformation. Others, who are still mired in their ego, may only be able to judge what they see externally, and therefore are more focused on the result instead of the true inner process. You may likely have enough of your own ego trying to poison your efforts, so guard against oversharing if there is a chance it will sabotage your progress.

The biggest part of your transformation to a healthier lifestyle will involve a shift to greater balance. This shift alone may cause you to focus more on your physical health by adding exercise, a healthier diet, and/or a proper amount of rest. You may consider the effects of your work; are you required to work too many hours? Or is your job in some other way causing mental stress and taking time away from family, friends, and personal enjoyment? You might consider if a change within your current job or to a new job is most beneficial to your overall wellness. When our greatest focus is upon the quality of our life, instead of mere survival or to pacify the ego, we begin to take ownership of our choices and know that there are always options.

If in pursuing the elimination of certain harmful habits or establishing new healthy habits you feel that you would benefit from outside professional support, then this may be a good option for you. If you want medical, holistic, or psychological assistance for issues of dependency, addiction, or extreme weight loss, there are many practitioners available. Use your discernment to connect with someone who is qualified to support your overall objectives.

"Beliefs consist in accepting the affirmations of the soul; unbelief in denying them."
– Ralph Waldo Emerson

Healing Through Wellness

Healing brings wellness, but wellness can also bring us healing on a deeper level. If we were to heal from a sickness or injury, we would say that by overcoming that situation we may now experience wellness; with wellness being a state of existence that is free from physical ailment. But flip the script and consider that the ailment came into our physical existence for the purpose

216

of healing us on a deeper level. If we look deeply, we might notice that our life was not reflecting sufficient wellness in one or more areas, and therefore we were given the gift of an ailment in order to heal the deeper issue.

If we are only concerned with healing our sickness or injury so that we can rush back to our normal state of unconscious living, we may temporarily experience a physical wellness, but we have not utilized this experience to address and overcome our deeper need for healing. Some of the deeper issues that can lead to disease or injury deal with a lack of: life balance, self-love, inner peace, trusting your intuition, connection to spirit, forgiveness or a release of past trauma, etc. These are all issues of spiritual wellness that must be maintained in order to foster healing on a deeper level. Sustaining this level of healing will go a long ways toward eliminating the need for many of the physical ailments we experience. The existence of negative energetic qualities in the body system will lead directly and predictably to certain ailments, while their persistence over many years will create other more pervasive diseases.

In our human form we do live within some limitations and are always in the process of growth and healing. It is uncommon to effectively eliminate the need for or consequence of disease over an entire lifetime. However, depending on one's state of spiritual consciousness, I would not say that it is impossible. The point here is that personal and spiritual growth will ultimately have a very positive impact on your overall holistic wellness.

When we have good physical health we often say that we are fortunate, while those with poor health are unfortunate. As opposed to judging something as fortunate or unfortunate, we may rightfully express gratitude for whatever process of healing we are experiencing. I may be grateful because I am presently able to

217

live within a place of physical health, and continue my focus on fulfilling my higher spiritual purpose. It is not a matter of luck or chance, our energy is an intelligently designed maintenance system. I may also be grateful when in a position of requiring a physical healing, as I know that my energy systems are telling me to shift my focus from where it was previously into the place that addresses my immediate needs for overall wellness. Something was allowed to become unbalanced, dysfunctional, or was otherwise leading to some breakdown. With proper awareness I may now move into a state of spiritual alignment, and take the steps necessary for my healing.

What has been true for me over the last several years is that by using my awareness to detect a deficiency in my energy level, I am able to shift my focus into healing mode. Even though it means that I may have to shut down my present activity level, by doing so I find that my period of downtime is very short, and it does not lead to more severe problems. Once again, present moment focus on overall wellness is extremely valuable.

You probably have heard of situations when someone gets sick or incurs an injury, where in the course of their diagnosis or healing of that problem, they become aware of a much larger ailment that would not otherwise have been detected or cured. Having to deal with a physical ailment may be protecting you in some unknown and unseen way. At other times we have various ailments that we continue to ignore, and we often will not address these until we are "forced" to do so. You may suddenly have an "accident" that is serious enough to force you to heal those ailments you previously ignored.

Truth is that there are no accidents. We always attract that which we need for our highest healing and growth. The only choice becomes how we choose to understand and learn from this universal gift. That is why the word gratitude is most appropriate. Notice I don't say: fun, enjoyable, happy, etc. This is certainly a disruption from our normal productive lives, and sometimes a painful one at that. But it does serve a higher purpose, and it does support your personal growth and healing when you choose to work with it in this way.

Meditation as a healing tool

Meditation is becoming universally recognized as a valuable technique and daily practice to help alleviate stress and its effects on the health of the body. *Time Magazine* reported an article called "Strongest study yet shows meditation can lower risk of heart attack and stroke." This refers to a scientific study in the American Heart Association journal which provided the following conclusion: "A selected mind-body intervention, the TM (Transcendental Meditation) program, significantly reduced risk of mortality, myocardial infarction, and stroke in coronary heart disease patients. These changes were associated with lower blood pressure and psychosocial stress factors. Therefore, this practice may be clinically useful in the secondary prevention of cardiovascular disease[10]."

Stress is really just a disconnection from wellness (spirit). We have moved away from our inner peace in order to attach to some outside disturbance or imbalance. Meditation is the practice of reconnecting to spirit and going within to a deeper alignment with who we truly are. We are not the problem, situation, or event that triggered the stress attack. That is just an energy manifestation that is happening around us. While we must deal with the issues involved by taking the necessary steps, we must not

---

[10] Time Magazine, article from November 14, 2012, discussing the results of the American Heart Association study, website link: http://circoutcomes.ahajournals.org/content/5/6/750.full

get caught up in identification with this trigger. Meditation is a tool to help us remember who we are, to envision a positive outcome to our problem, and to receive our higher guidance. Therefore, *Just Breathe!*

The key to wellness is balance, which is only really possible when aligned with spirit. When one is controlled by ego their focus cannot be on peace, harmony, balance, and unity. Therefore, they will naturally create emotional drama, mental stress, and physical fatigue. This is why you find so many who try to settle for escape instead of healing. They develop addictions that attempt to cover up the pain of their dysfunctional lives. While it may temporarily distract us, it creates additional problems and does not heal the real problem in our life – a disconnection from our higher Source.

If you are willing to pursue inner healing and more conscious living, you are much more likely to create the conditions that support wellness on a holistic level. Follow your higher guidance to develop healthier habits, and greater life balance. Your wellness supports you and those around you on a higher path. By utilizing your higher awareness and consciousness in support of wellness, you are on your way to living your highest personal and spiritual potential.

Chapter 5 Exercises

Exercise 1:

In this exercise, take a specific period of time (like a week) to elevate and sharpen your awareness of your energy levels.

Energy flows all around us all of the time, expanding and receding as we allow it to be impacted by emotions, memories, activity levels, balance, and exchanges with other people. As we become more aware of our energy levels we can more successfully make choices that lead to our wellbeing and empowerment. Granted, this is very subjective, but that is ok because this is only relevant for you and accordingly is rightfully based upon your own interpretation.

Notice what thoughts, words, or actions affect your energy level, either up or down (better or worse). A sufficient energy level keeps you feeling happy, satisfied, stronger and healthier (mentally, emotionally, and physically); you feel like you can forge ahead with life's challenges. An insufficient energy level will either have you retracting from the normal challenges or otherwise feeling dissatisfied and disempowered. Do not judge either of these situations as good or bad, merely observe and document what is happening when your energy shifts.

With greater focus on your own energy levels you will naturally take more responsibility for your own wellbeing, and you will better understand what choices are more or less empowering for you. This is taking ownership of creating your life in a way that is most beneficial to you, instead of merely responding to the energy that comes to you from other people.

Exercise 2:

Take an objective look at your holistic health. Determine if you have a strong desire to shift and elevate your level of wellness; either to improve the health of your physical body, your mental focus, your emotional peace and stability, or your spiritual practice and connection. Document your goals and the steps you can take to begin on the road to greater wellness.

Know that this is a process that is changing the way you see and feel about yourself. You are shifting to healthier habits, so only you can decide what steps and goals are appropriate for you. Consider the five basic health factors listed above and begin to create an action plan that supports your experience of greater wellness. Research what you can on your own, and for goals that require a significant shift in lifestyle, consult a physician or other qualified health professional.

Make short term goals that are readily attainable for you, and then progress at a comfortable pace. Be enthusiastic and disciplined for the qualities you are now manifesting. This still needs to be in balance with your overall life responsibilities, but honoring yourself enough to create healthier habits is very empowering. If you are particularly goal oriented, monitor your progress, but the important thing is the shifting of unhealthy habits and patterns to those that support growth and healing. Be empowered to create your optimal health.

CHAPTER 6:
EMBRACE

"Your only obligation in any lifetime is to be yourself."
– Richard Bach

Embrace the Truth of Who You Are

The truth is that you are a spiritual being, having a human experience. This simple statement has the power to completely transform the way in which you see your life, and therefore, your potential. Encompassed in who you thought you were, as simply a human being striving for survival against all odds, is the program of struggle, suffering, limitation, fear, and defeat. This is largely a matter of perspective, but your life need not be so consumed by this false teaching.

You are spirit first and last (with a little bit of humanity/ego, in between), which having been created by Source, in its image (energy), you are therefore a part of the Divine energy that makes up all things. This is the understanding that the world needs to embrace. It is not just for a select few anymore, it is time for everyone to awaken to this truth. We have been falsely educated (whether or not it was consciously accepted) that we are

223

all sinners, and as such, without redemption, we face eternal damnation. However, my awareness says that "heaven or hell" is right here on earth, and your free will affords you the ability to choose to live in either state of existence.

By choosing to embrace your spirit you are supporting love, peace, unity, acceptance, joy, and a higher purpose in your life - the qualities of heaven on earth. While choosing to embrace ego you are supporting fear, lack, discrimination, judgment, hate, and disempowerment – the qualities of hell on earth. Without considerable inner training, each of us will continually vacillate between these two energetic states. With a greater understanding and acceptance of your inherent power to choose and create your life path, it is my sincere hope that we all will begin to spend more time in "heaven".

Sin is the same as error, which coming from the mind of ego, is a constant inevitability for mankind. So, does man often err? Absolutely, and this is true regardless of your beliefs. Is this error going to condemn you to an eternal "hell" after your physical death? Depending on your viewpoint of God, I guess you have your answer. From the standpoint of empowerment, when we know that we are connected to and part of Source, we know that we are capable of residing in a state of love, compassion, and peace, regardless of the errors we make within our ego-based perceptions and attractions. Our lives may now be more purposeful and consistent with our higher nature. It is a matter of awakening to our Divinity, rather than deferring our greatest qualities in hopes of some outside redemption, as judged by others.

I love this prayer, from the book, *A Course in Miracles*, "Forgive us our illusions, Father, and help us to accept our true relationship with You, in which there are no illusions, and where none can ever enter. Our holiness is Yours. What can there be in us that needs forgiveness when Yours is perfect? The sleep of forgetfulness is only the unwillingness to remember Your Forgiveness and Your Love. Let us not wander into temptation, for the temptation of the Son of God is not your Will. And let us receive only what You have given, and accept but this into the minds which You created and which You love. Amen."[11]

In order to fully embrace the higher truth of who we are, we must release the illusion that has taught us that we are separated from, and therefore less than Source. We are Source; we are love. Within our own beingness we are capable of creating empowering lives that serve others while fulfilling our Divine purpose. To choose disempowerment is to willingly handover your power to some other person or group of people, who have remained asleep and unconscious. Throughout history we have supported our own disempowerment, not only with religion, but many other institutions and situations. We can easily see how this can diminish our self-image, especially for those who do not "make the rules". This has created many of the traits that destroy a civilization, not support or expand it. If we continue to succumb to the power of ego-based organizations, that do not support and promote our individual rights and abilities to create and live our life according to our highest understanding and awareness, then we will continue to get the same results we currently have.

I hold out great hope for the transformation of our institutions as a result of the awakening of the masses. I offer great love and appreciation for the Ascended Master and Higher Beings, who through their great love for humanity, came to live in human

---

[11] A Course in Miracles, from the Foundation for Inner Peace, excerpt from page 350.

form to teach us about the higher principles of truth and love. I have tremendous gratitude for Jesus, Buddha, Krishna, and many others, who continue to support us while in spirit form. Know that these Masters have great love and hope for you apart from any allegiance to the many false teachings that have been attached to their name. If you are an awakened practitioner of a particular religion, and find great empowerment toward creating a life filled with the highest qualities of spirit for both yourself and all others, then you are on a beautiful path of growth and healing. However, it is not your religious affiliation that is important; it is the acceptance of your own Divine nature that is most significant.

If you are not experiencing this higher state of being, or if due to your disgust and disapproval of religion you have denied any existence of your spiritual nature, you may want to release any thoughts that are holding you back from true empowerment. We have a choice, right where we are, to choose our path. The path of personal growth does include utilizing our spiritual nature, in order to reach our higher understanding, awareness, and potential. If you are already perfectly content with every aspect of your life, then honor your path with appreciation, but remain open to the opportunities to expand your vision of what is possible and most supportive of others as well. We all have to judge for ourselves what it is that we are willing to receive and contribute in our lives.

So going forward from here, as one who is interested in personal and spiritual growth, embracing your Divinity is crucial. This is the truth of who you are, and all personal growth starts with truth and inner reflection. When you can honestly look at your life as one who is Divinely created, with capabilities and support beyond what you may have previously allowed or accepted, you will begin to open to a whole new level of potential. You will dream bigger, and know that you can create a life where your dreams can be fulfilled. You will align yourself with an energy and understanding that supports you in utilizing and developing your unique gifts. You will gradually expand your energy as you release self-imposed limitations as a false state of mind, as error. Forgive yourself for having accepted this error in understanding, for this is your path of transformation. You are healing and aligning with a perspective of yourself and others, which then supports your true empowerment.

If we cannot accept our Divinity, how can we see a new way of experiencing our life? If all that we have done or created has come from our education and self-belief, what radical thing can come into your life to change and improve what or who you think you are? Are you just going to suddenly decide to work harder, be smarter, or just be a "better person"? Believing that there is some Divine entity "out there" to "save" you, may be effective in motivating you through fear (in order to avoid some wrath or judgment), but it is not especially supportive toward fully recognizing the goodness and power in yourself and all others. So acceptance of your higher self is a way to understand and release the false teaching of limitation, lack, and fear that have created your current reality. This will guide you to a greater enjoyment and respect for life, and to discovering your true plan and purpose.

Beyond this initial level of awakening to the possibility of being Divine, is the concept of "Embracing" this as who you really are. The first reality of this statement is that you know that ALL people are Divine. So it is not that you are better than anyone else, it's that perhaps you are better than you or others thought you were. By embracing your truth you can more confidently go about the business of designing what you want to experience in your life, and then take the steps to fulfill your dreams. You will know that you have the capability and the tools to heal on an inner level, which then allows you to manifest more love, joy, and peace on the external. You will have healthier relationships because you have a profound love and respect for yourself and others, and you will be more compassionate, supportive, and accepting of the errors that others commit. Living in the truth of your Divinity allows you to take ownership of your life and all that you create, with courage, appreciation, and freedom.

"The desire to reach for the stars is ambitious. The desire to reach hearts is wise."
– Maya Angelou

Embrace the Shift

Shift is another term for "a process of significant growth." This process supports transformation, ascension, evolution, higher vibration, etc. For humanity, the shift implies moving from an ego-dominated approach to life, to a spirit-liberated path. The shift (should we choose this path) takes place in the relatively short span of time that we call our human life. It requires an awakening to our true identity, and then the motivation, intention, and daily practice leading to this higher existence. Exactly when this happens, or the specific experiences that precipitate our shift, is unique to each of us.

We all have the free will to awaken and shift, or not. Some who are stuck in their current mode of surviving and experiencing this human life will remain in this ego-state until they crossover. Even while shifting, we will function in various states of higher or lower consciousness. Personal and spiritual growth is an ongoing process of elevating awareness to higher vibrational states. Ideally we will experience this ascension in this lifetime, which not only supports us in living a more joyful and loving life, but it also benefits and assists others as well. Once we transition from this physical life, we move back into an energy form that is void of human (ego) consciousness, and we will reside in an energy field of pure love and light. From there, we will review and evaluate the details of the human life we just completed, and determine the next phase of our spirit's mission.

You may eventually decide to reincarnate as a way to complete the ascension that you did not accomplish while in your current human life, or you may decide to return for the purpose of lovingly and compassionately assisting other souls. This is why you cannot judge the value of anyone else based on appearance or egoic perception. Some highly evolved beings may be masquerading as the individuals you look down upon, but within their sphere of influence they are performing enlightened service.

Embracing this shift means to fully appreciate yourself, and all others on your path. Life is a journey, it is a process. Choosing to utilize your truth and higher wisdom to heal and develop into someone who is experiencing their human life from the perspective of spirit is worthy and amazing. So honor yourself on this path. You are taking responsibility for your life with respect to your individual wellness, as well as the positive impact you may have on the welfare of others. You not only know how much you matter to yourself and others, but you are living each moment within the awareness of what your choices bring into this world. You are shifting into one who is adding their light onto this planet. Remember, we all have a bright light within us.

Dr. Wayne W. Dyer wrote a wonderful book (which is also a movie) called, *The Shift*. The subtitle of the book is, "Taking your life from ambition to meaning." I highly recommend this book to everyone on this path. He aptly

229

describes this notion of shifting from ambition (ego) to meaning (spirit) during your physical lifetime, as a natural consequence of awakening to your higher truth. We all start out in this physical life learning the ways of ego. How best to survive and "take care" of ourselves, largely through selfishness and satisfying the desires of our ego. This may be especially true for the early education of men. I think you can clearly see that ambition, which is about competition, acquisition, false security, material gain, and winning at all costs, is not a position that is aligned with spirit or true higher meaning.

When in ego, we live this life, which really brings a great deal of suffering, in the hope of some superficial short term pleasure. For even if your ambition leads you to great wealth, fame, and position of power, the things that ego strives for, there is a great cost to this illusion. Those who do not receive the worlds acclaim have none the less sought this fool's gold at great sacrifice to their wellness, peace, joy, and love. Most of us ultimately reach a place where we have a true inner knowing that this is not the way to experience a joyful, fulfilling life.

According to Dr. Dyer's book, this is where we become increasingly interested in finding and shifting to bringing more meaning into our lives, which is the inner spiritual journey. It is this willingness and desire to shift in my own life that has led me to write this book. I believe that many more men are in this position of wanting to find and experience more truth and meaning in their lives, and are ready to prioritize their own inner healing and growth. In actuality, it is the simple pleasures which bring the greatest reward, which went virtually unnoticed or underappreciated because of our consuming lust for the things of ego.

This shift is preparing you to begin to reconnect with an awareness of the spirit that has always been with you and available to you. You are now focused on releasing the energies of ambition, conflict, and attachment. You no longer need to be "right" (which necessitates someone else being wrong), because you know that it is much better to be peaceful, happy, and secure within your own being. You function in a space of abundance that exceeds the accumulation of material wealth. You are happier with less "stuff", and now abundance includes inner peace, freedom, loving relationships, and the great joy found in helping others.

Embracing this shift with an open and receptive heart will carry you through the challenges of growth. You have the power, wisdom, Divine support, spiritual tools, and the intention of transforming your life to this higher perspective. Utilize all of these gifts and qualities, and feel the immense joy within your being. This is the true mission of your life. It is like matriculating into graduate school having just come from grade school. Your higher knowing is leading you to this significant shift.

"There is nothing stronger in the world than gentleness."
– Han Suyin

Sweet Surrender

The definition of surrender is: to yield (something) to the power of another. Normally we use this to mean that we are yielding to another person. In common terms, this will call into question our resolve, fortitude, and toughness. However, I say that as part of the process of shifting from ego to spirit, we are required to *embrace* surrender. Oddly enough, this will take more determination, courage, and strength than holding on to ego and challenging everyone you meet. We must, within ourselves, be willing and able to yield our ego nature to our true spiritual power, in order to transform and shift to a higher level of conscious living.

The word surrender is the perfect example of how so many things are completely turned around in this world. Something that has been branded as weakness is actually an example of strength. We must surrender our false perception of ourselves and the world. We must surrender our rigidness and closed-heartedness in order to allow our spirit to flow in and out of an open heart, and we must surrender our mind of aggression and selfishness to one of peace and cooperation.

Jesus said, "Blessed are the gentle, for they shall inherit the earth".[12]   What does this really mean? Do you think he was saying we should all be weak? No, Jesus, who represents the ultimate awakened human, was anything but weak. Rather, the word gentle denotes strength brought under control. He is suggesting that we be humble, which is a shifting from a perspective of false self-importance (ego) to a willingness to see the Divinity in all (spirit).

Much of what we are doing throughout this process of personal and spiritual growth is redefining the thoughts, words, and actions that have held humanity captive by our collective ego, which is our perceived separation from Source. We cannot heal, grow, and live within a conscious connection to our Divinity

---

[12] New American Standard Bible, Mathew 5:5, excerpt from the Sermon on the Mount.

while retaining our expressions of energy (thought, words, and actions) according to the old disempowering paradigm. During his time on earth, Jesus was trying to teach us about our Divine nature, thus supporting a powerful shift for mankind. Instead he was made out to be God, whereby once again, man would be subservient to a Divinity outside of themselves. This message was more advantageous to those in power, and has led to a great manifestation of ego control in the world (judgment, war, inequality, fear, guilt, etc.). Clearly, this is very disempowering to humanity as a whole. It is merely one example of man misinterpreting and manipulating the higher truth offered by a Master Teacher.

Embrace the surrendering of the ego within yourself; this is an amazing tool for liberation from false identification and for gaining tremendous inner strength. This does not take away from having great passion and determination for developing yourself to your highest potential. You will utilize great inner strength to break free from the crowd in support of your true path and purpose. Better to walk alone on the right path, than to follow the crowd on the wrong path. In truth this concept of surrender is an internal process for connection to Source and inner development. Yielding your ego in order to shift to spirit is something that is done within. Only the distractions and reminders of your false education reside without.

Strive for peacefulness, humility, and gentleness. These are Divine qualities that will support your happiness in the following ways: 1) by assisting you in energetically attracting others with these positive qualities into your life; 2) by strengthening your character, and establishing boundaries when dealing with those stuck in ego; you will then not automatically engage in an unnecessary and unfruitful battle; and 3) your nature will be much more compassionate and supportive toward love and kindness for others. By cultivating an inner strength in this manner, you will feel less inclined to require anyone else's approval, therefore, more inclined to be who you choose to be for the betterment of your life and that of all others.

Surrender inspires the energy of allowing, and allowing is crucial if we want to be in the flow of spirit. In so many ways, we get in our own way. Allowing is being receptive, which is a higher quality than force. If you are spending time consistently forcing your agenda on others (or yourself), you are not only infringing on their space, but you are also not open to the good that your spirit is offering you in your life. As an example of this, instead of working with the reality of what is, we fight everything and everyone in order to get what we think we "should" have.

If our spirit is always leading to our higher good, and we are attracting the things that we need, then we can allow life to be as it is with an attitude of peace and openness. This is not a passive activity; you are utilizing great inner strength and control, without having to engage in unnecessary confrontational battles. Emotions are better spent in joy and gratitude, than with anger and disappointment. From this perspective we can take the appropriate action with better clarity and wisdom.

Surrender your position of protecting your ego, and you will open up to a whole new set of possibilities in your life. In order to truly grow, we must be able to face our fears, and then overcome them. When we are protecting ourselves from the things that we fear, we are only preventing ourselves from achieving the life we have always desired, and were, in fact, meant to live. The fear that you run from is an illusion that you have created within, due to your false education and perception. So, surrendering to this fear, is actually allowing you to deal with it head on. Instead of avoiding this imaginary monster, you are allowing your awareness to consider the consequences of overcoming the thing that you fear. You may then break it down into smaller, easier steps that ultimately lead you to conquering your fear and moving forward. Often this is the very thing that leads us to fulfilling our highest purpose.

Surrender does not imply that you let people mistreat you and be happy about it. When we are allowing the shift from ego to spirit through the wisdom of surrender, we are in a stronger position to maintain our inner strength and empowerment in any situation. You can then decide from this stronger position, using your higher discernment, what is the most appropriate course of action for you. At the same time you are treating others with compassion because you know that they are either acting from a place of ego (disconnection to Source), or simply from a position of what they think is in their best interest. In any case they came upon your path in order to support you in some higher way. Surrender to the light of love that is always available to you.

"Our task must be to free ourselves by widening our circle of compassion to embrace all living creatures and the whole of nature and its beauty."
– Albert Einstein

Embrace Oneness

Oneness represents, within both your Heart and Mind, that you are connected to all that exists within creation. We have already well-established in this book that you are an extension of the Divine Source (God, Universe, Tao, or whatever you want to call it). As a spiritual being you are part of that which created you – everything is energy. This confirms upon you the capabilities and qualities of light, love, peace, harmony, wisdom, abundance, and wellness. I do not believe that Source created you to be anything less than itself. Our early development into the education of ego (or ambition, as Dr. Dyer wrote) is the consequence of the accumulation of misguided teachings throughout man's existence. Through our free will we have the opportunity to remember who we really are, and embrace the shift for greater alignment with our higher truth.

This higher truth about who we are is the exact same truth that identifies all other humans as well. We are all equally the "Sons" of a loving creator. This does not change or get taken away when we sin, which is a really good thing because we all make errors on a fairly regular basis. The Oneness that created and encompasses all of life offers us only light, love, and compassion for our struggles. Some of our choices lead to errors which then lead to consequences where we will experience suffering or "punishment" of some kind. This has to do with the established rules of mankind, combined with the natural laws of cause and effect.

Our consequences, for either good or bad, create an experience from which to further develop our awareness of our higher nature and the opportunity to heal, grow, and make more empowering choices in the future. There is no retribution offered by Source because you made an error in judgment, spirit always offers you the opportunity to awaken to truth, that you might choose to connect to your own Divinity, instead of ego. It's time to stop bringing God down to man's ego-based level. This is energy in its highest form, why would it be offended, vengeful, jealous, petty, etc., when the parts of itself make mistakes while in the process of fully transforming and awakening?

However, this same offering of love, light, patience, and peace, which is gifted unconditionally from Divine Source, is the very same qualities we are meant to share with all beings. From the standpoint of the energy of Oneness, all humans are brothers and sisters, all are equal, and all are deserving of our highest support. If this seems radical it is only because of our education in ego that has convinced us that we are separate from Source, and then based on the difference in our beliefs, wealth, geography, race, gender, and every other kind of discriminating criterion, we are separate from each other.

We can look for every reason to think we are different, but even on a human level we are all on this planet together, and when we do something to help ourselves at the expense of our brother, we all suffer. What affects one, affects the whole. In a shortsighted way, which is all the ego has, we may think we win; but from the standpoint of spirit, we continue to perpetuate the destructive energy that shields many people from their light, and threatens the survival of man and planet Earth. Even when we simply harbor fear, anger, or hatred of another person (or group of people), we are damaging ourselves by aligning with ego (darkness) instead of spirit (light). Instead of adding our light to the world we are withdrawing it. Then when people who feel this darkness in their heart for others teach it to generation after generation, it is quite clear why it seems like such a radical concept to love each other as brothers and sisters.

The truth is that people are living and teaching what they know. It is my hope in writing this book (and with my coaching work) that many of us begin to learn a new education and way of living. If we harbor anger, guilt, judgment, fear, greed, etc. within our own hearts, what makes us think that our expressions of energy (thoughts, words, and actions) towards others would be any different? The value and need for personal and spiritual growth is very real. And not just for yourself but for all of life.

When we learn who we really are, we can start to accept that we are capable of more love, peace, joy, and fulfillment. This ignites the fire to begin taking the steps for inner healing, and the transformation of how we feel about ourselves, including our circumstances, experiences, and potential. We begin to elevate our energetic vibration a little at a time as we connect more deeply with our higher consciousness in each present moment. This is the path which supports the embracing of Oneness. It is not an intellectual exercise. You don't just say to yourself, "I think that I will be more loving, kind, and patient to all people – beginning now." It is certainly fine to attempt to make an effort in this direction, but in the end you are limited by your own need for inner healing. We can only give what we are: if we are loving to ourselves, we give love; if we are peaceful within ourselves, we give peace; and if we are kind to ourselves, we give kindness.

You are a unique and beautiful facet of creation; you are One with All That Is. Oneness is your call to recognize the spiritual nature within each of us, in support of unity. This is a very high concept, which requires a level of significant healing and growth for each of us individually. As part of our own individual Divine life plan, we all have the purpose of supporting and fostering unity for all beings. Therefore, your Divine purpose always has the addendum of being beneficial to all others, as well as yourself. So embrace with great joy your opportunity to serve humanity. As good as it feels to help yourself, it is that much more rewarding and fulfilling to help others as well, and once enough people are living in this unified way, we will shift humanity into a powerful new age.

"Absorb what is useful, Discard what is not, Add what is uniquely your own."
– Bruce Lee

Utilizing your Past for Growth and Healing

If I was to suggest that you embrace your past, what does that mean? Normally we are told to let go of the past. There is a difference between embracing your past and being held prisoner by your past memories. To embrace something is to appreciate and honor it. Our past contains countless experiences, and whether an experience from our past was seen as good (pleasurable, supportive) or bad (hurtful, damaging), it no longer exists in your present. However, you attracted that experience in order to satisfy some higher need. It was not something that happened TO you, it happened FOR you. As a way to fully receive that which was given to you, use your higher awareness to understand the lesson or benefit of this gift. It is a piece of the puzzle that illuminates your spirit journey.

This process of truly understanding the purpose of a past experience will assist in your present growth and healing. You may come to accept the value of an experience in one or more of the following ways: 1) you will have a greater understanding of the consequences of your choices or habits; 2) you will be reminded of the value of using higher awareness and mindfulness in each present moment; 3) you will understand the requirement for you to live in your truth, and not give away your power to anyone else; 4) you may be reminded of the consequence of not loving yourself enough (or not being courageous enough) to take ownership of your circumstances; or 5) you may have been inspired (whether

239

consciously or subconsciously) to provide needed support to someone else, even at the expense of your own happiness.

In truth, all of our experiences provide the opportunity to benefit, both for us and any others involved. Once an experience is in your past, the only healthy thing you can do is embrace and accept it. While understanding the lessons on a higher level, you will more naturally have true forgiveness for yourself and all others. This is a required element of healing. Once you have learned what you needed to learn, then allowed true forgiveness in your heart, you are free to release the experience, both mentally and energetically. This is how we can embrace our past.

Some experiences will take longer to process in this manner. And they may have consequences that continue for an extended period of time. The spiritual lessons are still valid and relevant to your growth and healing. You must continue to work on shifting your perspective of both a particular experience and the ongoing circumstances that were the result of past choices. If you had a very difficult experience with another person, for example, the lesson may have ended with the outcome of the experience, or it may be ongoing and forging a higher perspective while you endure further interaction with this person. Chances are that this is a very significant teacher in your life, and you are being given the opportunity to transform and heal on a very deep level. Not the most pleasant experience, but in the long run it is potentially extremely valuable.

It is far more important to learn and grow from an experience than to judge it as good or bad. Just because something is not what we "wanted" does not mean that it is not what we "needed". With a perspective of higher consciousness, it is always possible to reap the benefits of all experiences. However, when stuck in our ego-mind, where everything revolves around our comfort and pleasure in the short-term, you risk the following: 1) residing unnecessarily in unhappiness (suffering) of your own mental doing; 2) missing the value in the experience; 3) making a difficult situation much worse; 4) finding fault and blame for someone else when the lesson was for you; 5) retaining the negativity of a situation beyond the experience, that clouds your present judgment, perception, and choices; and 6) creating a victim identity from the experience which undermines your empowerment for years to come. Embracing, learning, healing, growing, and releasing will ensure that you will not be required to re-live that experience, and it will prepare you to attract more positive situations in the future.

Since your past experiences have developed you to be the person you are now, your best option when dealing with or thinking about the past is to embrace it. The choices you make from this point forward are up to you. When living in awareness we are always taking the next step; we are always in the present. If your path involves personal and spiritual growth, this next step is more empowering than the last. In taking this next step forward you are moving from a position, belief, understanding, perception or experience from the past. We rarely, if ever, make quantum leaps on our human journey. That's not to say it is impossible, it just has not yet been widely accessible for most people. Your past is the foundation of your present moment leading you closer to your optimal future.

Our goal is to continue to evolve; change is unavoidable. Some of what we have experienced has taught us things that we want to further explore and pursue, or otherwise incorporate into our present growth. I am currently experiencing this phenomenon myself. Having spent three decades in accounting and business management, I am now moving onto a path that has me writing, teaching, and coaching/mentoring. To some my background may seem incongruent to my present service. Yet my past experience can have great relevance within a whole new context if I will only grow and adapt my mental framework and move outside of my comfort zone.

I can tell you firsthand that this is not an easy endeavor. With such a background in ego education we normally become engrained, stagnant, and comfortable in our established roles. They become our self-identity, not to mention the way others have judged us. Even with many transitional and evolutionary life experiences, and training in various spiritual practices, it is like escaping gravity. In order to shift to a higher calling, in fulfillment of what we are determining to be our true purpose, we must risk disturbing and uncovering much of what we previously accepted as truth.

This is an ongoing process where one day you are energized and powerful enough to soar with the eagles; then the next day your ego will try to convince you that you are small, insignificant, and incapable of achieving your dreams. This shows that this path takes endurance and patience, as well as a consistently applied practice. Sometimes there are temporary external shifts in energy that surround and affect your life, and you will need to ride these out without panicking – just stay the course. This is the challenge one takes in order to heal, grow, transcend, and serve a higher purpose.

A few years ago I began a period of significant personal and professional growth, by turning down an opportunity to continue in my previous career with the company who acquired a business in which I was part owner. I chose a process of personal and spiritual growth and healing that is redefining my potential for career and service. Had I stayed on the same career path, I would have had greater financial abundance (in the short-term), but I would have missed the much richer quality of joy, peace, wellness, and fulfillment available in my life. This was an example of shifting from ambition to meaning.

During this career transition, and as part of my new education, I have taken the opportunity to begin various processes and businesses as a way to determine my highest path for service. This has required that I face my fears and embrace a higher perspective of my own potential. I started my own small business bookkeeping firm; I accepted an opportunity (that came to me without any effort on my part) to teach classes on accounting and finance at a local community college; I began a partnership designed to provide transformational life coaching, and then, most recently I started my own publishing company.

Each experience and venture is not an end to itself, but each is playing a role in developing my passion, skills, and interests to serve my highest fulfillment and purpose. You can see that after many years of primarily serving in an office setting as an employee and support service manager, I have consciously chosen to step into leadership, entrepreneurial roles in my work. I am gaining valuable experience in communication and teaching. Within this new empowering energy, I was inspired to write the book you are reading, as a way to share the wisdom I was given in support of growth and healing for men. Clearly the easiest path would have been to stay in the known; however, the great potential that resides within each of us is best served in loftier pursuits.

This is an example of how one can transition over a period of time with the appropriate tools, higher perspective, and a consistent conscious approach. It is my dream that this work will serve the world, while supporting me in a fashion that allows me to continue this career path. Yet, I continue to utilize the skillsets that supported me in the past. My writing, coaching, and

243

teaching about personal empowerment for men has grown from real world experience, and has great relevance to those in the workplace, including owners, managers, and employees (I am already working on an empowerment book for business). The mental makeup that made me naturally inclined to accounting, dealing with balance, structure, organization, logic, and practicality, assists me while communicating to others (especially men) who may process from a similar left-brained mental perspective. Additionally, as an entrepreneur, while I am required to learn many new facets of business, my financial background is a supportive foundation.

We don't throw away our past, we analyze it to understand our choices, inclinations, and skills. Then, through higher growth and healing, we can learn to recognize these things as gifts, and discover how to apply them in the most empowering way. We learn to overcome our perceived lack, and know that we are capable of greater things. My personal/spiritual growth as it relates to my career, and also to how I see myself, involves connecting to my higher source and trusting that I am supported as a writer, teacher, and coach. I have reinforced this with visualization, while experiencing the daily process of inner development and healing.

You too can follow your dreams wherever they take you. You are not limited by your past; you are only limited by a false self-image and your unwillingness to heal, grow, and evolve. Once you accept the truth of who you are, you begin to find ways to grow into who you are truly here to be. You begin to let in the light, and move out of the shadows that seemed to provide protection, but in reality diminished your joy and higher fulfillment. As you can see, I have taken the position of embracing my past as I make choices in the present which are creating my future. This has been (and still is) a step by step process of transformation and identifying, then pursuing, my dreams. There are no shortcuts, but if I can do it anyone can.

With respect to utilizing our past for growth and healing in the area of personal relationships, we all have had many experiences from which to draw useful data. From our upbringing, to our past association with family, friends, co-workers, and romantic partners, you probably have quite the mixed bag of lessons. All of our interactions are teaching us something of value, and we would be most wise to recognize this and apply these lessons for greater love, joy, peace, and fulfillment in the present.

The details of our experiences are all uniquely ours, yet the purpose of experience, for the process of growth and healing, is universal. In the past I have tended to have numerous shorter-term relationships as part of my life path. Others might be connected to only a few partners for a lifetime. No one way is better than another, and it is wise to refrain from judging anyone else's experiences as good or bad. Everyone is learning in the manner that is most effective for their life purpose and their connection to spirit. I could look back and be depressed that I did not have the one storybook lifelong connection. Or I could realize that in order to learn and heal on a deeper level, it was necessary and most beneficial for me to experience many different connections, and then utilize sufficient space in-between for much reflection and growth.

We attract others onto our life path according to our vibrational match and the learning opportunity that is most beneficial at the time. If the only way that someone can learn what they need to learn is through an experience that appears to bring suffering in one form or another, we need to honor that and support them, but that experience was unavoidable for them. This is also where accepting, allowing, and embracing come in as higher qualities.

Personal and spiritual growth is a purpose that we all share while in this human world. Whether and how we choose to develop this is up to each individual. While experiencing numerous relationships, I have also valued significant time on my own as a way for me to facilitate and support my internal growth. Relationship connections, which could be romantic, friendship, work associates, family, etc., are a strong way to understand your inner need for healing, as determined by how others are showing up in the external. However, to utilize this as a tool for growth it takes great awareness. We instead tend to identify ourselves more within the context of the relationship interaction than apart from it. Sometimes we are using relationships as a way to avoid dealing with our own healing and growth.

Our path of development is our own, and is independent of anyone else. Therefore, the most conscious way to be in relationship is to continue to work on your own growth, and allow the other person an opportunity to do the same, while you are sharing this healthy space together for enhanced love, joy, and peace. Sometimes we can do this, and other times we need to end a relationship in order to create sufficient space to support our healing and growth. Hopefully, we will utilize our mindfulness and connection to Source in order to develop a greater understanding of our Divine qualities, and then determine what are our true needs and desires in a healthy relationship. If we are not in this place of consciousness, we may instead reside in the suffering that ego is all too happy to offer, and then blame others for the experience or wallow in self-pity. As always, the choice is ours.

I have personally utilized all of the above at different times, as a way to learn from experience. I have learned that we can manifest experiences and circumstances within the teaching model of relationship that are virtually limitless. For both good and bad (joy and suffering) you can create things that you would have never thought possible. I believe that some of the most extreme experiences have the greatest potential for the deepest personal growth. So if you have experienced things in relationships that seemed to have caused an unreasonable amount of suffering, take heart and know that your level of inner healing can be absolutely transformative. Also know that there is nothing from which you cannot recover.

If you have chosen a difficult relationship from which to support your inner healing, the first thing that you will need to do is get in touch with your spirit. This is not only because this is where the healing takes place, but also because you need to begin to identify your life and value apart from the person, experience, and circumstance as quickly as possible. You must release the false perception of yourself that may have been very disempowering in the relationship. The truth is that you attracted the relationship to show you where you need healing, but the experiences that may have manifested are not who you really are.

You will need to take ownership, and create the opportunity to facilitate the healing within yourself. This is a process that will not always be easy, and will at times seem impossible. Your focus is on the short term, day to day if necessary, but taking the positive steps to regain or develop your self-love will eventually pay great dividends. Utilize counseling or coaching if so inclined. Having someone who sees the higher truth of who you are, from a place that is independent of your experience, can be very useful in supporting you to remember who you are.

247

Once you have done the work to remember your true identity, and have begun the process of personal and spiritual growth, embrace your experience for the indispensable gift that is was. Utilize the spiritual wisdom that was gained through this human ordeal. Release any judgment about the experience or the "teacher" that was involved. Forgive yourself for any guilt about having needed such a challenging experience. If at the time you could have handled things differently you would have. When you can do all of this, while shifting your life to greater awareness and consciousness, you will be able to make more empowering choices.

This is how you utilize your past experiences in personal relationships for growth and healing. Now that you are healthier within, you will attract relationships with healthier people. We are always in a process of growth and learning, however, these new people will support you within experiences that teach you in a way that may be more gentle, joyful, and peaceful.

"Nothing ever is, but is always becoming."
- Plato

Embrace your Spirit Journey

As you begin to honor your own inner truth, you will develop the greater awareness that will highlight and accent your particular life path. What was likely seen as a collection of judgments about your various circumstances, conditions, and "random" experiences, will form a cohesive picture from which to build upon. Your human life is an extension of your Spirit

Journey, which was conceived in some past timeless dimension, and will continue long beyond your physical form.

While limited to our awareness, consciousness, sense perception, and training, there is much more happening within and without you than you may know. Your experiences, and the people in your life who you have shared them with, are not a coincidence. They were either specifically designed by your spirit before birth, or they were an energetic attraction that fulfilled some higher need for healing and growth while in this incarnation. Obviously this denotes a level of accountability that many are still uncomfortable with. Whether you experienced suffering or joy, you created it on the level of spirit, and if you attracted a person who was either very cruel or very loving, you designed that for your benefit.

When you can start to grasp this truth, you will begin to *Embrace* your Spirit Journey. On the level of spirit it is always serving our higher good. On the level of our humanity it can feel like heaven or hell. When we learn and heal from our past, as a part of our personal and spiritual growth in the present, we can begin to understand how to move forward in the most conscious and empowering way. We will develop our higher knowing that will support us toward achieving our highest potential in the future. As always, this potential should not only assist us in experiencing greater love, joy, peace, and fulfillment, but also contribute in more meaningful ways to the world.

This Spirit Journey will lead us to define (remember) our higher purpose, and it will reinforce our knowing of who we really are, and who others really are. Everyone is on their Spirit Journey simultaneously. Therefore, it is very important to honor the path that others are on, just as we now honor our own path. If someone appears to be on a path of self-destruction, this is only true from our human perception and understanding. On the level of spirit they are attracting the experiences that are potentially leading to their healing and growth. However, this is on their timeline, not ours. Their progress or expansion may not even be evident to us in this lifetime. If we are peripherally affected by their life path, then there is something for us to learn and/or contribute. However, it is not our path or purpose to personally take on their pain and unconscious behavior.

We are to judge only our own journey, and do what we can to facilitate the elevation of our own wellness, consciousness, and soul expansion. The best support we can provide others, and all of humanity, is to heal ourselves, and recognize the Divinity in everyone. While woven into the Universal tapestry, your Spirit Journey is unique to you. This is why it is required for you to take ownership of your life, and to understand the power of your choices. You can choose to be empowered by identifying and applying your specific gifts, skills, and passions, in connection with your unique purpose in service to the world. You can choose to see yourself as an extension of Divinity, whereby you more naturally will express the higher qualities within yourself to others.

On the other hand, you can choose to deny any such "Spirit Journey" as your reality. You can move onward in your human life and react to the "good" that may come with temporary happiness; and react to the "bad" experiences with fear, anger, sadness, etc. This is disempowering in that your state of satisfaction and fulfillment in life seem to have less to do with you, than what is happening to/around you. Many people live this way, but to my mind, it cannot be as fulfilling and rewarding as understanding the power that you have to create a life of meaning and purpose.

However you choose to live, how you perceive your life will have a great impact on your potential, not only for creating what you want, but also with respect to having a positive impact on others. Regardless, your human life will flow with what feels like ups and downs, joys and sorrows. With a spiritual perspective, your highs and lows may be less severe, but they will still exist. We are challenged on many levels. When we are taking accountability for our own healing and growth, we must overcome many deep-seated doubts and fears. This is because we are extending ourselves beyond the so called "comfort" of our past limited self-belief and false education in order to experience something that is extraordinary to the ego, but attainable through spirit. Since we develop in a process that goes deeper and deeper, if we are growing we are continually challenged.

Instead, if we choose to deny our spiritual presence, we are very susceptible to a greater possibility of severe experiences in suffering, due to our unwillingness to understand the higher purpose in the experience. We may, therefore, repeat these difficult lessons throughout our life. Additionally, we may likely be less attentive to our own inner healing and balance, which will not only exacerbate our own fear and stress, but also lead us to mistrust and mistreat others.

Embrace your Spirit Journey because it is your highest path of understanding and evolution, designed specifically by your Divine spirit. Do not choose this as an easier path – because on a human level it is not. Since we are interested in achieving our highest personal and spiritual potential we seek the highest path. We utilize this unique journey for the purposes of learning and healing from our challenges, and for loving and serving ourselves and others with great aptitude and appreciation.

"Turn your wounds into wisdom."
– Oprah Winfrey

Embrace your Challenges

With wisdom and awareness you will utilize your past in a way that brings healing, growth, and the opportunity to create a life that is in alignment with who you truly are. However, this is not to say that you will no longer experience challenges in the present. So, as part of your ongoing development you will benefit most by embracing any new challenging experiences.

You are now working within a new and higher understanding of the purpose of all experience. If something comes into your awareness that seems to be bringing less than the joy and peace that you have intended to create, you now have an opportunity for spiritual practice. Something outside of our physical senses and perceptions is always at play. Your choices still lead to consequences, so the first thing to consider is: what choices have I made that may have brought about this experience? Are there new choices that can be made in order to create a new, more enjoyable outcome? If so, utilize your higher awareness to correct a situation, for the benefit of all involved.

Sometimes we feel challenged when we have expectations of others that don't work out the way we planned. Every experience is teaching us something, when we choose to receive the lesson. Much like a road map leads you to a destination, spirit uses our experiences to guide us on our path to truth and healing. Other people will ultimately do what they feel is in their best interest, whether they are honoring their spirit or ego. Support your inner peace and other people by accepting this fact. If you were relying on another person for some kind of support, and suddenly they are unavailable to you, know that you are being shown one of two lessons. Either this was something that you are better off doing yourself, or a different person or alternative is opening to you which will bring even greater benefit. This perspective is solution oriented and based in spiritual principles. There is no wasted time in needless suffering or ill will.

Another possibility is that through spirit you have setup an experience that will foster new growth and understanding. There is something that you need to learn or recognize on a deeper level that will either bring further education in truth, or reinforce wisdom previously attained. In any case, it is something that you need in order to continue to shift to your highest level of consciousness. Do your best to quickly gain awareness of this truth. Refrain from the desire to judge an experience that may feel challenging at the time. If your energy around this situation feels heavy and uncomfortable, you already know that it is something that you are required to deal with. So to focus on labeling the experience, and residing in your suffering, is not productive or supportive to your growth and healing.

Don't forget to breathe deeply and slowly, as a way of releasing the heaviness you are experiencing. This helps to relieve stress and assist the flow of energy that was temporarily restricted. Next, if something has already happened that can't be undone, allow and accept it. Your goal is to move with spirit to the highest solution, and in order to do this you must not get stuck in the "I am pissed off that this happened" mindset. Those who are not focused on consciousness will live in that space, which only causes further suffering. With the remembering of who you are, you now know that this is a choice. But for many others it is a habit and a trap.

When you can stay connected to spirit, you will be supported in the handling of any challenge and in cultivating the healing and growth that follows. In your meditative space, ask for guidance and assistance. You may ask Source, "What do I need to do, or how do I need to shift, in order to create the best and highest solution for all involved? Please guide me to a full realization of the wisdom, guidance, and healing that this experience is showing me." Shine your light and love on the experience with the knowing that all is moving in a higher direction. You are not being asked to be happy or joyful about the circumstances that have manifested, only appreciative for the opportunity to transform, heal, and grow. This is why we embrace our challenges. You are shifting your mindset to the solution and benefit, and away from the thoughts that are disempowering. You are not being punished; you are being awakened on a deeper level.

It is usually easier for us to embrace experiences that feel good, and that is okay as well. All experiences are gifts that may teach us valuable lessons. As described above, some teach us in a way that will require us to transform our way of thinking and being in the world, in order to live more consciously in alignment with our higher truth. Other experiences will feel more gentle and peaceful, and will support and confirm the shift in inner healing and alignment that has already taken place. We embrace these opportunities as well, not only because they feel good, but also in the knowing that they are reflecting the healthy connection to spirit that exists within us.

As would seem reasonable on any level, we want to create as many of the good feeling experiences as possible. As we develop along our path of spiritual practice, leading to living our highest potential, we will naturally do this. Your experiences will reflect an ever-increasing connection to spirit, and therefore the gifts of

254

spirit will manifest as your external reality more and more frequently. Since we are not yet living ego-free in this world, we still need lessons to remind us that the path of ego leads to suffering, and that the option of choosing a spiritual perspective is always available. As I've said, however, even difficult experiences may be handled in a positive way that brings further growth and healing.

So, shift your perspective about what is good or bad in the way of experiences, and embrace the gift that awaits. You have attracted both the person and the circumstances that manifested as the outer experience. Take ownership of this opportunity for the value it has to offer. Don't label it, and don't blame others, instead shift into a personal experience of ownership and spiritual practice. This is part of your new training. Can you work through a challenging experience with love, acceptance, and gratitude? Can you transform this experience into a teaching tool that supports your advancement? This, then, is true personal and spiritual growth. As you can master the difficult situations you will move into the space of claiming and creating miracles in your life.

"Too often we underestimate the power of a touch, a smile, a kind word, a listening ear, an honest compliment, or the smallest act of caring, all of which has the potential to turn a life around."
– Leo Buscaglia

Embrace those on your Path

As we fully embrace our Oneness with all of life, we also want to embrace all of those wonderful souls who have supported us on our path in this life. The experiences that are so incredibly valuable to our growth and healing, largely involve some connection and contribution by another person. Therefore, we want to develop an appreciation for their impact and benefit to us. Just as we are now recognizing ourselves as an extension of Divine Source, we must always remember that this is their truth as well.

As part of Oneness we learned to recognize all people as Divine in nature, as spiritual beings having a human experience. This truth is always independent of their expressions of energy (thoughts, words, and actions) that may clearly reflect a disconnect from their spirit. Like us, they are moving in and out of varying levels of awareness and consciousness. For this, our intention is to offer the same compassion, love, and support that Source offers us. In our state of transformation and development, this is not always easy.

"Oneness" is not just a concept for someone you may never meet; it applies to those you deal with every day. Some interactions are pleasant and some are not. When we are connected to spirit we can recognize their Divinity as well as ours. When we are controlled by ego and disconnected from spirit, we will project this onto others and refuse to recognize their light. Remember, while at times we all err (or sin), we none the less retain our spiritual and Divine essence. So we not only need to forgive ourselves when we act poorly, we must forgive others as well.

Also remember that we have attracted them onto our path as a vibrational match for the higher purpose of healing and growth. On the level of spirit this may mean that we have agreed to offer them something (love, light, support, wisdom, understanding, encouragement, the lesson of their consequences, etc.), and they have agreed to offer us something. This is true regardless of whether the experience feels good or bad to us. We may even be fulfilling some karmic debt between us and the other person going back to a previous life. We are connected to this person for some higher reason, so let's embrace it for what it is. Let's function from the place of our connection to spirit in order to support the lessons, growth, and healing that are necessary, and because this connection between the two of you has occurred, it was necessary.

Just as the energy of our experiences varies, so does the energy of our inter-connection with others. Some people naturally feel very light, joyful, and supportive. They are reflecting this energy within you. Other people feel very dark, heavy, and harmful. They are reflecting the places in you where darkness resides. We all have a balance of light and dark, though we are striving to enhance our light. They also may be offering you an opportunity to choose to love and honor your higher self, or to revert into ego mode for further lessons through suffering.

Always use your highest awareness and discernment when connecting with anyone. Sense the impact they have on your energy, it will always lead you to truth. You can then either open or protect yourself, as is most appropriate for the relationship. While we are all here to serve and love, our highest priority is to live in spirit, so it is always up to you to decide how much energy you are willing to share with another. Do not disempower or deplete your life force energy for anyone else.

What about our family? As I mentioned in the "Educate" chapter, we all have chosen our own unique life circumstances from which to learn, grow, heal, and expand our soul. We chose these things from a place of spirit prior to incarnating into our temporary human life. This would clearly include our original family and upbringing, not only for genetics but also for our early ego education. Some people will have on-going interaction with parents and siblings, and others will have chosen to disconnect early in this life. Regardless of what it looks like from the outside, all have chosen a path that suits their spiritual needs, and all parties to this connection were in agreement prior to birth (on a spiritual level).

Embrace your family as you would any other person on your path. They have offered the potential for great learning, and therefore are a benefit to you. On the level of spirit, they are teaching you to honor your true self. Sometimes they express their energy in ways that will support, obstruct, or even contradict our higher truth, and it is up to us to choose for ourselves what is most empowering. In doing so we may emulate them or radically deviate from their example. Like anyone else, their actions may have not always reflected a connection to their spirit, and consequently they may have made many errors which you perceived to be unloving, unkind, unjust, and even cruel.

However, they may have also made many sacrifices, from their standpoint, that you have not recognized while your main focus was on judging them for their sins, or only being concerned with how things were impacting you. The truth is that they were acting from their place of awareness and consciousness. To the extent that they were unable to overcome their false ego training, they likely would have projected this onto you. Remember, your life path is not primary to them. They have their own path and purpose, so we must learn to not take everything so personally. When it comes to family, it seems that this higher awareness is particularly challenging to us.

As you develop your own higher understanding and inner healing, you may now look upon others with compassion, forgiveness, and love for who they truly are, even if they cannot see this within themselves. The bottom line is that you chose them according to your specific needs and desires for spiritual growth. You have the opportunity to take ownership of this situation for your highest benefit.

Learn to accept others as they are, and then make your own choices as to how you are to be in the world. If someone shows you something that is light, loving, and supportive to your wellbeing, then incorporate those qualities into your development. On the other hand, if someone offers you examples of darkness, disempowerment, fear, etc., then understand that you can decide not to accept or imitate those harmful qualities in the design of your life. When you are living consciously you have the power to choose your own highest path. Do not judge or condemn those who, while stuck in ego and false identity, chose differently.

Make a conscious effort to express appreciation to those on your path who are sharing their light and energy. While all people are equal and valuable, only certain souls chose to share part of their journey with you. Offer them kindness and encouragement as they are negotiating life's circumstances along their own path. There are many ways in which we can share our light with these individuals. You can offer a kind word, a hug or handshake, a smile, or sometimes just acknowledging someone with eye contact.

From an intimate partner, to family member, to friend, to work associate, to any casual encounter with a stranger, we can offer them our light in some fashion. Doing so will elevate the higher consciousness on the planet, and it does not cost us a cent.

Embrace all who enter your path, for they all have the potential of sharing love and light, and offering you valuable gifts. Take ownership of your own development, based upon consciously choosing to receive only that which is empowering, and supports a higher purpose. Show compassion and love to all, but you decide who is best suited to spend your time and energy with, and you decide how much to give without jeopardizing your own wellbeing. We are meant to live as in-spired humans, and in this space we would all support each other in love, kindness, cooperation, and unity. With the power of your inner development and connection to Source, create your world to reflect this reality.

Chapter 6 Exercises

Exercise 1:

Embracing the truth of who you are is essential to living an empowered life. **Write about your current thoughts, beliefs, habits, experiences, or conditions that may conflict with your own empowered higher truth.** These are things that you have accepted in your life that are actually someone else's truth (whether or not they are empowering or disempowering to them is not relevant for you).

After meditation/prayer, determine what is required of you to shift into a reality of honoring yourself enough to live your truth. Do you need more inner strength; a better understanding of your higher truth; to take more ownership of your life; or do you need greater belief in the truth that you matter?

All of your experiences have been trying to teach you to honor the truth of your being. By now the consequences of not doing so should be very obvious. Recognize and then work to heal (through greater awareness and education) the causes of resistance that are keeping you from believing in yourself.

Those people who appear to be preventing you from living your truth need to see your inner strength and clarity of purpose; they will then fall in line or fall away from your life. Either way you will be creating greater love, joy, peace, and wellness.

Exercise 2:

Reflect on the people in your life, those who are currently sharing your path. While living in your highest truth, contemplate how you can develop and express a more supportive connection that honors each of you. Focus on giving your love and attention without giving away your power. Determine the ways in which you can improve communications or otherwise lend a helping hand, then begin to implement this into your daily life.

Now consider some person or group of people not so directly connected to your daily life. Think about people who may not be living their highest capacity for any number of reasons. Is there space in your life to assist in some small or big way to brighten their day or life? Remember, on the level of spirit we are all one, so what we do for another we do for ourselves. **After contemplating and meditating on this, journal your conclusions and begin to implement them into action.**

CHAPTER 7:
REWARD

"You never change things by fighting the existing reality. To change something, build a new model that makes the existing model obsolete."
– Buckminster Fuller

Shifting your Reality

The key question in any spiritual discussion is, "Who do you think you are?" Everything you believe will flow from there. As you have read thus far in the **Empower Model** teaching, I am sharing and reiterating that you are the energy that comes from Divine Source (God, Universal Energy, Tao, etc.). You are part of Source, you emanate from Source, and you have within you the qualities (energy) of Source. Most important, if you *knew* you were a piece of the Divine Source, your reality would be very different.

In the world's training many have accepted one of two belief systems to frame their reality (in simplified terms I have summarized the following): 1) that we are sinners and less than a God, that is separate from us (Religious Model); or 2) neither God nor soul exists, our human life is all we have (Humanist-Atheist Model). People in the Religious Model seem to have little tolerance for those who have different *beliefs* then them. This is because their primary reward in this life comes from the truth of their beliefs, which distinguish them and validate their faith. Those who subscribe to the Humanist/Atheist Model have less tolerance for the *actions* of other people. This is because they are primarily concerned about how things impact and affect them personally (physically and materially) in this lifetime.

In the Religious model, while God created us, He created man to be essentially unworthy of His powers, status, and characteristics. All people are judged by how they accept and obey "God's Will" according to the interpretation of men. This God, who sits in judgment, apparently causes death and hardship, or blessings and miracles, according to what has been written and preached. However, if we accept His plan for "salvation", we will be spared an eternity in hell (with an evil entity called Satan) once our human life ends.

The Humanist-Atheist model teaches that all we have is this one human life. Our rewards are based upon a combination of our own determined effort and good fortune. Our suffering may be based primarily on poor effort and misfortune. This good or bad fortune may be largely dependent upon our birth circumstances, or the things that "happen" to us in our life. A good life is one in which, comparably speaking, there is comfort, wealth, good health, beauty, and intelligence. However, in large part the opportunity for these things are a matter of genetics and upbringing. Everything is judged by how our human body and personality (ego) are affected during this lifetime.

In the Religious Model I believe that there is an element of personal accountability and ownership that is missing. Our ultimate empowerment seems to come from a source outside of ourselves, and is a matter of human interpretation. Some may make changes in their lives that support a higher connection that brings peace and love, while many others will feel entitled to judge and condemn the "non-believers", without the personal responsibility of being loving, compassionate, and accepting of all people. This would strongly suggest that they are not aligned with a spiritual connection that comes from heart space and exhibits Divine qualities.

What is most relevant to an empowered loving life is to connect with all others in an empowered loving way. Therefore, to sincerely believe that a person who is otherwise kind and loving to all, will none the less go to "hell" because they do not have the same belief system, is quite disconcerting. To love your brother as yourself is non-negotiable to spirit, and it is not conditional upon whether they share your race, religion, economic status, etc. What is the point in serving a system of ancient rules and dogma in order to win a proverbial "ticket to heaven" after we die, if we do not value ourselves and all others whom God has created?

In the Humanist-Atheist Model we are born on some date in history, we live an unknown number of years, and then we die – and that's pretty much it. So we might as well get all we can for ourselves in this life. We may try to do as much good as we can while we are here, but ultimately that is limited by our level of wellness, and how we view ourselves, and our connection to others.

This view may have more to do with sustaining our drive for selfish desires, and supporting the fear of lack that exists in the world, than the Religious Model. This is completely ego made, denying the existence of anything unknown by the physical senses. It has really no choice but to judge the value of people based upon

265

what they achieve, accumulate, or how they outwardly live their life. People will struggle and fight (if they deem it necessary) with each other to make sure that they get theirs, not only for the sake of survival, but also to feed an insatiable need for self-worth, image, and worldly success. That in essence is their "heaven".

This model may be a counter balance of the Religious Model, which was seen as too restrictive and hypocritical. At least here people think that they are empowered, but it usually only really goes as far as their external conditions can substantiate. Their sense of empowerment may lead to more choices, yet many of the choices lead to fulfilling selfish desires, which are ultimately unsatisfying and void of meaning and real contribution. However, the more liberal minded in this model often have a greater tolerance for other viewpoints than many in the Religious Model.

Again, according to the Humanists, we are born into certain circumstances regarding – our parents (genetics), race, geography, socio-economic status, gender, etc. We have "good" or "bad" conditions from which to make the most of the life we were dealt, which is pure chance and not originating from any unseen higher energy or intelligence. All of the pleasure and purpose to be gained will take place within this life span. So we avoid thoughts of death, which we greatly fear.

We are missing the depth of our connectedness to all others, because we are not considering our energetic connection and shared origin. Therefore, any ideas of unity are largely an intellectual exercise, or we only acknowledge as significant those who directly affect our own life (family, friends, co-workers, etc.). We tend to make it our purpose to live comfortably, and stay within the tracts of conformity and the known. We are missing the inner peace and love that comes not from achievement or

266

outside perception, but from inner acceptance and approval, knowing that we are connected to a higher Source and purpose. If we are overly concerned about how all external circumstances affect our joy and suffering, we often miss the greater lesson about utilizing our experiences for the greater value of personal and spiritual growth.

Sometimes we get a good laugh when we parody these examples in the movies. Again, let's take a look at the character Ricky Bobby (Will Farrell) in the movie, *Talladega Nights: Ballad of Ricky Bobby*. He combines the excesses of both models. As he rises in success and fame by going from a pit crewman to winning NASCAR races, he completely loses himself in his inflated pride and material possessions. Additionally, he offers prayers (during grace) to "baby" Jesus, to help him win the next race so that he can collect all the money. As silly (and funny) as this example is, this is the dream for many people who have not recognized their true identity and highest potential. If only they had more money and more stuff, then they would be happy, but enough is never enough for ego. After all, someone or something could take it away, then what? Of course this is what happens to Ricky Bobby; he has to lose everything that he thought was important in order to get back to the things that really matter.

Are these models truly the most empowering? I am not condemning anyone for believing in either model. We all have free will, and if you are perfectly happy while functioning within either of these models, then do what is right for you. If not, you might consider shifting your reality to the Spiritual Model, which considers both the personal and spiritual aspect of our being. What is most critical is to honestly look at the education you have received from others, and determine for yourself if this way of thinking is bringing the most empowerment in your life. Also, is it supporting the ascension and evolution of life going forward?

267

Some of what was taught in the old models was purely about power, greed, manipulation, and control. However, at the same time, many good and decent people have lived within these models with very pure intention and concern for their fellow humans. Only you can decide if there is a way to shed the limitations held by either model that may bring higher benefit for personal and spiritual growth and healing.

I do not believe that you have to prostrate yourself before some unapproachable Deity, defined differently by different people. Nor do I believe that it is wise to eliminate the deeper meaning, purpose, and value from your life path. I know that for some, who are on the path of awakening to their highest personal and spiritual potential, the idea that we are as Source is a radical departure from their previous conditioning. If it helps, Divine Source (God, Universal Life Force, Tao, etc.) is a term used to encapsulate the unfathomable, undefinable benevolent energy or life force that exists everywhere. If we think of it as some omniscient power that rules over everything (as has been taught) we really would have no basis in claiming to be Source.

The idea is that you come from the Source that created all life, you are here on purpose, and you have within you the characteristics to co-create your life (with spirit) and fulfill your true higher purpose. This higher purpose supports all of the following: 1) developing inner strength and healing; 2) true self-love, joy, and peace for yourself, which also supports all of your relationships; 3) an opportunity to more readily utilize your unique gifts and skills toward a deeper satisfaction and fulfillment in your life; 4) a greater recognition and willingness to serve and support others within your purpose; and 5) the expansion of your Divine spirit and light into the world to promote wellness, equanimity, and harmony for all.

The greatest gift that comes from Source is not the gift of salvation, and it is not the gift of being born into wealthy circumstances. It is something we all share – that we are created with the qualities and characteristics of Source, and are given this opportunity to experience life in human form. Ultimately we are energy, and as such, we can flow with the current of our Divinity or we can live within the mental conditions that block this flow. Due to the collective unconsciousness on the planet we have made it more difficult to choose to develop, and then flourish, according to our spiritual gifts. Yet with the assurance of free will, any one of us can decide to apply our Divine qualities and create a new reality for ourselves at any moment we choose.

It is time to shift our "reality". This starts with accepting who we are. Even in a conceptual way at first. Your life is created by your thoughts, later these thoughts manifest into your experiences. Most people who believe only in their physical senses, would be limited to projecting their past experiences as their present (and future) reality. So you have to take a different mental approach in order to begin to create a different reality. You first must be willing to consider that you are capable of greater things in your life than what you have already learned or experienced. Greater than the limitations you and society have placed on your life. This is not about blame, but the truth is that many of us have been crushed by our fear and false perceptions. Accordingly, it is extremely difficult for most people to believe in a world that is not filled with fear and lack, and where we are capable of having the love, peace, joy, and prosperity that we all desire.

This is the position we start from in this human life. So even with Divine capabilities our free will is at a disadvantage without the right education and training. This is the purpose of the information that I have been guided to share in this book. It

269

is also why I have never said that this transformation is easy. There is often as much to unlearn as there is to learn (sometimes more); it is an on-going retraining and daily practice. But the **REWARD** is worth it.

Start to shift your mind toward an understanding that you are a Divine being, and not just some sinner or human form who is merely trying to survive, and is destined to struggle until you die. Even if you have a higher, more optimistic opinion of yourself, you can still be functioning less than optimally while dealing with this predominant mental-ego energy. What you begin to recognize is that while we all have conditions to manage, and we all must interconnect and relate with others, how your mind either unites with your spiritual possibilities or attaches to the lower ego constraints will make a significant difference in your reality. You do not have to be so concerned with the reality of others; your shift in mindset is to focus on your own empowerment (which always leads to the betterment of all).

We have our own unique circumstances, desires, gifts, and skills, so your job is to identify what supports your highest love, joy, and fulfillment – while adding your light to the world. When you focus on giving the best you have to give, while utilizing your special gifts and talents, you are on the way to a higher fulfillment. Conversely, when we are doing the least amount possible, merely for the sake of what we can get out of it, no amount of wealth or acclaim is fulfilling. You came into this life not only for something to gain, but for something to contribute. What you give to others is expressed in every moment. It is not some grand gesture to donate money (unless that is within your heart to do). You do not need money in order to contribute to the world; you need to live your highest truth.

When you accept your own Divinity you know that you have the same characteristics as Divine Source, which is unconditional love, peace, compassion, kindness-encouragement, truth, acceptance, limitless abundance, and creativity. Your job on the planet is to orchestrate these gifts in your own life, as a way to share them with all others. So when you are shifting to this new reality, you are beginning to live your Divine qualities. You are beyond thinking you "should" live this way, and you are moving through "trying" to live this way. You are now on the path to *knowing and accepting* that you "are" these things. Now, you are being and expressing what you are, which is fully sustainable. To be anything less would be unsatisfying. You ARE love, you ARE peace, you ARE compassion, and yes, you ARE limitless abundance and creativity.

You do not have to choose to compromise these qualities in order to make money and pay bills, be in a relationship, get and keep a job, be healthy, etc. You are shifting to a reality that was setup from the beginning (from Source) to offer great fulfillment, spiritual advancement, love, peace, and unity. Not only is this world available to us, but it was intended to flow to us and from us with ease. Your efforts and struggle cannot duplicate this gift. It is not Divine Source's plan, but instead the false ego training that has created a hell on earth, a world filled with great struggle, not for true fulfillment, but merely for survival.

What does this mean for you? As one who is beginning to conceive of the possibility of creating a new more empowered reality, you have to start the process of personal and spiritual growth from where you are – from your current circumstances and perception of reality. Much of this book has described this process, which includes: Higher Education, accepting on a deeper level that You Matter, developing Inner Peace, taking Ownership for your life and choices, supporting Holistic Wellness, and

Embracing higher truth. All of this material applied with intention, awareness, and diligence will connect you with your higher spiritual nature, leading you to great personal and spiritual growth and living your highest potential.

Your goal is to heal, grow, and shift throughout this journey that is your life path. Your life will naturally and rightfully look different than anyone else's. You will recognize your love, joy, and fulfillment in relation to the development and transformation of your higher awareness and inner healing. This includes your inner thoughts and feelings, and the creation and acceptance of your outer actions and manifestations. You are on a path of ascension that is your own. Anytime you judge your success or happiness (or lack thereof) based on anyone else's life, you are coming from ego. This path is about transforming from ego-control to spiritual-freedom. So always embrace your own progress within your own circumstances and development.

As you accept and live *who you are* to a greater degree, you will begin to experience things that you never truly thought possible. This started with the shifting and expanding of what you previously saw as your reality. You may have had fleeting dreams to be or do something that seemed extraordinary, but this was quickly squashed and abandoned as "crazy talk". This particular dream was actually a seed of truth, which was in need of the proper care and development in order to blossom.

Now you recognize thoughts that bring a feeling of enthusiasm as a message from spirit, you are being guided to a possibility that may be cultivated. When you open to the Divine guidance that is now captured by your awareness, you will open doors to higher fulfillment. As you start down this path, utilizing your conscious empowerment, you will be supported in creating your desired circumstances and experiences in alignment with your spiritual purpose and nature.

As a model for the highest empowerment and fulfillment, I support the Spiritual Model, as opposed to the Religious Model or the Humanist-Atheist Model. However, with respect to walking your highest path and creating your own reality, all models are more of a framework. Your life is unique unto itself, so while you may resonate with certain examples of those who live within a certain belief system, you have to decide what meets the highest ideals of empowerment for you.

Creating your own reality always starts with honoring yourself by finding *your* truth and living in integrity. Even with the suggestions in this book, you get to decide what feels right for you. When you find the truth that supports your highest love, joy, peace, and fulfillment for yourself, while at the same time shines the light of love, kindness, compassion, and support for all other beings, then you are on an enlightened path. If you are on a path that seems to require you to support yourself or others, but rarely both, you are not living your empowered life. If in order to survive and meet your physical needs, you feel required to experience great struggle, stress, and suffering, again, you are not in your highest alignment.

Your highest truth always supports you and others on the highest level. So if your belief system is preventing you from living in this reality, you may want to reconsider who you think you are. There is always a process of growth, healing, and exploration to finding and then following your truth. Be persistent and take ownership for your own development. Decide for yourself what you want your life to look like, go within to feel what you feel about this, and then take the steps to create your ideal reality. Do not just react to what other people seem to be

273

putting upon you. This is your life, not theirs, so live in your reality.

"Try not to become a man of success but a man of value."
- Albert Einstein

Be the Hero in your Life

You are the most important person in your life. You are the only one that can create your life path, and decide how you want to experience it. Whether or not you ever realized that you have this power, it is true. Others will influence you on your path, for purposes of teaching you this truth. However, on the level of energy, you chose them (as they chose you) through the attraction of like vibration. How you react to, and process these experiences throughout your life, is ultimately up to you, and this will define your level of consciousness.

When we go through life without fully participating in the creation process, we may feel like life is what happens to us. Maybe we will feel lucky or unlucky, mostly satisfied or mostly dissatisfied. Either way, we are not taking control of the enormous power within our being. For some people this brings a general fluctuation of good and bad experiences, no real rhyme or reason, but overall a feeling of a lack of true fulfillment. For other people this will manifest into tremendous suffering and sense of powerlessness. This is the ongoing mentality of the victim. Their sense of a lack of power is so extreme that they actually find a warped sense of power by claiming themselves a victim. This diminishes their incentive to take personal responsibility, in order to heal and grow.

When you are tired of being the victim in your life, you may decide to become the hero in your life! With enough education (re-training) and awareness, we eventually tire of playing the victim. They say, "Don't let the man hold you down!" Well guess what, the "man" is you. Choose to be your own hero. What is a hero? There are some people who have chosen to serve in roles that traditionally require what we call heroism. You may think about law enforcement officers, fire fighters, military personnel, etc. These jobs are potentially life threatening, but this is not the only definition of hero.

To be a hero you must be responsible, courageous, and serve the higher good. Being a hero is not about your job, which is more a reflection of your purpose and skillset. Instead, a hero is defined by who you are on the inside. This inner truth will translate into how you treat yourself and all others.

You are responsible for taking ownership of all that occurs in your life. You will accept a higher role in every interaction, and then utilize your awareness to determine if your expressions of energy (thoughts, words, and actions) are of the highest quality. If in any moment you slip into ego mode, you can make amends and/or use the experience to further facilitate your own healing and growth. You are accountable for everything in your life. You understand that you are creating your life, and in no way defer that responsibility to others, although you are humble enough to ask for help when you need it. Functioning as a hero does not make you responsible for the perception, understanding, and consciousness of other people. That is their responsibility. However, you will be kind and compassionate, while protecting your energy.

275

You must be courageous in order to be the hero in your life. A hero speaks his truth, even in the face of non-acceptance or disapproval. A hero will face his fears, knowing that this leads to his greatest growth, joy, fulfillment, and contribution. A hero is independent enough to walk his own path, and since we each provide a unique footprint, regarding our purpose, gifts, and energy, this path will be forged for the first time by you. A hero is courageous enough to trust his inner guidance, and act accordingly.

To be a hero you must serve a higher purpose than ego. You will know that the most significant part of your journey of personal and spiritual growth is the opportunity to live in your highest fulfillment while giving your light, love, and gifts to the world. You give because of who you are, not because of what you hope to receive. Since we can only give what we are, having developed your Divine characteristics means that you are able to give – love, peace, joy, truth, compassion, skillful service, and gratitude, in support of others. As a hero you are living consciously in spirit, with awareness and purpose.

A hero adds their light into the world; they shine from within. The world needs true heroes. It makes no difference who you were before, what you do for work, or your level of education or wealth. Anyone who lives their life on purpose can offer their higher gifts when connected to their spirit. You can be a hero in your work, whether you are a doctor, mechanic, engineer, janitor, artist, school teacher, police officer, or anything else. It's not what you do, but how you do it.

Doing your job on purpose means that you are giving your best effort and highest intentions, in support of your personal fulfillment and service to others. Since we need people to serve in all of the different jobs in order to maintain a society, aren't all jobs important? So finding a way to develop and utilize your unique gifts to better yourself and contribute to the world is the best that any of us can do. As a hero this is how we look at our careers, and this is how we respect all others who are fulfilling their roles.

Another way to fulfill your role as a hero is in how you treat those close to you, especially family and friends. The first and most important thing is to be the example and embodiment of the qualities of the hero. The greatest impression you will have on people will come from the way they see you treat yourself and others. It is the consistency and authenticity of your energy, words, and actions. If you offer them your truth and wisdom, but then not follow your own advice, or scream at them for making a mistake, you are not serving spirit and you are not being a hero. Offer your greatest example by pursuing your own healing and growth; they will then be more inclined to pursue this path for themselves when they can see the positive results in you. While we will naturally have greater love for all people, there are also the souls that you have chosen to play a significant role in your life. Offer your love, attention, and compassion, even if they do not always offer you the same.

If you have children, nourish their spirit, and support their healing and growth. Don't ignore or neglect them by thinking that your life (or theirs) is too busy or important. While not your only purpose and service to the world, chances are that nothing you accomplish will be more significant than raising your children to be healthy, loving, contributing adults. Recognize and support the development of their unique gifts. Whether or not you were a sports star in high school (for example), has nothing to do with your child. Don't try to relive or live vicariously through them. Encourage them to be independent of you, while subtly keeping a watchful protective eye. Build a trusting relationship (as best you

277

can) so that they might feel more comfortable in asking for advice or guidance. As the hero in your life you can be the model for them to be their own hero in their life.

Be willing to be a leader. We all have the ability within ourselves to do this. If we come from our place of consciousness and integrity, it will manifest differently for each of us according to our circumstances and gifts. First and foremost, lead yourself. While developing your higher knowing of who you are, you will naturally follow others for the purpose of learning, healing, and growing. Oftentimes, we become too content to be the follower. Always the follower, never the leader; or always the student, never the teacher, eventually shows a lack of personal accountability and ownership, because I assure you, no matter who you are, on some level you are here to lead others.

Your audience may be different than someone else's, but you are no less important, and you have something of value to contribute. Develop your inner strength and confidence and find your area of positive influence and contribution. This is not about recognition or publicity; it is about personal growth and reaching your potential in service to the world.

Heroes are regular people, which mean all of us are potentially heroes. But regular in this case, means conscious, and therefore striving to live the Divine qualities that are inherent within each of us. We must be functioning on our higher spiritual level and not consumed by ego-control. We must be responsible for all we create, attract, and experience. We must pursue our truth and the higher qualities of our spiritual nature, which will take courage within and without. We must also recognize that, ultimately, we are here to serve ourselves and others with integrity, humility, compassion, and purpose. I encourage you to take this higher role to heart. We do not need "Superman"; we need a world full of Super Men.

"Love and compassion are necessities, not luxuries. Without them humanity cannot survive."
– Dalai Lama

Living your Divine Qualities

Within the process of understanding *who you really are*, is the context of opening up to limitless possibilities, or at the very least, beginning to overcome some of our falsely perceived limitations. Growing, healing, and transforming will guide us to create the reality that for us will reveal our highest potential and purpose. At this level of awareness, we begin to bring our human nature into alignment with our spiritual nature.

When we are awakened to the existence of spirit, we can feel when we are in alignment or not. It is not necessarily the external experience that answers this question, it is more about what we feel and how we deal with our external experiences. Regardless of where we are in our journey of personal and spiritual growth, we will always attract opportunities to heal and grow on a deeper level. The Universe provides what we need, not necessarily what our ego wants. It is our awareness of this truth that continues to support our continued growth and transformation.

As spiritual beings having a human experience, we embody the qualities of the Divine while functioning within a world stuck in the darker, denser energy and perception of ego. Our first (and ongoing) step is to "remember" our true nature (the only nature that existed prior to our human birth), but our ultimate purpose is to live and become these qualities as humans. This is the evolutionary tract that each of us can either contribute to or delay. The greatest reward both for you and for humanity is to transform and evolve into this higher level of being.

Examples of the divine qualities that we inherited from Source are: love, peace, harmony, compassion, joy, abundance, creativity, wisdom, etc. These are energetic qualities of expression, not just intellectual concepts. We are all "Sons" of Source, equal in this inheritance. This is true for all, regardless of a lack of awareness or awakenedness that may cause someone to act in ways that seem contradictory to their Divinity. We cannot judge one to be worthy and another unworthy. We all are on our individual path, and we all err from time to time, but we all come from and return to the same Source. Can we agree that the qualities listed above represent a higher level of being? If so, I ask you to consider that you have the potential for living these qualities in your life. Whether or not you accept that you are a Divine child of the Universe, I would like you to have a goal of embodying these ideals, for the benefit of all.

I have said that everything is energy. This includes you, me, all other living creatures, and all objects that we can perceive. Qualities are also expressions of energy. Therefore, love, peace, joy, compassion, etc. are all energies. All things vibrate to a different (higher or lower) frequency. We will always attract the people, things, and experiences that are a vibrational match to us. So within our inner development it is our purpose and potential to match our vibrational frequency to the higher qualities we wish to live.

In this life we have primarily been taught to believe in and express the quality of fear, which vibrates at a much lower frequency than any of the Divine expressions. Fear is the primary energy of ego, and it translates into all of the suffering and limitations we experience as humans. The various faces of fear include: lack (of every kind), sadness, hopelessness, anger, jealousy, judgment, stress, hate, violence, and suppression of our light. Our energy which started out pure, having just come from spirit, has been inundated by this lower form of energy which permeates society. Within our being we attached to these qualities by lowering our frequency, to the point where this state of being may now feel natural to us. However, this is in fact very disempowering and far less than how we are meant to live.

On the other hand, spirit is the opposite of ego, just like love is the opposite of fear. Love is the primary energy that translates into all wellbeing and limitless possibilities that are our human potential. The various faces of love include: peace, joy, abundance, wellness, unity, compassion, wisdom, and light. As we shift to a higher (inner) connection, we begin to raise our energetic vibration to be in alignment with our Divine qualities. This is how one becomes as love, or peace, or joy, or compassion. It is then not about the mental and physical effort of acting loving or peaceful in certain situations. You are actually becoming these qualities within yourself first (as vibration), which is then more easily and naturally expressed to all others.

This is your goal and the higher purpose of spiritual practice. As Source called itself "I AM" in the Bible, we are to use the "I AM" statement in confirming and claiming our power as one who is created in the image of Divine Source. Our I AM Presence signifies the Divine Presence within us. Therefore, I AM love, I AM peace, I AM abundance, are declarations of the truth within your being. These are the qualities that you are realizing in your life as you shift to a new reality and consciousness.

281

In our highest attainment we become the qualities that we desire to experience in our life. This is the process of co-creation with Divinity. If you want more loving relationships, you must become and express the energy of love. We may have requested, "I want a soul mate, or a partner". What that usually means is that we want to share the energy of love with a person who is closely connected to our life path. We want to give and receive intimate love, but, if we can only give what we are, don't we first need to allow and manifest our inner quality of love, through healing and growth? Additionally, we can only attract that which is a vibrational match to us. So if we are riddled with ego and emotional scars in need of healing, who do you think we attract to "love" us? Certainly not someone who is capable of loving honestly and openly. Instead we attract the opposite of that, someone who will teach us the need to heal and love ourselves.

Our inner thoughts are saying we are not worthy of true love, we are not enough. Yet we are expecting that someone will show up and make us suddenly love ourselves. Can you see how this is doomed to fail? This is spiritual truth, and it must become a part of our awareness and consciousness, so that we can apply it in order to create the circumstances and experiences we desire.

As long as we are going to create our experiences anyway, why not apply spiritual truth as a logical approach to getting what we really want? While there are countless things that we fear in our human lives, probably the most devastating to us, especially in the U.S., is the fear of a lack of money. We know we need money to survive on the physical plane, so without it we may encounter great suffering. Therefore, with the goal of having enough money (which for most people is impossible, since the more we have the more we spend), we are willing to circumvent or sacrifice everything if necessary. We are willing to deny our own happiness, toil and struggle, create stress and illness, lie and cheat, and ruin our relationships and reputation, and more. We will spend our lives chasing our tail, and miss out on some of the very qualities we had hoped that money would buy us. No one on their death bed says, "I wish that I had worked more hours, made more money, or bought more stuff."

Most of us determine what kind of lifestyle we want, calculate how much money we need to make, and then decide what kind of work we will do in order to make this amount of money. Beyond our basic necessities, we are essentially working to buy, maintain, display, store, and insure our stuff. Do we need all of the stuff, or is it just making our ego feel better? What if we appreciated who we are without all of the stuff, would we need to make as much money?

In any case, the plan is backwards. First, define your gifts, skills, joy, and passion. Then research to understand the work (service) that best utilizes your gifts, skills, etc. Next determine the steps necessary to develop yourself to be marketable within your chosen work. And finally, honor yourself fully by offering quality service with the highest integrity. This is a recipe for finding great fulfillment and enjoyment in work that provides for your financial needs and offers a valuable service to humankind. There are shortcuts to just making money, but in the end the price is steep. I believe that a comprehensive developmental approach is best and most satisfying. Live within your means, offer quality service, and maintain a balanced life that supports your wellness on all levels. Boom! You are now rich!

However, from the level of spirit and energy there is more to say on the subject. Everything is energy, including money (currency). We have been taught very strong attitudes and beliefs around the concept of money; mostly that you have to work *hard* to get it, and that it is in *limited* supply. So we say and think that "getting and having enough money is very difficult and there is not enough to go around, in fact it takes great sacrifice in order to have enough." What kind of energy are we creating about money when our mind is constantly reinforcing this belief system? That's right; we are feeding our fear and creating the exact conditions that we believe in. This works for any attitude around abundance.

We need to know that on the level of energy, attracting money is no different than any other quality. The difference usually comes in the fact that our false training about money is so deeply ingrained that it seems to be one of the last things we are willing to shift. We may be able to see that we are worthy of love, peace, joy, etc., and the shift seems doable with retraining and practice, but abundance around money, not so much. My suggestion is to begin to shift your perception about money. It takes awareness, practice, and faith, but start visualizing and feeling what it is like to be the energy of money and abundance. The truth is that when we are in alignment and a vibrational match, there are literally unlimited ways that we can attract our desire.

One key to receiving money is gratitude. Being and expressing the energy of gratitude brings riches beyond money. So maintain an attitude of gratitude, in both your inner and outer work, for the abundance that is available, and manifesting in your life. Energy is always in process of manifesting when the right conditions exist. Another energetic key is generosity. So, whenever and however possible express this energy to others. All energy flows in and out, this is true for the energy of money, love, peace, etc. You must be willing to both give and receive. So do not block this flow because of false limiting beliefs in lack, by not appreciating, or selfishly hoarding what you have.

The Universe wants us to have an abundance of all of the Divine qualities it has ordained to us. This requires that we be connected with these things on a higher vibrational level, which naturally allows them to flow into our lives. It is important to remember that they are to be shared with all others. This is a gift available to us for living our human lives in a spiritual way, connected to our spirit. Since we have been gifted with many blessings, it is necessary and natural for us to support those in need who have not yet awakened to their inheritance. The flow of our Divine gifts must support us in doing Divine work. When you are on the level of creating and claiming these Divine energies in your daily life, you will find great joy and fulfillment in sharing them with others.

"Everyone has a purpose in life…a unique gift or special talent to give to others. And when we blend this unique talent with service to others, we experience the ecstasy and exultation of our own spirit, which is the ultimate goal of all goals."
– Deepak Chopra

Discovering your Purpose

There are many ways to think about our purpose. First I will talk about the way in which most men think about it, and that is as your occupation. This represents the work or service that we offer the world, and it represents the primary way in which we receive money. So this is very important to us. I spoke earlier about the importance we place on our jobs with respect to the money it earns; we often choose our jobs because of the paycheck, instead of the higher qualities of our service.

When we put more emphasis on the inner value of our work, both for ourselves and others, we will find more satisfaction in the performance of the job. We also will likely find that, in the end, we will prosper more financially as well. Instead of thinking about the things we need to buy, and therefore the money we need to earn, leading to our career choices, we may want to approach it from the other direction.

If your work represents the expression of your purpose, and your purpose is to do whatever you can to make money, are you truly fulfilling any real purpose? Perhaps, you are merely facilitating your survival or superficial lifestyle. Or maybe you found a job that was once interesting, and challenging, but years (or decades) later it has become unchallenging, monotonous, and boring. From a higher level of consciousness, your purpose represents utilizing your unique gifts, skills, joy, and passion. You always have the opportunity to express the highest qualities of your being within the context of your work. However, if you need to make a change in order to once again find purpose and fulfillment, you will need to accept your higher value (that you Matter), and you must take ownership of the circumstances and experiences in your life.

One of the rewards for growing, healing, and developing your higher awareness, as described in the ***Empower Model,*** is that you are now in a greater position to tackle real life issues (like your career) from the standpoint of consciousness and accountability. The famed psychologist Joseph Campbell coined the phrase, "Finding your bliss." Your bliss is something that resonates deep within your knowing and feeling as enthusiasm and truth for you. It is an instant and steady jolt of pure joy and fulfillment. Regarding the work you do for others, as it represents higher qualities, find the thing that offers this bliss. **Our truth is our purpose.** We are all naturally drawn to certain activities that are needed in the world, and sometimes our purpose is right under our nose. We just need to expand our awareness, and follow our inner guidance with courage.

As I look back at my career in accounting, I recognize that I had marketable enough skills in order to be employed and earn a reasonable paycheck. While there was some satisfaction in that, it never really felt like my bliss or life purpose. It was certainly practical in supporting my lifestyle, but on a deeper level it left me unfulfilled. We are not here to just go through the motions enough to survive, we are all here to flourish and share our true light with the world.

However, as a manager or co-worker, I always enjoyed assisting and encouraging people on a personal level. I did not know it at the time, but I was coaching them. I had a deep caring for others, and an ability to see objectively through their self-imposed drama in order to offer some supportive wisdom and guidance. Energetically, people were comfortable sharing with me their personal stories. As I progressed through my career, I began to feel that I was there (in that work environment) as much for my ability to hold a supportive energetic vibration that helped to keep people functioning together, as for my accounting skills.

Now, when I look back throughout my life, it is very clear how people felt comfortable with me on this level, and I would naturally coach them. This certainly did not mean that I had all of the answers for them or myself. It just meant that there was an innate gift and skill that could be developed further, as a way to serve others. A seed, if you will, to be nurtured and cultivated.

It has taken me a very long time to recognize my bliss was to do this coaching work. I was doing it for free; and they say, "Do the thing you love to do even if you were not paid to do it."

Now, eventually if you want to do it as an occupation (and you are not independently wealthy), you have to create and develop a way to shift in that direction, and exchange the value of your service for the value of money. The beauty in this is that your energy, interest, passion, inner guidance, and persistence, is so much stronger when performing work that is fulfilling your purpose. If you want it, you will find a way (you will co-create it with spirit).

After a period of transition and personal growth, I am now beginning to serve in an occupation that is more in alignment with my higher purpose. With greater awareness (and outside coaching) I may have been able to make this shift earlier in life. However, I am grateful for the transformation that has occurred, and I love my work!

I would also like to share something else that I discovered in this transitional process. It truly is transformational. By this I mean that it is not just about a job or career change. When aligning to our higher purpose we are often required to experience a great shift within our being. This is especially true if you have spent a significant amount of your life functioning within a somewhat disempowering belief system, or if you have spent many years settling for less than this higher fulfillment. In addition to all of the personal and spiritual growth and healing, as talked about in this book, a great deal of faith, effort, and resolve is required.

We must truly carry out our daily action plan, which is in alignment with spirit, but is very challenging to our ego. I have found in my experience that I had to commit to greater self-reliance for everything I was learning and creating. Even when I found assistance from others, I was responsible. At times when I tried to collaborate or handoff a task along this journey, I found that no one else was available to do the work. This is never a cause to be disappointed in others. It was always a message that I was responsible and capable for the specific task or action myself. So, in order to make this kind of shift, which is ultimately so very rewarding, I was required to maintain an extremely high level of ownership. In the end, I learned that, yes, I am fully capable of trusting myself and creating my highest dreams and fulfillment!

The important thing is to find your bliss and recognize the inner joy you receive in service to others. Some recognize their purpose as children, and for others (like me) it becomes a second career later in life. Only you can define what your purpose is for you. It may feel amazing to you, but crazy or unachievable to someone else, and that is ok, as always, trust your own inner knowing. Remember, other people are looking at it from their ego (their dream), and you are now moving into alignment with spirit. People around you may be fearful about this shift, which is causing you to change, grow, and trust yourself. Don't be upset with them, for they are merely expressing the ego (fear) that is controlling them, and this is likely mirroring a part of you that is still overcoming your fear.

As you develop your own healing and growth, this outer and inner resistance will decrease. Most people, who really care about you, but don't understand your path, will be more supportive once they see your passion and productivity. You are showing them something new, and beyond their fear they are actually proud of you. You are fully honoring yourself as you move along this journey. Additionally, you will connect with many new people that support you on your path and provide needed assistance.

Oftentimes we must develop this new purposeful work while performing a job that "pays the bills". You are in a transition which is not only potentially creating a way to fulfill your purpose in your career, but you are also (first and foremost) going through the personal and spiritual transformation necessary to support you in your new endeavors.

You may think that you are just finding a new way to work, but really the shift is much deeper than that. You are healing from the things that kept you from finding this purpose sooner; you are expanding your mind and energy in order to create something that is specific to who you are and what you have to offer the world; and finally, you are placing a higher level of ownership and trust upon yourself than you likely ever have done before. Sorry, there are no shortcuts here.

Did you notice that I never mentioned a paycheck or a business plan? This comes later in the process. First things first; the inner shift precedes the external business steps. Remember, you make the shift to purpose first, and the money will follow. So in the meantime, if you need to keep (or get) a "day job", honor that too. So long as this job is not contrary to your growth and development, do this job with integrity to the best of your ability. If your job is in direct conflict with your higher principles and purpose, you may want to find a different temporary job. To the extent that you can live within more modest means, you have the advantage of more options.

If you are already serving in a career that resonates as your life purpose, congratulations! Honor this blessing with your highest integrity, intention, energy, and gratitude. Know that in order for you to continue to serve on the highest level, while also experiencing all of the Divine qualities available to you, you will need to maintain sufficient balance in your life. Sometimes we are so enthusiastic about our work that we forget to take care of the other aspects of our life. We must sustain wellness on all levels, and as always, be connected to our present moment awareness that may be moving us to new growth and expansion.

Living your purpose ultimately resonates as your expression to the world through all aspects of your life. Our occupation is an opportunity to contribute to the world as our primary focus of service, according to our specific and unique gifts, skills, and passion. However, our highest purpose is to live in a state of being that is connected to our spiritual qualities at all times. We are then residing in the continual flow of the receiving and offering of this higher energy, as an expression of who we are.

When we are connected in this way, we are filled to overflowing with light and love, and we are sharing our gifts as a natural extension of our abundance. When we feel an energy deficit, we have the tools to replenish. This starts with an awareness of our own state of energy. We can go within to release our fear (ego) and reconnect with our higher Source. We can also find the light of support in the many associations that we have developed with others who reside primarily in this abundance. We are recognizing our external challenges for the truth they represent, and we process them internally as a tool for further healing and growth. We then emerge with an expansion of our energy that illuminates our path in alignment with our purpose.

Your purpose is to truly love and honor yourself as one who is blessed with a spiritual presence that is always available to support you. Connect with your spirit and continue the process of personal and spiritual growth. Your purpose is to serve others as a natural extension of your Divinity. Your highest reward is in your contribution and service to the world. Your purpose is to love and accept all other people. We are all in various states of awareness as to our own Divinity, so if someone acts in a way that is contrary their higher nature, offer them love and compassion and show them a better path.

Your purpose is to be free from the crippling fear that was forcibly fed and constantly reinforced into your conscious and subconscious mind. Release any guilt for having accepted these lies as truth, and forgive all others who taught them in error. We are all in the process of remembering our truth, and we are all in a different place in this journey. Your purpose is to live with an abundance of love, light, peace, joy, prosperity, wholeness, and wisdom. Deny no one these qualities for themselves, for their supply does not infringe on yours. Spirit is unlimited, so always be grateful for what you have, and joyful in the abundance of others.

"It is not what we get. But who we become, what we contribute…that gives meaning to our lives."
– Anthony Robbins

The Essence of the Journey is Giving Back

So why do we go through all of this healing, growth, and transformation? I hope that by now I have explained in an effective and compelling way the answer to this question. To state it succinctly, we do this to create a better life for us and others. There is no denying that effort, strength, courage, and persistence is required on the human level. Somehow, it often seems easier to settle for a fraction of the love, joy, peace, and potential for greatness that is available to us, and at times, we have all settled in this life. After all, if we choose to, we can just ride out this life within our comfort zone, making little if any progress, and having a minimal impact in the world.

We come into this life with certain human qualities, characteristics, and circumstances. Regarding our making a mark in human (ego) terms, we each have certain advantages and challenges (comparatively speaking). If we utilize our advantages and minimize our challenges we will likely survive, and maybe even find relative material comfort and acclaim. So, someone born with a superior physical body may become a star athlete, someone born with a superior intellect may attain great knowledge, and someone born into great wealth may be able to enjoy the comforts of their affluence. Congratulations, as far as that goes, on your choice of conditions to be born into, but how did you further expand and develop these and other gifts? How are you utilizing your gifts by contributing, sharing, and connecting with the world?

These are all human conditions and therefore temporary, and while they are often admired by others who wish they had these gifts, they are really only a blessing when they benefit other people as well. Most people live and develop in circumstances that do not reflect these superior attributes. Their advantages may be much more subtle or undiscovered, and their challenges may be fairly pronounced. So whether you are quite advantaged, but searching for deeper meaning and a way to be a more valuable contributor to the welfare of the world, or whether you are searching to understand your gifts as a way to sustain a more empowered life and to help support others in need, a shift to a more spiritual perspective is most appropriate.

I am convinced that as spiritual beings having a human experience, we are only truly fulfilled and living our purpose when we are giving back to the world. I believe that this is also our greatest reward for having experienced this journey of a human life. When I say "giving back to the world", I mean a willingness to recognize all beings as equal and Divine, and then utilizing your gifts as best you can while serving with a pure heart. As our life paths differ, some people's reach will effectively impact only those closest around them, and this is the way that makes the most difference in the Divine scheme of things. Others will develop the capability and means to reach millions in a beneficial way. It is not a competition, work within your own personal potential and highest integrity. Developing ourselves and ascending to a place where we have truly loving intentions for all beings is something that anyone can do, and this will have a great impact in shifting the consciousness on the planet.

How many of you have been in a dark place, feeling sorry for yourself, when you suddenly accepted an opportunity to do something for someone else? If you are like me, it always lifts me out of my ego focus. Not only because it changes the channel in my mind, but also because there is a recognition of my value in assistance to others, and this always feels good. Apply this in a much larger scale, where you recognize and define your purpose as assisting people as part of how you live your life. Now the focus of your job is to do what you do with the intention of benefitting others, and not just to pay the bills. Your focus in your closest relationships is to offer peace, kindness, encouragement, acceptance, and understanding, so that others may feel better about themselves while on their specific journey. The same is true when interacting with strangers; we can be kind, smile, and send loving thoughts, as a way to brighten their energy.

You see, through our inner work we are now becoming healthy and whole; living our spirituality in our humanity. The focus is no longer just on us, consumed by our drama and the dissatisfaction with ourselves or other people. We now have the bandwidth to care for ourselves and others, easily and effortlessly. And again, in the times where this is challenging for us, we have the tools to self-heal. Truly, we now heal our energy for the benefit of all. That is what makes this path so significant and rewarding.

We start out in the spirit world, and then are born into our human circumstances. We are educated in the world of ego (or ambition, as Dr. Dyer states it), where we forget most of the truth we came in knowing. Then we struggle to varying degrees trying to find a way to experience the Divine qualities now hidden within us, and further veiled by a physical world based in ego. At some point we can no longer deny the futility of searching for our higher purpose within this system, and we begin to shift from ego-control to spiritual-freedom.

We are now healing and growing from all of our past challenges, and we recognize that they were trying to teach us our truth all along. As we move into this space of higher awareness and purpose, we are now living more consciously. As a result, we are now giving back in love and service to others. Our life never felt better or more significant, as we live out our human days with the full expression of spiritual truth. Finally, we return to the spiritual world of pure light and love, having shed our human form.

This is truly the circle of life. This is a life lived on purpose. In this context do we really care about our job title or the value of our personal assets? Did we help one person recognize their light in the midst of their darkness, if only for a moment? Is this not rewarding? We who have this wisdom and Divine love in our heart have this opportunity every day. It is not about believing me, you may not agree with everything I have written in this book. The important thing is to recognize your own truth in a way that brings such inner healing that you are willing to shine your light into the world, for the benefit of ALL. I already know that you are Divine.

Your true life has been waiting for you, so don't hold yourself back any longer. You have been searching for your greatest love, joy, and fulfillment, and the world has been waiting for your greatest contribution, and they both are attainable with inner development and expansion.

I wish you great success in a life lived on purpose. Let's be a positive factor in shifting our own lives, and uplifting the path of men, leading to the ascension of energy on the planet for all people. If all of this seems like such serious business that there is no room for fun, that may be more my writing style than the truth of the matter. All of the people that I know on this path say that they have never previously experienced so much pure joy, fun, and laughter.

As you begin to heal and release the weight of your old reality, you understand that it is self-imposed. You can now live more consciously and make empowering choices, and that will definitely lighten you up. Instead of succumbing to the negativity that is promoted every day in the news, you will see and be the light that shines so much beauty in the world.

Namaste

In case you are unfamiliar with the Sanskrit word "Namaste," here is a simple but profound definition:

"I bow to that Divine light within you and within me"

I think that the longer version gives you an even greater perspective of the word Namaste:

"I honor the place in you where the entire Universe resides, I honor the place in you of light, of love, of truth, of peace, and I honor the place in you where, if you and I are in this place, then there is only one of us."

This word represents a knowing that we are all made from the One Divine Consciousness. When you feel these sentiments for yourself and all of life, you will feel comfortable using this word as a greeting to others or in your own personal meditation or private reflection.

Know that my affection for you and all of humanity is of the highest order. So with palms together, in front of my heart chakra, I reverently say to you with a slight bow – **Namaste!**

Chapter 7 Exercises

Exercise 1:

Make a list of up to 10 ways in which you can be the hero in your life; ways to take more responsibility, show more courage, and serve the higher good. Give strong consideration to implementing the steps to make this happen.

Exercise 2:

Contemplate and meditate on the ways that you can use an approach to living more consciously as a way to contribute more to the world. Journal or document the ideas that come to mind, and pick one or two things that you can begin to do today.

ABOUT THE AUTHOR

The Empower Model for Men is the first book by Scott E. Clark. Mr. Clark is the Owner of Bodhi Publishing Company, LLC, (and Bodhi Life Coaching) in Phoenix, AZ. Through writing, mentoring, and teaching, his primary focus is to assist others in recognizing and developing their own personal empowerment, leading to happier, healthier, and more fulfilling lives.

This book represents a joyous step and transformational shift for Mr. Clark, who previously worked in the corporate world for thirty years in accounting and business management, and was a certified public accountant. Even while working in this structured, left-brain capacity, he was always interested in personal and spiritual growth. He found great satisfaction in supporting and guiding others toward resolving their personal issues. With a natural interest in helping others, and an ability to listen and then offer objective wisdom, people seemed to easily open up to him and appreciate his support.

Through his extensive experience in the corporate workplace, as well as his own personal relationships, Mr. Clark has gained great insight into the spirit vs. ego dynamic that is common to all people. Through a multitude of life experiences, spiritual training, and consistent self-reflection and inner development he now recognizes his higher purpose as a teacher and messenger of wisdom and truth in support of the growth and healing of others. He wants everyone to know that it is never too late to find your purpose and experience the amazing life you are here to live.

The combination of personal healing and growth that has opened a greater channel to spirit, along with his propensity to approach life from a logical and practical perspective, makes Mr. Clark an ideal teacher of higher wisdom for men. He is a proponent of leading a balanced life, which not only includes our focus on maintaining health and wellness on various levels, but also balancing and developing our inner strength as much as the outer. As the world is shifting to resolve long standing issues of inequality, violence, and greed, which have been the byproduct of a world focused on fear (ego), he believes that men are ready to take a more active role in their own growth and healing, and live more conscious lives that lead to greater unity on the planet.

In addition to fulfilling his professional goals, his great joy is in being a father, and new grandfather. He loves to work out at the gym, maintains a regular meditation practice, and is a baseball fanatic; he also likes reading/writing, watching movies and TV, and spending time with family and friends. He continues to grow and expand his spiritual connection and practice, and is learning to just flow wherever life leads, while staying open to the unlimited possibilities.

Mr. Clark is grateful for those who have taught him to connect with his spiritual truth, leading to the potential for awakening to the amazing life that is available to each of us. The wisdom that is shared in this book has resonated with him as being received from spirit. He is thankful to all who have guided and supported him in the writing of this book. Mr. Clark is hopeful that this wisdom finds the place of understanding and awareness that connects with the higher truth of his readers, and that it supports them in the process of their personal and spiritual growth and healing. **The world awaits your Light!**

www.ingramcontent.com/pod-product-compliance
Lightning Source LLC
Chambersburg PA
CBHW062150080426

42734CB00010B/1636